100 Literacy Hours

YEAR 5

Published by Scholastic Ltd,
Villiers House,
Clarendon Avenue,
Leamington Spa,
Warwickshire CV32 5PR

© 1998 Scholastic Ltd

AUTHOR
Chris Webster

EDITOR
Lorna Gilbert

ASSISTANT EDITOR
Lesley Sudlow

SERIES DESIGNER
Joy White

DESIGNER
Mark Udall

COVER ARTWORK
Val Biro

ILLUSTRATIONS
Robin Lawrie

© 1998 Scholastic Ltd Text © 1998 Chris Webster
2 3 4 5 6 7 8 9   8 9 0 1 2 3 4 5 6 7

British Library Cataloguing-in-Publication Data
A catalogue record for this book is available from the British Library.

ISBN 0-590-53917-5

Contents

ACKNOWLEDGEMENTS

The publishers gratefully acknowledge permission to reproduce the following copyright material:
Bantam Doubleday Dell Publishing Group Inc for the use of 'The Fun They Had' by Isaac Asimov from *Earth Is Not Room Enough* by Isaac Asimov © 1957, Isaac Asimov (1957, Doubleday).
Carcanet Press Ltd, Manchester for the use of 'The First Men on Mercury' by Edwin Morgan from *Poems of Thirty Years* by Edwin Morgan © 1982, Edwin Morgan (1982, Carcanet Press, Manchester).
Curtis Brown, Ltd New York for the use of 'Shrewd Simon Short' by Alvin Schwartz from *A Twister of Twists, A Tangler of Tongues* by Alvin Schwartz © 1972, Alvin Schwartz (1972, J.B. Lippincott, Bantam Skylark).
Janet Perry for the following units: 'Alliteration', 'Investigating Homophones' and 'Idioms' © 1998, Janet Perry.
Peters Fraser and Dunlop for the use of 'Potato Clock' by Roger McGough from *Sky In The Pie* by Roger McGough © 1983, Roger McGough (1983, Kestrel Books).
Scholastic Inc, New York for the use of an excerpt on Betsy Byars from *Meet the Authors and Illustrators* Volume One by Deborah Kovacs and James Preller © 1991, Deborah Kovacs and James Preller (1991, Scholastic Professional Books).
Chris Stephenson for the following units: 'Establishing Roots', 'Note-taking', 'Skimming and Scanning', 'Note-making', 'Dictionary Work' and 'Detecting Bias' © 1998, Chris Stephenson.

Every effort has been made to trace copyright holders and the publishers apologize for any inadvertent omissions.

Introduction

INTRODUCTION

ABOUT THE SERIES

100 Literacy Hours is a series of year-specific teachers' resource books that provide a core of material for the teaching of the English curriculum within the context of the National Literacy Strategy *Framework for Teaching* and within the structure of the Literacy Hour. Each book offers term-by-term lesson plans, complete with objectives and organization grids and accompanied, where relevant, with photocopiable texts and activity sheets. The materials are ready-to-use, and their adaptable format enables them to be used as flexibly as possible. The 100 hours provided offer a balance of both reading and writing, and of range: fiction and poetry and non-fiction. However, it is expected that you will wish to personalize the material – altering the order, interleaving lessons plans with complementary materials from your school's existing schemes, consolidating work by using the structure of a lesson plan as a model for a lesson with different content, and so on. The loose-leaf format of each book, with hole-punched, perforated, tear-out pages, makes the integration of other tried-and-tested and favourite material into the core very easy.

USING THIS BOOK

The materials

This book provides 100 literacy hours for Year 5, presented as 'units' of between 1 and 5 hours. There is a balance of reading and writing units, most of which are linked in order to demonstrate and reinforce the close relationship. The bulk of the 100 hours is fully supported with detailed lesson plans and integrated photocopiable resources. The remainder of the hours are plans for suitable follow-on or follow-up hours linked to some of the units. These can be found at the end of the unit to which they refer and are presented as grids outlining objectives and organization. Together, these materials should be regarded as a core, as a starting point for developing your own personalized folder for the year.

Adapting and personalizing the materials

During the trialling of these resources, wide differences in ability were found in classes of the same year group in different schools. This means that the *precise* content of the plans and resources will almost certainly need modification to suit the children in a particular school. One way to do this is as follows:
■ Separate the pages of the book and place them in an A4 ring-binder.
■ Adjust the level of the photocopiable resource sheets to match the needs of the children in your year group.
■ 'Trade' materials with higher or lower year groups so that the average level matches that of the target year group.
■ Add your own favourite teaching materials in the appropriate places.
■ Substitute materials for others if necessary (for example, if you have a set of books which you wish to use instead of one of the ones recommended).
   You have now created a tailor-made folder of plans and resources for your year group!

Preparing a scheme of work

All schools are required to write detailed schemes of work, and these materials have been designed to facilitate this process.
   The termly Overview grids provided on pages 16–21 have been compiled by extracting the 'Objectives' grids from each teaching unit and putting them together to provide you with what are, essentially, medium-term plans. These grids are photocopiable so, should you wish to alter the order of units and/or add your own, they can be copied, cut and pasted to make your own plans. On page 22 there are also photocopiable blank objectives grids for you to use when inserting your own material.

ORGANIZATION OF TEACHING UNITS

Each term is divided into teaching units comprising between 1–5 hours. Each of the main units has either a reading or a writing focus (although there is, of course, overlap) and a fiction, poetry or non-fiction content.

The units are organized as follows:

OBJECTIVES GRID

Outlines the word-, sentence- and text-level objectives of the unit.

UNIT	SPELLING/VOCABULARY	GRAMMAR/PUNCTUATION	COMPREHENSION/ COMPOSITION
READING NON-FICTION Persuasive writing: 'Are Today's Kids Turning Into Couch Potatoes?'	Develop vocabulary through reading.	Investigate language conventions and grammatical features of persuasive text.	Read a persuasive article and understand ways in which it seeks to persuade. Distinguish between fact and opinion.

ORGANIZATION GRID

Outlines the key activities for each part of each hour.

INTRODUCTION	WHOLE-CLASS SKILLS WORK	DIFFERENTIATED GROUP ACTIVITIES	CONCLUSION
HOUR 1: Read the article. Discuss type of text and any difficult vocabulary.	Revise and extend knowledge of discursive connectives.	1*: Guided reading and discussion. 2 & 3: Reading Comprehension, parts A, B & D. 4*: Guided reading and discussion.	Discuss the 'Ten Rules for Potential Couch Potatoes'.
HOUR 2: Re-read the text and analyse how the writer seeks to persuade us.	Investigate the features of persuasive text.	1: Reading Comprehension, all parts. 2 & 3*: Guided reading and discussion. 4: Reading Comprehension, parts A, C & D.	Discuss answers to the questions on the Reading Comprehension sheet.

UNIT LESSON PLANS

Each unit of lesson plans is written to the following headings:

Resources

Provides a list of what you need for teaching the whole unit.

Preparation

Outlines any advance preparation needed before the hour(s) begins.

Synopsis

Gives a synopsis of the story, where whole published fiction texts are used as the basis of units.

Each hour is then set out as follows:

Introduction

Sets out what to do in the whole-class shared reading/writing session.

Whole-class skills work

Sets out what to do in the whole-class word- and sentence-level skills sessions. (See page 11 for further information about whole-class skills work.)

Differentiated group activities

Sets out what each group does in the guided group and independent work session. (See page 12 for further information about differentiated group work.)

eg
pg 25

Conclusion

Sets out what to do in the whole-class plenary session.

Follow-up

Some units lend themselves particularly to follow-up hours. These are indicated in the lesson plans and are provided as grid plans at the end of the relevant unit.

Further ideas

Provides ideas for extending what is done within the hours of the unit.

Photocopiable sheets

Photocopiable resource and activity sheets that support each unit. These can be found at the end of each relevant unit and are marked with the photocopiable symbol ▨ .

Many of the sheets have more than one application and are therefore used in several units.

READING UNITS

These teaching units have three aims:
■ to develop basic reading skills across a wide range of texts – fiction, poetry and non-fiction
■ to develop skills of comprehension, inference, deduction and literary appreciation
■ to encourage enjoyment of reading.

Using the texts

All shorter texts are provided on the photocopiable resource sheets. The following longer texts will be needed (half-class sets are recommended for fiction and group sets for non-fiction):

■ *Why the Whales Came* by Michael Morpurgo, Mammoth, ISBN 0-7497-0537-X
■ *A Thief in the Village* by James Berry, Puffin, ISBN 0-14-032679-0
■ *The Cartoonist* by Betsy Byars, Red Fox, ISBN 0-09-942601-3

All the texts are intended for use as *shared texts*; that is to say, texts for whole-class and/or guided group reading. Use of appropriate teaching methods enables children to read and understand texts beyond their *independent* reading level.

These methods include:
■ preparation, for example giving the background to a story, prior study of difficult words
■ an initial reading to the whole class with children following the text
■ re-reading in groups with less able groups supported by the teacher
■ differentiated follow-up activities which allow more able children to respond independently to the text while further support is given to less able readers
■ guided reading, in which the teacher takes children through the text helping them with phonic or contextual clues (less able readers), or higher-level reading skills (more able readers).

Additional suggestions are given, where relevant, in the detailed lesson plans, for example use of different versions of the same story.

It is assumed that children will be following a programme of guided reading alongside their reading of these shared texts.

Managing the reading of longer texts

In those units where the whole of longer texts is read, it is assumed that sometimes the chunks of reading allocated to the Introduction session (whole-class shared reading) may need to be undertaken outside of the session or lesson time. It could be included in guided group reading, or in other shared reading time or as homework. Recording and making copies of an audio tape of the text will enable those children who cannot read the text independently to have access to the story.

Responding to texts

Since the mid-1980s, a complete methodology for teaching children how to respond to texts has developed, and is becoming well established from KS1 to KS4. The materials in this book try to exemplify as many types of responses as possible, so that, as well as providing specific lessons, they also offer models which can be adapted for use with other texts. Some examples of responses to texts are:

- cloze – fill in gaps in a text
- sequencing – place a cut-up text in order
- design a storyboard – such as plan a film version of the text
- use drama techniques to explore a text – for example role-play, hot-seating
- design a newspaper front page about an aspect of the text
- comprehension questions answered orally or in writing.

Written comprehension

The majority of written tasks set in these materials encourage a creative response to reading. These often reveal children's comprehension of the text as clearly as any formal comprehension, and, like the oral and dramatic activities, they are just as effective in developing comprehension skills. However, children do need to practise formal written comprehension of different kinds, and activities for this have been provided in many of the units. Note that the main purpose of the comprehension material is to develop understanding of the texts, not to provide detailed numerical assessments. Marking should therefore be kept simple. On most occasions, the marking can be done orally in a concluding session. You might take each question in turn, asking for responses from the children and discussing them. The correct answer (or answers) can then be identified and the children can mark their own answers, simply placing a tick if they have got it right. Queries can be dealt with immediately. You can look at the comprehensions later to see at a glance which children are doing well at basic recall, which are doing well at inference and deduction, and most important of all, which children are struggling with basic understanding. These children should then be given further support during the next guided reading session.

WRITING UNITS

These units provide a series of structured writing experiences throughout the year leading to a more integrated, creative and open-ended approach in Term 3 which draws together and puts into practice previous skills taught and developed. The idea is to provide 'props' for learning and then to remove them gradually in the hope that children will be able to write with increasing independence and creativity. Examples of

props are the many 'templates' to support writing. These include sentence and paragraph prompts for fiction, and page-layout templates for certain types of non-fiction (see 'Words in Windows' unit, Term 2). Other kinds of props are the Story Planner (see 'Science Fiction Cards' unit, Term 2) and the Redrafting Checklist (see 'Redrafting Simulation' unit, Term 2). Regular use of these will help children to internalize the prompts they contain, and so help them build independence as writers. Towards the end of Term 3, the 'Writing Simulation' unit ('Ban the Bypass) provides a context for children to write in a range of forms for a range of purposes and audiences, so bringing together in a creative way, the wide range of skills covered throughout the year.

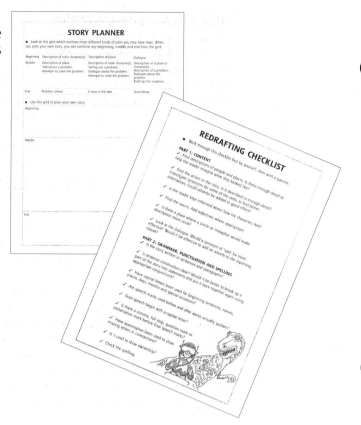

Cross-curricular writing

The best opportunities for most non-narrative writing occur in other curriculum areas. Therefore, when the necessary skills have been introduced through one of the non-fiction units, they should be applied to another curriculum area soon afterwards. It would be well worth holding year-group meetings specifically to 'map' opportunities for non-narrative writing across the curriculum.

REFERENCE AND RESEARCH SKILLS UNITS

Within each term there are two 1-hour Reference and Research Skills units. The purpose of these units is to focus attention on important skills that may otherwise not get appropriate time within the context of other lesson plans.

In this book for Year 5, the Reference and Research Skills units deal with the following skills:
Term 1:
Dictionary work (roots, prefixes and suffixes).
Note-taking.
Term 2:
Skimming and scanning.
Note-making (quotation and adaptation).
Term 3:
Further dictionary work (using a range of dictionaries).
Detecting bias.

WORD PLAY UNITS

At the end of each term there is a Word Play unit. The purpose of these units is to demonstrate that playing with words is not only 'OK' and fun, but also a powerful learning tool. The Word Play units for Year 5 deal with the following:
Term 1:
Alliteration.
Term 2:
Investigating homophones.
Term 3:
Idioms.

SPEAKING AND LISTENING

Speaking and listening is also an essential part of literacy, and development of skills in this important area has been integrated into the units for both reading and writing. Speaking and listening is *the* most important way of developing higher-order reading skills. Children must be able to explore texts through discussion, role-play and other forms of oral 'comprehension' before they can do justice to more formal written comprehension. 'Brainstorming' sharing ideas, helping each other to check work and so on, will all help children to write more effectively. The challenge for the teacher is to ensure that this discussion is clearly focussed on the task and not merely idle chatter.

TIMING OF THE LITERACY HOUR

A brisk pace is an important feature of an effective Literacy Hour. The following suggestions, based on experience in trialling these materials, will help to keep things moving:
■ Train pupils in efficient classroom routines (see below under 'Differentiated group activities').
■ Don't talk too much! Keep explanations brief. Get children on task as soon as possible, and give further clarification and help in the context of the activity.
■ Don't let skills sessions overrun, unless there is a good reason which has been previously planned for. Skills will be revised and practised several times throughout the year within the context of other slots in the Literacy Hour and outside of it.
■ When starting group activities sessions, give a clear message about what you want children to have achieved in the time allocated, and encourage them to work efficiently such as not wasting time decorating a border before starting writing and so on.

Introductory session

Most often, these sessions involve the reading aloud of a shared text. Where possible, children should follow the reading in their own copy of the text. Using an overhead projector is the best way of doing this (see below). It allows a shared text to be used as a focal point for the whole class in the same way as a Big Book. Find ways to make them interactive by involving children in reading, asking questions and so on. Give appropriate background information and briefly discuss vocabulary and ideas. However, in all this, do not lose sight of the need to keep the pace of the lesson moving!

Whole-class skills work

It is during these sessions that the majority of grammar, punctuation, spelling and phonic skills are taught. The main principle is that the skills arise from the shared text and will also be used in the related writing unit. Over the year, key skills should be revisited many times so that children's mastery of them will grow incrementally. A word of warning: many grammatical concepts are difficult and abstract, so do not expect children to grasp them all at once. Expect it to be a slow process in which their understanding develops over several years. For example, many children may not achieve mastery of writing in paragraphs until they reach their teens – but they will not achieve it at all if a start is not made when they are much younger.

Although the materials in this book include spelling activities based on spelling rules and patterns arising from the texts, they cannot take the place of a programme of individualized spelling for children. Children could collect a list of words they need to learn in a spelling book. This could be supplemented at least once a week with words from a standard list to make a list of, say, ten (or more for more able/older children). Children then learn their lists using the LOOK/SAY/COVER/WRITE/CHECK method. Pairs of children can test each other on their own lists. Any words not learned can be carried over into the next list.

The same book can be used backwards to collect new items of vocabulary. Again, these should be a mixture of words which children have come across themselves, and words introduced during teaching (for example, character adjectives, synonyms of 'said').

Differentiated group activities

For most group activities, three levels of differentiation are suggested, usually shown as four groups to reflect a normal distribution of ability:

Group 1:	above average pupils.
Groups 2 & 3:	average pupils.
Group 4:	below average pupils.

In the average KS2 class, group sizes would be between 7–8 (with some trade-off between groups according to the spread of ability in the class). This is fine for organizational purposes, and working with the teacher, but too large for most collaborative activities. These groups will therefore need to be subdivided into smaller groups of fours or pairs for many activities. There will also be occasions when mixed-ability groups are most appropriate for the activities (for example, the drama units).

Children need to know which main group they are in and be able to subdivide into fours or pairs quickly and efficiently. To help this process, teachers could name the groups, for example 'Home Group', 'Small Groups', 'Pairs', and train children to get into the appropriate group immediately the group is named.

When this routine is firmly established, children should then be given the experience of working with children from other groups, for example opposite sex pairs, fours made up of pairs from different 'Home Groups' and so on. It is also important to give them the experience of working in mixed-ability groups for appropriate activities.

The teacher should try to divide teaching time equally between all groups over the course of the week – the more able need help just as much as the less able if they are given suitably demanding tasks.

[NB: An asterisk (*) after the group number is used on the grids and in the lesson plans to show which groups the teacher should be working with during the group activities session.]

Finally, it is important to stress that even when a teacher is working intensively with one group, the first priority is always the overall work rate of the whole class. The following tips will help:

■ Train children to work independently. Tell them that you cannot help them while you are working with a group – their turn will come. In the meantime, they must find out for themselves, or ask a friend or a classroom assistant.

■ When working with a group, sit in a position so that the rest of the class can be seen.

■ Break off group work immediately to deal with lazy or disruptive children. They will soon learn that they are under supervision even when you are working with a group.

Concluding sessions

The key objective in most of these sessions is to review the teaching points of the lesson and ensure that the work of *selected* children, pairs or groups is shared with the class for discussion and evaluation. Enough should be heard to exemplify the variety of work produced, but not so much that it becomes boring, or takes too much time. Keep a record of who has presented what to ensure that all children have the opportunity to present their work in due course.

Finishing off

When the time arrives for the concluding session, children will be at different stages of their work. Some will have finished, but many will still have work to do. The following strategies are recommended for dealing with this situation:
■ Expect children to be *on task* during the time allocated for writing.
■ Encourage them to work at a reasonable pace.
■ Make expectations of each group clear: 'I expect you to write at least a side during the next 20 minutes' (Groups 2 & 3). 'I want one paragraph of four or five lines written very carefully and checked over by the end of this session' (Group 4).
■ Give frequent time warnings such as 'We will have to stop writing in ten minutes'.
■ For key pieces of writing plan either a) homework to finish them off, or b) another hour of careful redrafting and presenting.
■ Discourage time-wasting activities such as decorating margins. Pictures should only be encouraged when they have a specific part to play (as in many non-fiction writing activities).

PHOTOCOPYING

Please note:
■ Where there is instruction to copy material from copyright texts, *you need to ensure that this is done within the limits of the copying licence your school has.*
■ If pupils are using their own exercise books or paper for answers, then all photocopiable resources are reuseable.

USE OF OVERHEAD PROJECTOR

Having the use of an overhead projector (OHP) is ideal for whole-class work. Photocopiable texts and skills activities can then be copied onto acetate to make overhead transparencies (OHTs) which can be projected onto a screen or a bare, white or light-coloured wall. For best effect, try to clear a whole section of wall from floor to ceiling and have it painted white. A partial black out would be an advantage. You will then be able to project a huge impressive text or picture. It can also be used to project backgrounds for drama improvisations. Where an OHP is not available, photocopiable sheets should be enlarged to at least A3 size.

INFORMATION AND COMPUTER TECHNOLOGY

Word processors have revolutionized the way we write, making redrafting less of a chore, and allowing documents to be well presented. However, the benefits of word processing only begin to be felt when the user has acquired a reasonable typing speed. It is therefore recommended that all children should use both hands on the keyboard and spend enough time practising so that they do not have to search for letters. To achieve this, word processing should be 'on the go' at all times. In most classrooms this will mean that a rota will have to be set up. When children have mastered the basics of word processing, they should be encouraged to make judgements about choice of fonts and page layout. The 'Words in Windows' and 'Writing Simulation' units provide good opportunities for this.

ASSESSMENT

Regular and ongoing assessment of children's achievements and progress is, of course, essential. These materials assume that you and your school have satisfactory methods and systems of assessing and recording already in place and therefore don't attempt to suggest an alternative. However, what these materials also assume is that your current procedures are based on clearly stated teaching objectives. Therefore the objectives grids at the beginning of each unit should be invaluable in providing you with a framework for ongoing assessment.

In addition, to facilitate individual children conferencing at the end of each half-term, a photocopiable record sheet has been provided on page 15. Specific targets for reading and writing can be set for each pupil at the end of the previous half-term and recorded on the sheet in the left-hand column. Interim progress towards these targets can be assessed when appropriate and noted in the middle column. Then, at the end of each half-term, during the conference, pupil and teacher together can record achievement and agree further targets for the next half-term.

HOMEWORK

The amount of homework should be increased throughout the Key Stage. In Year 5, it might take the form of:
■ Finishing off work that could not be finished in class. *Note:* be careful how you manage this. Less able pupils are often the slowest workers, and could end up with the most homework. If there seems to be a lot of finishing off needed in children's own time, consider revising lesson plans to allow more time in school.
■ Preparation – for example finding texts, such as cereal packets, newspapers and so on, to be used in the next day's lesson; making notes or plans for storywriting; research such as interviewing or surveying family members.

PUPIL ASSESSMENT GRID

Pupil's name:				Class	Year group
Term	1	2	3	1st half	2nd half

	TARGET(S)	INTERIM PROGRESS (inc dates)	ACHIEVEMENT AT END OF HALF TERM
Reading			
Writing			

OVERVIEW: YEAR 5
TERM 1

	UNIT	SPELLING/VOCABULARY	GRAMMAR/PUNCTUATION	COMPREHENSION/COMPOSITION
HOUR 5(+5)	READING FICTION Modern fiction: *Why the Whales Came* by Michael Morpurgo.	Explore the vocabulary in the text. Make a glossary.	Revise punctuation and the setting out of dialogue. Use the past continuous tense.	Read novel by significant children's writer. Analyse features of a good opening. Record personal responses in a reading log. Carry out an in-depth study of one character in the story. Respond to characters.
HOUR 5	WRITING FICTION Guided writing: 'Harwell Hall'.	Recognize and use similes and metaphors. Use synonyms to add variety to writing.	Understand how dialogue is set out and how it is punctuated. Revise adverbs.	Understand how to use story structure effectively. Understand the terms 'climax' and 'anti-climax'. Redraft work to make improvements.
HOUR 3	READING NON-FICTION Historical recount: 'John Cabot'.	Explore technical vocabulary used to describe Cabot's ship. Explore vocabulary quoted from original sources.	Recognize the past tense. Understand the 1st-person form and match verbs accordingly. Understand use of punctuation, in particular, commas.	Read a recount and identify features of recounted text. Understand purpose of note-taking.
HOUR 3(+1)	WRITING NON-FICTION Historical recount: The *Titanic*.	Develop and use vocabulary from reading and other media forms.	Write in paragraphs. Extend work on verbs: use of past and present continuous tenses and auxiliary verbs.	Read a number of historical sources as models for research and writing. Identify features of recount texts. Make notes and use for writing.
HOUR 1	REFERENCE AND RESEARCH SKILLS Dictionary work: Identify roots, derivation, spelling patterns.	Widen vocabulary and develop awareness of spelling patterns. Identify word roots and name prefixes and suffixes in specific examples.	Sort words with the same root and use them appropriately in sentences.	Compile own collections of words with the same root.
HOUR 3	READING POETRY 'The First Men on Mercury' by Edwin Morgan.	Investigate irregular plurals (plurals by vowel change) eg *man/men*.	Understand the difference between direct and reported speech. Revise the setting out and punctuation of dialogue.	Read and understand the poem.

NB 5 (+2) = Number of hours in unit (plus number of follow-up hours)

OVERVIEW: YEAR 5
TERM 1 (CONTINUED)

UNIT	SPELLING/ VOCABULARY	GRAMMAR/ PUNCTUATION	COMPREHENSION/ COMPOSITION
WRITING POETRY 'It Can't Be – Can It?' by Chris Webster.	Explore synonyms of key words in the poem. Explain the differences between various synonyms.	Analyse the verse form.	Read and understand poem. Choose words with exactly the right shade of meaning.
READING PLAYS 'Jurassic Classroom'.	Understand and use vocabulary related to drama conventions.	Mark up a text to support reading aloud. Identify statements, questions, orders and exclamations.	Understand the conventions of playscripts. Use appropriate gesture and expression to communicate character/action. Make notes.
WRITING PLAYS 'Washing-up woes'.	Recognize (and use in own writing) idiomatic phrases, clichés and expressions. Understand when they are appropriate to use in speech and writing.	Understand the difference between the punctuation and setting out of dialogue in a story and in a play.	Write a playscript using layout conventions correctly. Write convincing dialogue. Write production notes for a playscript.
READING NON-FICTION 'Crippen Hanged'.	Investigate unfamiliar vocabulary. Develop of knowledge of prefixes.	Revise simple present and simple past tense. Know past tense of irregular verbs. Identify the past tense in recounts.	Understand a crime report and explore the issues raised.
WRITING NON-FICTION Police report.	Check spellings.	Understand the need for arrangement of subject and verb.	Recognize the features of recounted texts. Write a report in the appropriate style.
REFERENCE AND RESEARCH SKILLS Note-taking.	Use simple abbreviations.	Formulate questions and note relevant information.	Discuss the purpose and some of the methods of taking notes. Take notes in different formats.
WORD PLAY Alliteration: 'Shrewd Simon Short' by Alvin Schwartz.	Be aware of the use of adverbs to qualify verbs.	Understand the use of punctuation as an aid to the reader.	Explore the use of alliteration.

OVERVIEW: YEAR 5
TERM 2

	UNIT	SPELLING/ VOCABULARY	GRAMMAR/ PUNCTUATION	COMPREHENSION/ COMPOSITION
HOUR 2	READING FICTION Science fiction short story: 'The Fun They Had' by Issac Asimov.	Extend vocabulary from vocabulary in text. Investigate antonyms. Identify vocabulary that indicates in which culture the story was written.	Construct sentences in different ways.	Investigate key features of science fiction genre. Discuss appeal of science fiction.
HOUR 3	WRITING FICTION Science Fiction Cards.	Extend vocabulary from vocabulary in text.	Revise and extend writing of dialogue.	Apply skills of story writing learned in 'Harwell Hall' unit (Term 1) but with more imaginative content. Use a planning grid.
HOUR 3	REDRAFTING SIMULATION Two stories: 'Virtual Jurassic' and 'The Titan'.	Identify misspelled words in own writing.	Revise use of apostrophes, questions marks, speech marks. Revise and extend use of conjunctions. Construct sentences in different ways. Use punctuation effectively to signpost meaning.	Review, edit and evaluate writing. Investigate how to redraft the content and format of writing.
HOUR 3	READING NON-FICTION Information genre: 'Venus'.	Collect, define and spell correctly technical words from reading.	Combine sentences in different ways, while retaining meaning.	Read non-chronological information text. Prepare for reading by identifying what is already known. Identify features of information genre. Critically appraise information texts.
HOUR 2	WRITING NON-FICTION Information genre: Words in Windows.	Secure knowledge of information book related vocabulary.	Construct sentences from notes. Use conjunctions.	Plan and write non-chronological information text. Prepare for reading by identifying what is already known and what they need to find out. Make notes.
HOUR 1	REFERENCE AND RESEARCH SKILLS Skimming and scanning.	Identify key words and locate them in lists and texts.	Organize information into sentences and paragraphs.	Understand and use the processes of skimming for the main idea and scanning to locate specific information.
HOUR 4	READING POETRY Classical narrative poetry: 'The Lady of Shalott' by Alfred Lord Tennyson.	Identify and understand archaic words. Revise terms 'simile' and 'metaphor'. Introduce term 'figurative language'. Explore spelling patterns of rhyming words.	Explore grammar of poetry. Interpret punctuation appropriately when reading aloud. Read a classical narrative	poem and understand genre. Perform poem. Discuss imagery. Use structure of poem to write additional verses.

OVERVIEW: YEAR 5
TERM 2 (CONTINUED)

	UNIT	SPELLING/ VOCABULARY	GRAMMAR/ PUNCTUATION	COMPREHENSION/ COMPOSITION
HOUR 2	WRITING POETRY Ballad: 'The Spanish Armada' *Anonymous*.	Investigate interesting and unusual words, including archaic ones.	Understand the grammar of poetry. Use punctuation to help convey meaning when reading aloud.	Read ballad and understand distinctive features. Retell story in a different format. Use structure of ballad read to write own ballad.
HOUR 3	READING FICTION Traditional story: 'The Laidley Worm of Spindlestone Heugh'.	Look up difficult and archaic words in a dictionary. Investigate spelling of words with *-ful* suffix. Investigate doubling consonants when adding endings.	Revise different kinds of nouns. Recognize archaic syntax.	Read a traditional story in its earliest written version. Investigate different versions of the same story.
HOUR 2	WRITING FICTION Write a 'choice' story.	Investigate hard and soft 'c' spellings. Use known spellings as basis for spelling words with similar patterns.	Develop grammatical awareness through redrafting process.	Write own story based on traditional tale and using structure identified in reading.
HOUR 2	READING NON-FICTION Explanatory and recount texts: 'The Mechanical Television'.	Develop subject-specific vocabulary. Make a glossary for technical words.	Revise verb tenses.	Prepare for reading by establishing prior knowledge. Read a text that combines explanatory and recount genres and investigate and note features. Formulate questions for further research.
HOUR 2	WRITING NON-FICTION Explanatory text: 'Future TV Brainstorm'.	Collect, define and spell technical words. Invent words. Understand how language develops.	Understand how writing can be adapted for different audiences by changing vocabulary and sentence structure.	Write explanatory text for two different audiences. Use brainstorm technique for developing ideas.
HOUR 1	REFERENCE AND RESEARCH SKILLS Note-making: quotation and adaptation.	Understand meaning of words *quote, adapt, acknowledge, bibliography*.	Adapt text and quote from it.	Understand what is meant by 'in your own words'.
HOUR 1	WORD PLAY Investigating homophones through poetry.	Distinguish between homophones.	Consolidate the conventions of 'Standard English'. Write extensions to poems using known structures.	

OVERVIEW: YEAR 5
TERM 3

HOUR 2
HOUR 2
HOUR 2
HOUR 2
HOUR 5
HOUR 2

UNIT	SPELLING/ VOCABULARY	GRAMMAR/ PUNCTUATION	COMPREHENSION/ COMPOSITION
READING POETRY Older literature: 'The Cat' by W Adolphe Roberts.	Find meanings of unknown words. Identify rhyming words with different spellings.	Explore the grammar of poetry. Use punctuation to help convey meaning when reading aloud.	Explore the challenge and appeal of older literature. Investigate the sonnet structure. Compare prose and poetry texts. Explore figurative language.
WRITING POETRY Blank verse: Extract from 'The Prelude' by William Wordsworth.	Develop vocabulary from reading.	Use 1st person in letter writing.	Read an extract from a narrative poem by a well-known 'romantic' poet. Use poem as model for writing own poem in blank verse. Perform poem. Revise simile and metaphor.
READING NON-FICTION Persuasive writing: Are Today's Kids Turning into Couch Potatoes?'	Develop vocabulary through reading.	Investigate language conventions and grammatical features of persuasive text.	Read a persuasive article and understand the ways in which it seeks to persuade. Distinguish between fact and opinion.
WRITING NON-FICTION Friendly persuasion.	Investigate the vocabulary of argument, debate and persuasion.	Examine types of argument. Revise discursive connectives.	Write a persuasive article.
READING FICTION Short stories from a different culture: *A Thief in the Village* by James Berry.	Revise use and spelling of possessive pronouns. Make a glossary. Investigate how words can be transformed in a variety of ways for a variety of purposes.	Revise person: 1st, 2nd, 3rd. Investigate differences between standard English and dialect.	Read and investigate stories from other cultures. Identify features of life from text. Compare to own experiences. Identify point of view and how this affects reader response. Understand difference between 'author' and 'narrator'.
WRITING FICTION From blurb to book.	Identify and define descriptive vocabulary used in advertisements. Use dictionaries and thesauruses.	Investigate use of punctuation to signpost meaning.	Read and understand purpose of book blurbs. Write a story based on a blurb.

OVERVIEW: YEAR 5
TERM 3 (CONTINUED)

UNIT	SPELLING/ VOCABULARY	GRAMMAR/ PUNCTUATION	COMPREHENSION/ COMPOSITION
REFERENCE AND RESEARCH SKILLS Use a range of dictionaries.	Explore spellings, meanings and derivations of words and phrases.	Recognize and mimic format and layout of entries in different types of dictionary.	Understand purpose and use of different types of dictionary. Compose own dictionary extract.
READING FICTION Modern fiction: *The Cartoonist* by Betsy Byars.	Identify and understand vocabulary from another culture. Understand and identify simile and metaphor.	Recognize non-standard English and its function in reflecting a culture. Analyse sentence construction and use of punctuation.	Read American fiction by significant children's author. Understand different points of view. Explore irony and sarcasm. Investigate characterization. Write in the style of a particular author.
WRITING FICTION Stories from memories.	Use dictionaries to explore meanings of unfamiliar words.	Demonstrate awareness of grammar and use appropriate punctuation in own writing.	Read author's account of own writing. Plan and write a story based on own experience.
WRITING SIMULATION Ban the Bypass.	Develop new vocabulary from text. Use dictionaries efficiently to explore meanings of unfamiliar words.	Understand conventions of formal letter writing. Revise use of connectives. Investigate the grammar of newspaper writing.	Read and comment on issue presented in newspaper article. Draft and write letters for real purposes. Construct a persuasive argument. Write a newspaper article. Write a discursive essay.
REFERENCE AND RESEARCH SKILLS Detecting bias.	Recognize emotive language.	Study the function of rhetorical and other questions in arguing a case. Consider and compare form of headline and letters to the press.	Read and evaluate letters to a newspaper. Compose a persuasive reply.
WORD PLAY Idioms.	Enrich vocabulary by understanding purpose of idiom and use of dictionary of idioms. Make a dictionary of idioms.	Understand how writing can be adapted for different purposes and audiences.	Collect and discuss idioms. Distinguish between literal and figurative.

OBJECTIVES GRIDS:
BLANK TEMPLATES

Use these blank photocopiable grids when inserting your own material.

UNIT	SPELLING/ VOCABULARY	GRAMMAR/ PUNCTUATION	COMPREHENSION/ COMPOSITION

UNIT	SPELLING/ VOCABULARY	GRAMMAR/ PUNCTUATION	COMPREHENSION/ COMPOSITION

UNIT	SPELLING/ VOCABULARY	GRAMMAR/ PUNCTUATION	COMPREHENSION/ COMPOSITION

UNIT	SPELLING/ VOCABULARY	GRAMMAR/ PUNCTUATION	COMPREHENSION/ COMPOSITION

Term 1

WHY THE WHALES CAME

OBJECTIVES

UNIT	SPELLING/VOCABULARY	GRAMMAR/PUNCTUATION	COMPREHENSION/ COMPOSITION
READING FICTION Modern fiction: *Why the Whales Came* by Michael Morpurgo.	Explore the vocabulary in the text. Make a glossary.	Revise punctuation and the setting out of dialogue. Use the past continuous tense.	Read novel by significant children's writer. Analyse features of a good opening. Record personal responses in a reading log. Carry out an in-depth study of one character in the story. Respond to characters.

ORGANIZATION (5 HOURS)

	INTRODUCTION	WHOLE-CLASS SKILLS WORK	DIFFERENTIATED GROUP ACTIVITIES	CONCLUSION
HOUR 1	Shared reading of Chapters 1 & 2 of *Why the Whales Came* (approximately 30 minutes).	Analyse features of the story's opening.	1*: Guided reading and discussion. 2 & 3: List words and phrases which refer to the Birdman. Write a summary of the story about him. 4*: Guided reading and discussion.	After a brief plenary discussion, all pupils make an entry in their reading logs. Pupils read Chapter 3 for homework and make an entry in their reading logs.
HOUR 2	Briefly sum up what happened in Chapter 3. Shared reading of Chapter 4 (approximately 15 minutes).	Revise verb tenses using page 43 of the story. Introduce the past continuous tense.	1: List words and phrases which refer to the Birdman. Write a summary of the story about him. 2 & 3*: Guided reading and discussion. 4: List words/phrases which refer to the Birdman. Write a summary of the story about him.	After a brief plenary discussion, all pupils make an entry in their reading logs. Pupils read Chapter 5 for homework and make an entry in their reading logs.
HOUR 3	Briefly sum up what happened in Chapter 5. Shared reading of Chapters 6 & 7 (approximately 25 minutes).	Explain the template for the Birdman essay (photocopiable page xxx).	1*: Guided reading and discussion. 2 & 3: Begin the Birdman essay. 4*: Guided reading and discussion.	After a brief plenary discussion, all pupils make an entry in their reading logs. Pupils read Chapter 8 for homework and make an entry in their reading logs.
HOUR 4	Briefly sum up what happened in Chapter 8. Shared reading of Chapter 9 (approximately 18 minutes).	Use pages 106–107 as a focus for revising the punctuation and setting out of dialogue. Investigate stylistic features of dialogue.	1: Begin the Birdman essay. 2 & 3*: Guided reading and discussion. 4: Begin the Birdman essay.	After a brief plenary discussion, all pupils make an entry in their reading logs. Pupils read Chapter 10 for homework and make an entry in their reading logs.
HOUR 5	Briefly sum up what happened in Chapter 10. Shared reading of Chapter 11 (approximately 18 minutes).	Make a glossary for the book.	1–4*: All groups complete the Birdman essay.	Shared reading of Chapter 12 (approximately 9 minutes). Pupils make a final entry in their reading logs.

RESOURCES

Copies of *Why the Whales Came* by Michael Morpurgo (Mammoth, ISBN 0-7497-0537-X) – see note below, photocopiable page 29 (The Birdman – Essay Template), board or flip chart, OHP and acetate (optional), writing materials.

Note: The length of the selected text means that additional readings will be required outside of the five literacy hours suggested below. Additional readings can either be done at other times such as after lunch or just before school ends, or children can complete the readings as homework. The former will work with a half-class set, whereas the latter will require a copy for every child.

PREPARATION

If possible, prepare photocopiable page 29 as an OHT, or as an A3 enlargement. Provide enough photocopies of this sheet for one per pair of children.

It might also be useful to make OHTs of pages 43, 106 and 107 of the story, for use in whole-class skills work.

SYNOPSIS

Gracie and her friend Daniel live on Bryher in the Scilly Isles. They befriend the Birdman, a lonely old man who is misunderstood and shunned by the community. The Birdman warns them never to go on Samson Island, saying it is cursed. However, a secret fishing trip leaves the children stranded on Samson by fog. When Gracie returns home, she learns that her father is missing at sea. She believes the curse of Samson is the cause.

Soon after, the islanders hear about a stranded whale and plan to kill it along with the other whales in the bay for meat and ivory. The Birdman warns them that it was the Samson Islanders' greed in killing whales that caused the curse to come upon the island. Eventually, the islanders are persuaded to help the stranded whale. Shortly after, Gracie's father returns safe and sound. The Birdman is never seen again, but the curse of Samson Island is finally lifted.

Introduction

Introduce *Why the Whales Came* briefly by reading the 'blurb' on page 1, then read from the beginning of the story to page 32. This will take about 30 minutes. (Note that the length of the readings in Hours 1 and 3 will reduce the time available for the whole-class skills and group sessions.) Discuss briefly the children's feelings towards the Birdman at the beginning of the story. How do these feelings change by the end of the second chapter?

Whole-class skills work

Re-read the opening of the story and analyse its features. (Because of the length of the introductory reading, keep this session brisk and short.) Ask the children: How does the writer catch our attention? Discuss features such as: the use of dialogue in the opening sentence which draws the reader immediately into the story; the raising of the reader's curiosity (for example, who is the Birdman and why must Gracie keep away from him?); and the building up of suspense (we don't learn anything about the Birdman until the bottom of page 13). How effective do the children think this story opening is?

Differentiated group activities

1*: Guided reading and discussion with the teacher. The teacher selects appropriate short sections of the text to re-read, linked to the aspects under discussion. The following questions can be used as a starting point:
■ What are the first things we learn about Daniel and Gracie?
■ What do we learn about the place in which they live?
■ What do we learn about the Birdman? What are the different opinions of him as expressed by different characters?
■ What do we find out about the Birdman's history?
■ What is the first sign that the Birdman might not be so frightening after all?
2 & 3: Make a list of all the words and phrases which refer to the Birdman and write a summary of the story about him told by Gracie's father.
4*: Guided reading and discussion with the teacher. The teacher begins by helping the

children with basic reading skills, difficult words and so on. The next step is to ask questions to test basic comprehension. Some of the questions for Group 1 can then be adapted for use with Group 4, particularly those about the Birdman.

Conclusion

Briefly discuss the text read with an emphasis on personal responses, for example, how does life on the Isles of Scilly compare with life where the children live? How would they feel about the Birdman?

Explain to the children that they are going to create a reading log to which they will add an entry each time they read a part of the story. Each entry should contain:
■ a *brief* summary of the story in the text just read (just a few sentences).
■ personal responses to the text (as in the discussion above, for example) – emphasize that this is the important part and so it should be written in more detail.
■ a note of any difficult words and their meanings once these have been looked up.

Write this information on the board or flip chart for the children to copy, so that they will remember the main points each time they make an entry in their reading log.

Finally, ask the children to read Chapter 3 (pages 33–42) for homework and to make an entry in their reading logs, or arrange to do this activity later in the day if you prefer.

Introduction

Briefly sum up what happens in Chapter 3 of the story: Gracie and Daniel continue to visit Rushy Bay, sailing their boats and communicating with the Birdman through shell messages, but they still know very little about him. The children's teacher, Mr Wellbeloved, warns that war with Germany is imminent but Gracie's father dismisses this as nonsense. One evening, however, they hear Gracie's mother announce that war with Germany has been declared. As Gracie lies in bed that night, she can only worry about the Birdman out at sea in the terrible storm that blew up earlier that evening.

Next, read Chapter 4 (pages 43–53). This should take about 15 minutes. Briefly discuss Daniel and Gracie's first meeting with the Birdman. What impressions does the reader now have of the Birdman?

Whole-class skills work

Revise the basic past, present and future tenses in a brief question-and-answer session, then ask the children to investigate the tenses used on page 43 of the story. What do they notice? They will find that everything is written in the past tense, for example 'reached', 'stayed' and so on (this is the simple past tense). Point out that there is another form of the past tense which is also used on page 43: the past continuous tense. The first three words on the page provide an example: 'Daniel *was waiting…*'.

Explain that the past continuous tense is formed by adding the auxiliary (helper) verb 'was' to the present participle (the -*ing* form of the verb) 'walking'. Write this on the board or flip chart, together with a few examples. Then ask the children to find more examples in Chapter 4. Emphasize that they need to look for the pattern 'was + (verb)-*ing*'. Explain that 'was' used by itself is the simple past tense of the verb 'to be'. List their examples on the board or flip chart.

Differentiated group activities

1: Make a list of all the words and phrases which refer to the Birdman in Chapter 4. Write a summary of the story about him.
2 & 3*: Guided reading and discussion of Chapter 4 with the teacher. The teacher selects appropriate short sections of the text to re-read, linked to the aspects under discussion. The following questions can be used as a starting point:
■ Why are Daniel and Gracie worried about the Birdman?
■ What do they learn about the Birdman from the inside of his cottage?
■ What happens when they meet him for the first time?
■ What does the Birdman think about the children's news?
4: Make a list of all the words and phrases which refer to the Birdman from pages 48–53 of the story.

Conclusion

Hold a brief plenary discussion, focusing on how the children would feel if they met the Birdman face to face. Then ask the children to make an entry in their reading logs.

The children will need to read Chapter 5 for homework (or during another part of the school day) and make an entry in their reading logs.

HOUR 3

Introduction

Briefly sum up what happened in Chapter 5: The children tell everyone about the timber washed up on Popplestones and the islanders gather the wood and hide it before the Customs Officers arrive. A Customs Officer searches Gracie's house and discovers the Birdman's cormorant carving hidden by her in the attic. Gracie's parents are suspicious and so Gracie tells them that she and Daniel made it and intended it as a Christmas present for them. Daniel confirms that he and Gracie made the bird carving.

Next, read Chapters 6 and 7 (pages 65–84). This should take about 25 minutes. Discuss what Gracie and Daniel might be feeling about the thought of spending the night on the strange island.

Whole-class skills work

Introduce The Birdman – Essay Template on photocopiable page 29. If possible, display the sheet as an OHT or A3 enlargement. Explain that the template gives suggestions for each paragraph of an essay about the Birdman, including starter sentences and chapter references which the children can use to help them in their writing.

The template will encourage the children to investigate how the Birdman is represented in the story, through looking at text relating specifically to him, his relationship with other characters and the children's own responses.

Differentiated group activities

1*: Guided reading and discussion (see Hour 1) of Chapters 6 and 7.
The following questions can be used as a starting point:
■ How did the war begin to affect Bryher?
■ What was Daniel's main interest at this time?
■ What did Gracie's father do?
■ What happened when Daniel and Gracie took the boat out?

2 & 3: Begin the Birdman essay referring to the photocopiable template on page xxx. Encourage the children to refer to their notes on the Birdman (from Hour 1) and their reading logs. These groups should follow the template closely.
4*: Guided reading and discussion (see Hour 1) of Chapters 6 and 7. Discuss the questions listed above for Group 1, adapting them as necessary.

Conclusion

After a brief plenary discussion about what might happen to Gracie and Daniel, ask the children to make an entry in their reading logs.

The children should read Chapter 8 for homework and enter this in their reading logs.

HOUR 4

Introduction

Briefly sum up what happened in Chapter 8: Gracie and Daniel are marooned on Samson Island for the night after the fog descends. They decide that the Birdman must be on the island because of the fire they discover, but though they find his cottage, there is no sign of him. Inside the cottage, they find a huge animal horn but are unable to tell which creature it once belonged to. After eating a fish breakfast, the fog finally lifts and they are free to sail back to Bryher.

Briefly discuss the children's responses to the events in Chapter 8, then read Chapter 9 (pages 96–107). The reading should take about 18 minutes.

Whole-class skills work

Use pages 106–107 of the story as a focus for revising the punctuation and setting out of dialogue. Investigate the following:
■ the placing of speech marks
■ the placing of other punctuation, including commas before speech marks
■ the layout of speech – a new indented line is used for each new speaker.
Move on to investigate the stylistic features of the dialogue:
■ Look at the reporting clauses and note the additional description in some of them, for example *"Come here, Gracie dear," she said, her voice an unnatural whisper.* Talk about why

descriptions like these are used and what they add to the dialogue. Suggest some synonyms of 'said' and how these can be used to provide variety and avoid constant repetition.

■ Notice that some speeches do not have any reporting clause, for example *"Then run along in. Break's over. Bell's going."*
■ Evaluate how authentic or 'true to life' the dialogue is in the story.

Differentiated group activities

1: Begin the Birdman essay using the template on photocopiable page 29. The children should refer to their notes on the Birdman from Hour 2 and their reading logs. They may wish to add in or substitute details for those listed on the sheet.

2 & 3*: Guided reading and discussion (see Hour 2) of Chapter 9. The following questions can be used as a starting point:
■ Why are Gracie and Daniel keen to leave Samson Island?
■ Might Gracie's dream be significant in some way? Why?
■ Why do Tim and his friends attack Daniel?
■ What does Gracie think is the cause of her father going missing?

4: The children begin the Birdman essay, using their notes on the Birdman from Hour 2 and their reading logs. They could write their essay based on paragraphs 1, 2 and 5.

Conclusion

After a brief plenary discussion focusing on their responses to the ending of Chapter 9, ask the children to make an entry in their reading logs.

The children should read Chapter 10 for homework and enter this in their reading logs.

Introduction

Briefly sum up what happened in Chapter 10: Just before dawn, Daniel and Gracie secretly go to warn the Birdman of Tim's planned attack on his cottage. They find the Birdman on the beach struggling to move a beached whale back into the sea. The Birdman tells Gracie the story of the whales that became beached on Samson Island, and how the islanders' greed in killing them for meat and ivory brought the curse upon them. To lift the curse, the beached whale on Bryher must be returned to the sea, but Tim's gang arrives and they decide that the whales could be valuable. They run off to fetch the other islanders.

Next, read Chapter 11. This should take about 18 minutes. Discuss how the islanders are won over to helping the whales. What helps to persuade them?

Whole-class skills work

Discuss what information appears in glossaries and how it is usually set out (for example alphabetical order, words defined appear in bold). Tell the children that they are going to write a glossary for *Why the Whales Came*. Work as a group to collate all the difficult words they jotted down in their reading logs. Make a list of these words in alphabetical order on the board, flip chart or OHP. Next, share the various definitions given in the reading logs for each word and select the most appropriate to include in the glossary.

Differentiated group activities

1–4*: All groups work to complete the Birdman essay. Explain that the last paragraph is an opportunity to sum up some of the responses to the Birdman written in the children's reading logs.

Conclusion

Finish with a shared reading of Chapter 12 (pages 135–139). Briefly discuss the children's responses to the final events in the story, then ask them to make a final entry in their reading logs.

FOLLOW-UP

See page 30 which provides a grid plan for a 5-hour follow-up unit based on *Why the Whales Came*.

THE BIRDMAN – ESSAY TEMPLATE

Paragraph 1

■ Describe some first impressions of the Birdman (see Chapter 1). You could start with this suggested sentence:

The reader's first impressions of the Birdman are not very good. The very first line of the story…

■ Bring into your description one of the phrases jotted down earlier in the story, for example:

'Some said the Birdman was mad.'

Paragraph 2

■ Write about the Birdman's life story as described by Gracie's father in Chapter 2. Here is a suggested starter sentence:

Gracie's father describes how the Birdman came to be so strange. When the Birdman was a boy…

Paragraph 3

■ Describe what the Birdman is really like (see Chapter 4). Here is a suggested starter sentence:

Daniel and Gracie find out that the Birdman is not mad. In fact, he has many good qualities…

■ Describe what Daniel and Gracie learn about him from his cottage.
■ Describe what they learn about him when they meet him.

Paragraph 4

■ Describe the truth about the Birdman's story (the story of why the whales came), referring to Chapters 10 and 11. Here is a suggested starter sentence:

Daniel and Gracie find the Birdman trying to roll a whale back into the sea and he tells them what happened on Samson…

■ Explain how the Birdman helped to move the whales and how he felt when the job was done.

Paragraph 5

■ Describe how your personal feelings about the Birdman changed as the story developed (look in your reading log). Here is a suggested starter sentence:

My own feelings about the Birdman began with fear and dislike…

WHY THE WHALES CAME: FOLLOW-UP

OBJECTIVES

UNIT	SPELLING/VOCABULARY	GRAMMAR/ PUNCTUATION	COMPREHENSION/ COMPOSITION
READING FICTION Modern Fiction: *Why the Whales Came* – Follow-up.	Develop vocabulary from reading.	Understand the difference between direct and reported speech. Revise meaning of 1st, 2nd and 3rd person. Analyse language style.	Investigate how characters are presented. Respond personally to characters and plot. Revise characteristic features of folk tales.

ORGANIZATION (5 HOURS)

	INTRODUCTION	WHOLE-CLASS SKILLS WORK	DIFFERENTIATED GROUP ACTIVITIES	CONCLUSION
HOUR 1	Re-read Chapter 1. Discuss the characters which are introduced in the chapter.	Discuss how the Birdman Essay Template could be adapted for a different character, eg how the starter sentences and chapter references would differ, etc.	1–4*: Choose a character to write an essay about. Adapt the Birdman Essay Template.	Pupils share their essays. Aim to hear essays on a range of different characters.
HOUR 2	Re-read Chapter 9 and discuss the attitudes of Big Tim and his gang to the Birdman.	Revise the difference between direct and reported speech. Explore how dialogue is set out by studying the passages in which different people talk about the Birdman.	1–4*: Make a list of the main characters in the novel, then write what each one thinks about the Birdman. Which characters know him best? Adapt for each group according to ability.	Share ideas about the Birdman and the attitudes of the other characters towards him.
HOUR 3	Re-read Chapter 4 and discuss how it would be different if members of the class wrote themselves into it. Discuss what they would do that would be different.	Revise the meaning of 1st, 2nd and 3rd person. Rewrite a short scene from Chapter 4 in the 3rd person.	1–4*: Rewrite the chapter as it might have happened if you and your friend had been in it. Make the 'I' in the chapter yourself and change Daniel to one of your friends. Adapt for each group according to ability.	Pupils share their alternative versions of scenes in Chapter 4.
HOUR 4	Re-read the final chapter.	Examine the style and language of the novel: eg complex sentences, long passages of description, limited amount of dialogue, 1st person narrative etc.	1–4*: Write another scene for the novel which describes what happened to the Birdman. Adapt for each group according to ability.	Select some scenes to be read out to the class. Try to choose a range of different scenes. Ask the class to evaluate how effectively they capture the style of the novel.
HOUR 5	Re-read Chapter 10 in which the story of Samson is summarized. In discussion, add detail to the story by recalling information given earlier.	Examine the style of a folk tale: simple plot and characters, simple language with characteristic vocabulary.	1–4*: Write a folk tale version of the Samson story. Adapt for each group according to ability.	Share and discuss each other's folk tale versions. Which sounds most like a traditional folk tale?

HARWELL HALL

OBJECTIVES

UNIT	SPELLING/VOCABULARY	GRAMMAR/PUNCTUATION	COMPREHENSION/ COMPOSITION
WRITING FICTION Guided writing: 'Harwell Hall'.	Recognize and use similes and metaphors. Use synonyms to add variety to writing.	Understand how dialogue is set out and how it is punctuated. Revise adverbs.	Understand how to use story structure effectively. Understand the terms 'climax' and 'anti-climax'. Redraft work to make improvements.

ORGANIZATION (5 HOURS)

	INTRODUCTION	WHOLE-CLASS SKILLS WORK	DIFFERENTIATED GROUP ACTIVITIES	CONCLUSION
HOUR 1	Shared reading of 'Harwell Hall' on photocopiable pages 35 and 36. Explore the story's structure and discuss the terms 'climax' and 'anti-climax'.	Explore the use of similes and metaphors in description.	1*: Guided writing of a story. 2 & 3: Parts A & B of Reading Comprehension sheet. 4*: Guided writing as for Group 1, but following the template on photocopiable page 38.	Selected pupils from Groups 1 & 4 read out their story beginnings. The class evaluates them.
HOUR 2	Re-read the sections of 'Harwell Hall' that contain dialogue.	Revise the layout and punctuation of dialogue. Write interesting reporting clauses using alternatives to 'said'.	1: Parts A–C of Reading Comprehension sheet. 2 & 3*: Guided writing using story template. 4: Part A of Reading Comprehension sheet.	Discuss the answers to the questions on Reading Comprehension sheet.
HOUR 3	Re-read the section of the story where Jim and Jared explore Harwell Hall. Discuss how the author builds the suspense.	Revise adverbs. Investigate the use of adverbs in the selected section of 'Harwell Hall'. Investigate synonyms.	1–4: All groups write the middle section of their stories based on 'Harwell Hall'. *The teacher works with Groups 1 & 4.	Selected pupils from Groups 2 & 3 read the middle sections of their stories. The class evaluates their effectiveness of building up suspense.
HOUR 4	Re-read the ending of 'Harwell Hall'. Discuss why it is an anti-climax.	Find synonyms of words used in 'Harwell Hall' and explore the different shades of meaning.	1–4: All groups work on the endings to their stories. *The teacher works with Groups 2 & 3.	Selected pupils from Groups 1 & 4 read their alternative endings. The class evaluated their effectiveness in building up suspense and how their endings flow from the original story.
HOUR 5	Recap on the main points taught in Hours 1–4.	Give guidance on the process of redrafting.	1–4*: All groups redraft their stories, adding in more ideas of their own.	Selected pupils read out their stories.

RESOURCES

Photocopiable pages 35 and 36 ('Harwell Hall'), 37 (Reading Comprehension), 38 (Story Template), board or flip chart, OHP and acetate (optional), highlighter pens in different colours, lined paper with ruled margins, writing materials, thesauruses.

PREPARATION

Prepare photocopiable pages 35 and 36 ('Harwell Hall') and 37 (Reading Comprehension) for each pair of children. Provide the story template (page 38) for Groups 2–4 only, one per pair. If possible, prepare the story and story template as OHTs.

Introduction

Read 'Harwell Hall' on photocopiable pages 35 and 36. Discuss and explain the story structure, then write it on the board or flip chart as follows:

Beginning: Detailed and vivid description of a place.
Middle: Dialogue is used to introduce the characters.
            Details of the characters exploring the place.
            Gradual build up of suspense.
            A seemingly terrifying incident.
Ending: Anti-climax.

Now introduce the terms 'climax' and 'anti-climax'. Explain that 'climax' (from the Greek word for a ladder) refers to the build-up of suspense. An 'anti-climax' ending is one which brings everything down to earth again. Finish by discussing the ending of 'Harwell Hall' and asking the children whether or not they think it is an anti-climax.

Whole-class skills work

Explain that the children will later have the chance to write their own versions of the 'Harwell Hall' story, but first you are going to show them a way to make their descriptions more interesting. Teach them the terms 'simile' and 'metaphor'.
■ A *simile* compares one thing with another by using the words 'like' or 'as', for example 'His muscles were tough as steel'.
■ A *metaphor* compares one thing with another directly, for example 'His muscles of steel'.
    Explain that similes and metaphors are 'figures of speech' which are used to make descriptions more vivid. Figures of speech are used less frequently in prose than in poetry.
    Now give out one copy of the 'Harwell Hall' story (pages 35 and 36) per pair and ask the children to go through the story again, picking out the following features:
■ use of adjectives
■ use of similes and metaphors
■ use of descriptive details (such as details which help to build up the total effect or 'picture').
    The children could mark each feature using a different coloured highlighter pen.

Differentiated group activities

1*: Guided writing to produce a story based on 'Harwell Hall'. The children should use 'Harwell Hall' as a model for structure and style. Focus on writing the beginning of the story, using strong, vivid description. The picture of Harwell Hall on photocopiable page 36 will help to stimulate ideas.
2 & 3: Complete parts A and B of the Reading Comprehension sheet on photocopiable page 37.
4*: Guided writing as for Group 1, but Group 4 should follow the template on photocopiable page 38 closely. The picture of Harwell Hall will provide a valuable starting point for description.

Conclusion

Ask selected children from Groups 1 and 4 to read out their story beginnings, followed by a brief discussion. Is the setting clearly and vividly described? Have they used similes and metaphors? Is the beginning written in an interesting way that makes you want to read on?

Introduction

Ask the children to recap the story of 'Harwell Hall', then re-read together the sections containing dialogue.

Whole-class skills work

Use the passage of dialogue in the second paragraph of 'Harwell Hall' to revise the following:
- how dialogue is set out on separate indented lines for alternate speakers
- the punctuation of dialogue
- writing interesting reporting clauses using synonyms of 'said' and adverbs.

(Hour 4 of the previous unit contains similar coverage of the features of dialogue.)

Differentiated group activities

1: Complete parts A–C of the Reading Comprehension sheet on photocopiable page 37.
2 & 3*: The children write their own versions of a story based on Harwell Hall, using the template on photocopiable page 38. They should be encouraged to expand on sentences and add in extra description.
4: Complete part A of the Reading Comprehension sheet. Part C can be used for discussion if time allows.

Conclusion

Now that all the children have worked on the Reading Comprehension exercise, go over the answers with the whole class.

Introduction

Re-read the story and focus on the part where Jim and Jared explore Harwell Hall. Explain that the author is building up a climax of suspense. In other words, the feeling of suspense gets greater and greater. Discuss with the children how the author does this. For example, he achieves it by describing the strange things Jim and Jared find in some of the rooms and by describing the growing darkness and the noise of the storm – all this leaves the reader expecting something terrifying to happen.

Whole-class skills work

Revise adverbs by asking the children 'What is an adverb?' and inviting their responses. Sum up with the following definition:

An adverb is a word that describes a verb. Many adverbs end in -ly, for example *quietly, slowly, nervously, threateningly* and so on.

Explain that adverbs can be used to add detail and build up certain effects. Ask the children to investigate how the author uses adverbs in the part of the story where Jim and Jared explore Harwell Hall, for example *'anxiously'*, *'slowly'*, *'warily'*, *'urgently'* all help to build up an atmosphere of tension. Now ask the class to suggest some other suitable adverbs that could be substituted for these words.

Differentiated group activities

All groups continue to work on their own versions of the 'Harwell Hall' story, focusing on the middle section at the levels suggested below.
1*: Write the middle section of their stories (see Hour 1) with a particular focus on building up suspense.
2 & 3: Write the middle section of the story using the template as a guide.
4*: Write the middle section of the story following the template closely. The room plan of Harwell Hall on photocopiable page 36 will be helpful in stimulating ideas for this group.

Conclusion

Ask selected children from Groups 2 and 3 to read the middle sections of their stories. The rest of the class should evaluate how effectively the suspense is built up.

Introduction

Read the ending of 'Harwell Hall' and remind the children that this kind of ending is called an 'anti-climax ending'. Discuss why the ending is an anti-climax – from the start of the story, the author builds up an atmosphere of great tension and includes an event that seems terrifying at the time, so that the reader thinks something really frightening has happened. The ending, however, shows that this event was something perfectly ordinary. Briefly discuss the children's opinions of the story's ending.

Whole-class skills work

Revise synonyms by asking the children to give their own explanation of what a synonym is. Sum up with this definition:

Synonyms are words which have the same, or very similar, meaning, for example: 'wet' and 'damp'.

Next, remind the children that synonyms can be used to add interest and variety to their writing. Write these words from 'Harwell Hall' on the board or flip chart:

old	afraid	faint	small
strange	loud	went	said

Ask the children to suggest synonyms for these words, using thesauruses to help. Choose one word and its synonyms as suggested by the children, then use a dictionary to help identify the different shades of meaning.

Differentiated group activities

All groups work on the endings to their stories at the levels suggested below.
1: Write an alternative ending to 'Harwell Hall' so that the build-up of suspense leads to a successful climax. This group should be expected to include vivid description and detail and to focus on maintaining the tension built up so far.
2 & 3*: As for Group 1, but the children can include a less detailed, simpler ending.
4: The children write an alternative short, simple ending to their stories. They should focus on building towards the climax of the ending rather than including detail in their descriptions.

Conclusion

Ask selected children from Groups 1 and 4 to read some of their alternative endings. The rest of the class should evaluate how effective the endings are in terms of building up to a climax of suspense and how successfully the endings flow from the original story.

Introduction

In a question-and-answer session, recap on the main points taught in Hours 1 to 4:
■ What is the structure of the story we have been writing?
■ What have we learned about description?
■ What have we learned about dialogue?
■ What special kind of ending have we tried to use?
Jot down the points made by the children on the board or flip chart.

Whole-class skills work

Explain to the children that they are going to have the chance to redraft their versions of the 'Harwell Hall' story. Give them guidance on the redrafting process as follows:
■ Stage 1: read through the story and look for places where the description can be made more detailed and generally improved.
■ Stage 2: proofread the story for spelling, grammar and punctuation mistakes. Look particularly for the skills covered during the week as listed on the board or flip chart.

Differentiated group activities

1–4*: All groups redraft their story working in pairs. The teacher should work briefly with all the groups, but needs to give particular attention to Group 4 and some of the less able children in Groups 2 and 3. Explain that this is an opportunity for the children to rewrite their story and add in more of their own ideas.

Conclusion

Invite selected children to read out their whole stories.

FURTHER IDEA

Examine the beginnings, middles and endings of several horror stories, focusing particularly on the build-up of suspense. Compare short ghost stories such as *The Signalman* by Charles Dickens with popular longer ghost stories such as those found in the *Goosebumps* series.

HARWELL HALL

The storm was getting worse, so we had no choice but to
take shelter in the old house. 'Harwell Hall' the sign said,
and over it, somebody had written 'Keep Out!', but the
house itself was more forbidding than any sign. Though the
lower doors and windows were boarded up, the upstairs casements
swung in the wind as though a hidden hand was opening and shutting
them. Tiles had slipped off the roof in places, revealing the gaunt roof timbers
like a skeleton beneath flesh. At the entrance to the house stood two menacing
statues like hunched demons waiting to pounce. The house was a rotting
carcass, no longer fit for any human to inhabit.

A gust of driving rain finally made up my mind. "Come on," I shouted,
"let's get inside!"

"No way am I going in that...house of horrors!" replied Jared nervously.

"It's just an old house," I said, "and it beats getting wet!"

I walked cautiously past the 'Harwell Hall – Keep Out!' sign and down the
path to the front entrance. I saw Jared hesitate, then he shouted, "Jim, wait!"
and came running after me.

One kick on the front door, and the rotten wood gave way. Anxiously, we
stepped inside. It was dark, and there were cobwebs everywhere, but nothing
to be afraid of except a faint scurrying sound – mice probably. Slowly, we
moved down the hall and went through an open door into another room. It
looked as though it had once been the lounge. There were some chairs draped
with covers, a small table and a shadeless lamp, which thankfully gave a dim
light when I switched it on. Everything of value had been removed years ago.

"What's that?" asked Jared, suspiciously. He pointed to a small object on
the floor. I picked it up. It was a child's doll, but the strange thing was that
there was no dust on it. Everything else was thick with dust, but the doll was
quite clean. Uneasily, I suggested trying another room, trying not to appear
frightened.

Warily, we walked to the next room which was the library. There were rows
and rows of shelves, mostly empty except for a few dusty, mildewed books
scattered here and there. Suddenly, our eyes were drawn to something else
that seemed strange. Lying on a table was an open book, but the absence of
dust on the pages showed that it had been recently read. The title of the story
book was *Haunted Harwell Hall*. I began to read it, but before I had read more
than a few sentences there was a loud crash, sudden darkness and a weird
howling of wind that sounded like a cry of pain. I dropped the book and we
ran from the library. "Let's try to find some candles – I don't like this
darkness!" wailed Jared.

We tried the kitchen, but there were no candles there – or anywhere else.
It was dark now, and we felt exhausted, so we went upstairs. We found no
beds – only a damp old carpet. The wind wailed and the shutters creaked and
banged wildly as though we were caught in a gale at sea, but somehow I
finally fell asleep.

I was awoken suddenly by a sobbing noise. At first, I thought it was the
wind, but the more I listened, the clearer it seemed to be. I nudged Jared.

"Can you hear that?" I whispered urgently.

"What?" he mumbled, still drunk with sleep.

"It's a sobbing sound...listen!"

Suddenly he froze, and I knew he had heard it too.

"It seems to be coming from the next room," he whispered.

My thoughts began to race: the doll, the book, the story of the haunting of Harwell Hall...we were caught in the middle of some terrifying, ghostly event.

We clung to each other like two people in a shipwreck and hardly dared to move all night long. We fell asleep without knowing it, and awoke cold and stiff the next morning, wondering if it had all been a dream.

"Dream or not, let's get out of here!" I said, shivering.

We picked ourselves up and started for the door. It was then that we heard the footsteps. Tiny child's footsteps – and the sobbing. We stopped in our tracks. The door handle turned. We froze, filled with terror.

And in walked a little girl – not a ghost, but an ordinary live little girl of about six years old. She looked just as frightened as we were.

"Will you take me home?" she sobbed. "I got lost in the storm and had to stay here all night, all by myself!"

Jared and I looked at each other feeling rather stupid. It's funny what darkness and a few cobwebs can do to your common sense!

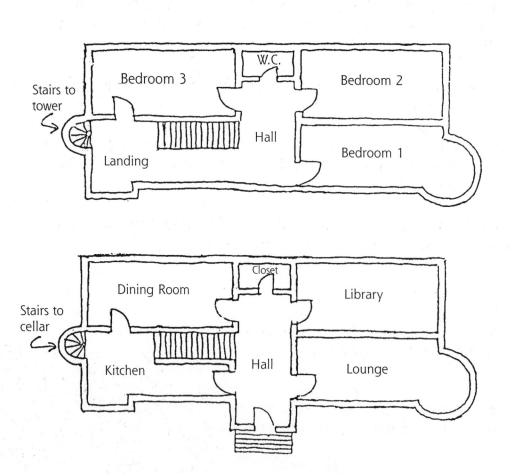

READING COMPREHENSION

PART A

■ Why did Jim and Jared take shelter in Harwell Hall, even though it looked so frightening?

■ What do we learn about the different personalities of Jared and Jim? Write a few sentences to describe each character.

■ What did they find in the hall, in the lounge and in the library?

■ What happened in the middle of the night? What did they think had caused it?

■ What did it turn out to be the next day?

■ Explain 'anti-climax ending' by referring to the way this story ended.

PART B

■ Read the description of Harwell Hall and explain why it is so effective. Refer to use of adjectives, similes and metaphors and what effect these have.

■ Which details does the writer focus on to develop the general description of Harwell Hall?

■ Which details does the writer focus on when describing the inside of the house? Two of these details were used later in the story. What were they used for?

■ Find four reporting clauses with adverbs. Write them out again using different adverbs which still make sense.

PART C

■ If you were caught in a storm outside a house like Harwell Hall, what would you do?

■ Have you ever experienced a real life anti-climax? Describe what happened.

STORY TEMPLATE

Beginning

The storm was getting worse, so we had to
take shelter in the old house. It was a...

Describe Harwell Hall in your own words. Make your description as
detailed, vivid and interesting as you can.

*A gust of driving rain finally made up my mind. "Come on," I shouted,
"let's get inside!"*

Write a short conversation between two characters who are friends
(make up names for them). Think about how you set out the
dialogue.

Middle

One kick on the front door, and the rotten wood gave way.

Describe some rooms inside the house and some objects the two
characters find there. Describe how they find a place to sleep when it
gets dark.

I was awoken by...

Describe a sight or sound that seems terrifying at the time, but turns
out to be something ordinary the next day. Describe the characters'
fear and what they say and do about it.

End

Somehow we got through the night...

Explain how the characters investigate the sight or sound of the
previous night and find something quite ordinary. End with the
phrase: "But it was only a..."

JOHN CABOT

OBJECTIVES

UNIT	SPELLING/VOCABULARY	GRAMMAR/PUNCTUATION	COMPREHENSION/ COMPOSITION
READING NON-FICTION Historical recount: 'John Cabot'.	Explore technical vocabulary used to describe Cabot's ship. Explore vocabulary quoted from original sources.	Recognize the past tense. Understand the 1st-person form and match verbs accordingly. Understand use of punctuation, in particular, commas.	Read a recount and identify features of recounted text. Understand purpose of note-taking.

ORGANIZATION (3 HOURS)

	INTRODUCTION	WHOLE-CLASS SKILLS WORK	DIFFERENTIATED GROUP ACTIVITIES	CONCLUSION
HOUR 1	Read the 'John Cabot' recount on photocopiable pages 42 and 43. Discuss content and genre, identifying features of recount texts. Explain difficult vocabulary.	Take notes from re-reading of text for the purpose of sequencing information. Extend work on 1st and	1–4*: All groups resequence the appropriate version of the photocopiable recount (prepared by the teacher) by cutting and pasting.	Re-read the original 'John Cabot' recount while the children check their work. Conclude by emphasizing the chronological nature of historical accounts.
HOUR 2	Re-read 'John Cabot'. Identify Cabot's route using the map. Identify the parts of Cabot's ship using the picture.	3rd-person forms. Use 3rd-person recount text to write 1st-person log/diary.	1*: Reading Comprehension – all parts. 2 & 3: Write entries for Cabot's log. 4*: Reading Comprehension, parts A & C.	Pupils from Groups 2 & 3 read out entries from Cabot's log. Discuss the differences between recount and diary writing. Evaluate pupils' use of technical vocabulary.
HOUR 3	Pupils read aloud sections of the 'John Cabot' account. Discuss what punctuation is and what purpose it serves.	Explore the various uses of commas.	1: Write entries for Cabot's log. 2 & 3*: Reading Comprehension, parts A–C. 4: Write entries for Cabot's log.	Go over Reading Comprehension answers. Sum up key features of historical recounts.

RESOURCES

Photocopiable pages 42 (John Cabot: 1), 43 (John Cabot: 2) and 44 (Reading Comprehension), paper and pencils for note-taking, blank A4 paper, scissors, glue, a world map and a large map of Newfoundland, a large desk diary.

PREPARATION

Prepare three versions of 'John Cabot: 1' (photocopiable page 42) for resequencing as follows:

■ Version 1: cut up the paragraphs, shuffle them and stick them down in random order on another sheet of paper. Make enough copies for one per child in Group 4.
■ Version 2: as for Version 1, but in addition, cut paragraphs 2, 3 and 6 into two

sections each. Make enough copies of this sheet for each child in Groups 2 and 3.
■ Version 3: cut all paragraphs into two sections each. Photocopy enough of these sheets for each child in Group 1.

Provide one set of scissors and glue per pair of children. In addition make a set of all photocopiable pages, allowing one between two children.

Introduction

Discuss briefly and simply the historical background to the 'John Cabot' account on photocopiable page 42, perhaps using the details in the first two paragraphs. Then read the full text, asking the children to listen carefully to what the piece is about and what information is given. (The children should not have texts to follow at this stage.)

Discuss the information provided in the text and the kind of writing it is. Establish that it is a *recount* and identify what the features of recount texts are, such as the inclusion of an introduction to orientate or guide the reader; the use of chronological sequence, temporal connectives and the past tense; the text is action-focused and so on. Explain some of the difficult vocabulary, particularly archaic language such as *'toneles burthen'* and technical maritime words such as *'caravels'* (a small, light, fast ship used by Columbus on his voyages), *'lateen'* (a triangular sail) and *'mizzen'* (the middle mast).

Whole-class skills work

Re-read the 'John Cabot' text and ask the children to take careful notes of the main features of the account and the chronological order of events. Explain that they will be using their notes to resequence the text in their group activities, so they must be accurate and as helpful as possible. Discuss what kind of notes would be most appropriate for this particular purpose, such as notes that highlight the chronological sequence, including important dates and cause/effect relationships.

Differentiated group activities

1–4*: All groups resequence the appropriate version of the 'John Cabot' account by cutting and pasting the paragraphs on their individual sheets. Group 1 should use Version 3, Groups 2 and 3 should use Version 2, and Group 4 should use Version 1 (see under 'Preparation').

Conclusion

Re-read the original account while the children check their work. How accurate was their cut-and-pasted version? Conclude by pointing out that this exercise was only possible because of the chronological nature of historical accounts.

Introduction

Give out copies of the 'John Cabot' text and illustrations (photocopiable pages 42 and 43). Re-read the text with the children following their own copies. Draw attention to the map and illustrations and help the children to relate these to the text. Use a large world map and map of Newfoundland to explain Cabot's route and point out named places from the account if necessary. Differences from Columbus' route can also be pointed out. Discuss the features of Cabot's ship using vocabulary from the account together with the picture.

Whole-class skills work

Discuss the idea of keeping a personal log or diary, and show the children the example of a desk diary. How might a log or diary entry differ from a recounted text? (It would be written in the 1st person, and may sometimes use the present tense rather than the past.) Discuss the sort of language that might be used and the style the entries could take, for example notes with little sketches, personal feelings and observations.

Differentiated group activities

1*: Complete all parts of the Reading Comprehension sheet on page 44.
2 & 3: Write entries for John Cabot's personal log of the voyage. Ask the children to select some important moments from the voyage and to elaborate the account from a personal point of view adding more imaginative detail.
4*: Complete parts A and C of the Reading Comprehension sheet.

Conclusion

Select children from Groups 2 and 3 to read out their entries from Cabot's 'personal log'. Discuss the differences between the impersonal historical account in the photocopiable and the more personal diary-style log. Evaluate how the children have used the technical vocabulary from the original text in their logs.

Introduction

Select children, in turn, to read aloud paragraphs or parts of paragraphs from the 'John Cabot' recount. Ask them to pay particular attention to the punctuation as they read. Discuss what punctuation is (a collection of marks and signs which break up words, phrases and sentences) and what purpose it serves (to help make meaning clearer).

Whole-class skills work

Discuss how commas are used, such as to separate:
■ words or groups of words in a list (for example *We saw lions, tigers and gorillas. We went to the zoo, played in the park and ate dinner in a restaurant.*)
■ two or more sentences which are joined together by words like 'but' or 'so' (for example *We wanted to buy a drink, but we didn't have any money.*)
■ a subordinate clause from a main clause in a sentence, particularly when the subordinate clause comes first (for example *When we left the zoo, we were very thirsty.*)
■ words or phrases that could be omitted from the sentence without changing its general meaning (for example *The animals, in most cases, were very well behaved.*)
■ the name of a person addressed in the sentence from the rest of it (for example *"Sasha, have you asked your mother?"*).
   Now look at the Cabot text and identify the various uses of commas.

Differentiated group activities

1: Write entries for Cabot's personal log (see Hour 2).
2 & 3*: Complete parts A–C of the Reading Comprehension sheet (page 44).
4: Write entries for Cabot's personal log. Suggest three entries for this group:
■ Leaving Bristol.
■ Sighting Newfoundland.
■ Looking around at Griquet harbour.

Conclusion

Discuss the children's answers to the Reading Comprehension sheet. Finish by summing up the key points of historical recounts:
■ They are chronological.
■ They are written in the past tense.
■ They are written in narrative (storytelling) style.
■ They are written in an impersonal voice.

FURTHER IDEA

Write a series of log entries which tell the story of Cabot's second voyage in which he hoped to reach Japan.

JOHN CABOT: 1

John Cabot (c.1451–1499) was an Italian navigator and explorer. He was born in Genoa but, as a young boy, moved to Venice and later came to live in Bristol in England.

Cabot had developed a theory that Asia might be reached by sailing westwards. He was therefore greatly impressed by reports of the discoveries of Christopher Columbus, who had set out in 1492 sailing westwards in the hope of finding a new route to India and the rich spice lands of the east. (In fact, what Columbus had found was not India, but America which he mistakenly named the West Indies.) Spices, especially pepper, cloves and nutmeg, were very expensive household necessities that were used to disguise the flavour of old, decaying meat. It occurred to Cabot that, because England was at the end of the spice trade route, the English would also be interested in finding a route to the Indies. So he persuaded the King, Henry VII, to finance an expedition. On 5 March 1496, Henry VII granted letters-patent to 'our well beloved John Cabote, citizen of Venice'. This granted Cabot the sole right to trade with any lands he discovered, so long as he claimed them in the name of the King of England.

On 2 May 1497, John Cabot set sail westward from Bristol to cross the Atlantic on the *Mathew* with a crew of only 18 men. This was a small ship of 50 'toneles burthen' which meant it could carry 50 tuns (or barrels) of wine. It probably had the same sail plan as Columbus caravels – a square sail on the fore and main masts, a lateen (triangular) on the mizzen (middle) mast, and possibly a square main topsail (see picture). He steered a north-west course and, seven weeks later at 5.00 am on 24 June, after a rough voyage, he sighted the rugged land mass of Newfoundland.

A big island rose out of the sea, 24 kilometres to the north which Cabot named Belle Isle. The *Mathew* was only eight kilometres from L'Anse aux Meadows where the Viking explorer, Lief Ericsson, had tried to establish a colony in 1001. It is a fascinating coincidence that the first two Europeans to discover North America hit the coast within a few kilometres of each other.

Cabot's way into the Strait of Belle Isle was probably blocked by ice, so he turned south in search of a harbour, and probably landed at Griquet harbour, a few kilometres south of Cape Degrat, where he took formal possession of the land for King Henry VII.

When Cabot went ashore, he saw no people, but observed signs of life such as snares and fishing nets, and a stick painted red and pierced at both ends. He also noticed dung and guessed that the natives kept cattle. After a brief survey, Cabot left and did not return. He probably wanted to avoid any hostile natives, and the area was also infested with mosquitoes which would have made life there very uncomfortable. However, because the weather was fine and warm, Cabot believed that he had really reached China (known as Cathay at this time).

Cabot was forced to return home by lack of supplies. He left the New World on 20 July, but on his way he sailed along the coastline from Saint-Pierre to Cape Breton, and found it to be a rich country, worthy of settlement. He saw tall trees suitable for masts, and what appeared to be cultivated fields. He also found that the seas were rich in cod.

Cabot reached Brittany on 4 August and landed in Bristol on 6 August. As soon as he had landed, John Cabot travelled to London to see the king and claim his reward. The king gave him £10. Despite Cabot's important discovery of the rich fishing grounds, King Henry and the Bristol merchants were disappointed by the results of his expedition; he had found no gold, silks or spices. But they were attracted by the mistaken belief that China and the riches of the Far East were only a few weeks' journey away.

Therefore, they planned a second voyage at once in which Cabot hoped he would reach Japan (then known as Cipangu). In May 1498, Cabot set off with five ships and 200 men, but was never heard of again. However, John Cabot will be remembered for his first voyage which laid the foundation for England's colonization of North America.

JOHN CABOT: 2

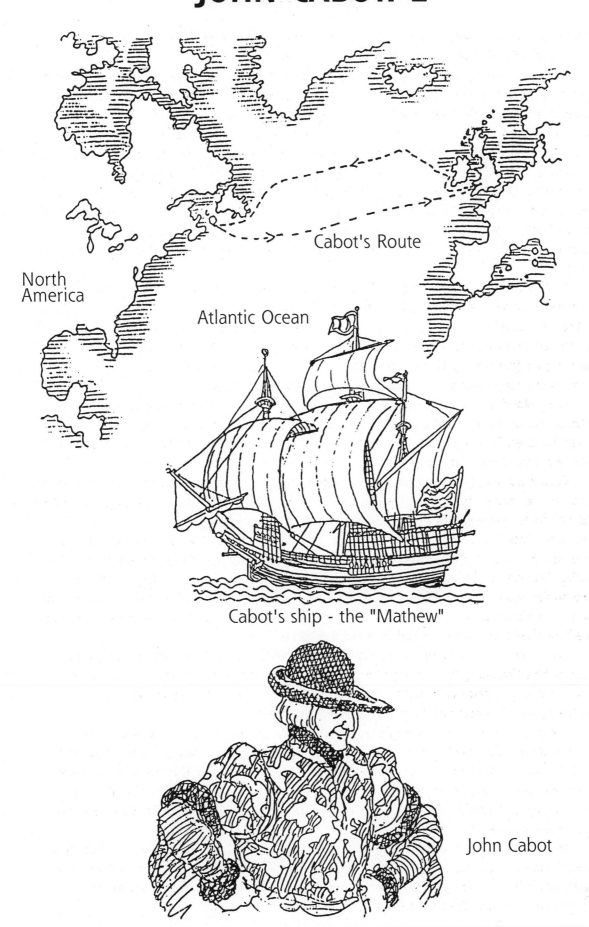

North America

Cabot's Route

Atlantic Ocean

Cabot's ship - the "Mathew"

John Cabot

READING COMPREHENSION

PART A
■ Why did John Cabot go to King Henry VII of England to back his planned voyage?

■ What are spices and why were they so important?

■ Work out how many days Cabot's initial outward voyage took.

■ Find Belle Isle on the map, and the Strait of Belle Isle. Why did Cabot not sail through the Strait of Belle Isle?

■ What evidence did Cabot find that people already lived on Newfoundland?

■ Why did Cabot not stay longer at Griquet harbour?

■ What was Cabot's overall impression of the country?

PART B
■ Work out how many days Cabot's return journey took. Which journey was the fastest? Can you suggest a reason for this?

■ What did Cabot think he had found?

■ What happened on Cabot's second voyage?

■ Write a glossary of any difficult words and nautical terms used in the text.

■ Find five verbs. What tense is used? Write out one of the verbs in full in both the past and present tenses.

PART C
■ Look at the reconstruction of the *Mathew*. Write a descriptive paragraph about the ship using information from the text and the picture.

■ Look at the illustration of Cape Degrat. How would you describe it? Would you think it was worth settling there?

PART D
■ What do you think John Cabot thought about his £10 reward?

■ No one knows what happened to Cabot on his second voyage. What sort of things could have gone wrong?

■ What was John Cabot's contribution to history?

THE TITANIC

OBJECTIVES

UNIT	SPELLING/VOCABULARY	GRAMMAR/PUNCTUATION	COMPREHENSION/ COMPOSITION
WRITING NON-FICTION Historical recount: The *Titanic*.	Develop and use vocabulary from reading and other media forms.	Write in paragraphs. Extend work on verbs: use of past and present continuous tenses and auxiliary verbs.	Read a number of historical sources as models for research and writing. Identify features of recount texts. Make notes and use for writing.

ORGANIZATION (3 HOURS)

	INTRODUCTION	WHOLE-CLASS SKILLS WORK	DIFFERENTIATED GROUP ACTIVITIES	CONCLUSION
HOUR 1	Establish what the children already know about the *Titanic* disaster. Read newspaper cuttings and other information on photocopiable pages 49 and 50.	Revise features of recount. Identify different types of information sources. Model note-making.	1*: Use sources to write a historical recount. 2 & 3: Write diary entries from the point of view of a passenger. 4*: Use photocopiable sources to write a historical recount.	Selected pupils from all groups share their writing. Discuss the differences.
HOUR 2	Re-read the newspaper cuttings on photocopiable page 49.	Explore and highlight the use of the past and present continuous tenses and the use of auxiliary verbs.	1: Write diary entries from the point of view of a passenger. 2 & 3*: Use photocopiable sources to write a historical recount. 4: Write diary entries from the point of view of a passenger.	As above. Recap on the features of recount texts.
HOUR 3	Show a clip from one of the *Titanic* films. Discuss books and films about the *Titanic*.	Develop vocabulary related to camera techniques in films. Relate to written texts. Compare film (fiction) with resources on photocopiable sheets (facts).	1–4*: Choose from various writing activities based on the photocopiable and other *Titanic* information.	Share some examples of different forms of writing based on the *Titanic* information and discuss the differences.

RESOURCES

Photocopiable pages 49 (*Titanic* Newspaper Cuttings) and 50 (The *Titanic*: 'Some Facts' and 'The Last Hours'), board or flip chart, OHP and acetate (optional), coloured felt-tipped pens, writing materials, a video clip from one of the *Titanic* films or documentaries, a video recorder and TV, a collection of books about the *Titanic* (optional, but see Introduction to Hour 3 for suggested titles).

PREPARATION

Make enough copies of photocopiable pages 49 and 50 for one between two children. If possible, also prepare the sheets as OHTs or enlarge to at least A3 size.

HOUR 1

Introduction
Establish, through a question-and-answer session, what the children already know about

the *Titanic* and from where they learned what they know. Make a list of the sources on the board or flip chart and discuss the similarities and differences of the sources in terms of content, format and purpose. Distribute and display photocopiable pages 49 and 50. Read the items relating to the sinking of the *Titanic*.

Whole-class skills work

Review the features of recount texts:
■ inclusion of an introduction to orientate reader
■ the use of chronological order
■ the use of the past tense and temporal connectives
■ narrative text, action-focused in style (for example tells a story, but one based on facts).

Review the information sources on photocopiable pages 49 and 50, identifying the kind of writing in each case and establishing how the information they provide might be useful in writing an historical recount of the *Titanic* disaster. Some ideas are listed below.
■ 'Unsinkable' is a *newspaper report* of a White Star Line spokesperson's *persuasive argument* for why the *Titanic* was thought to be unsinkable at the time. It is a useful source material for a recount, but all the detail is not needed. Pick out the main points.
■ '*Titanic* Disaster' is a *newspaper report* written just after the event to provide brief, factual information. It is useful, but not detailed enough.
■ '*Titanic*: Some Facts' is a *list of facts.* They could usefully be incorporated into a recount, but they are not a 'primary' source and, therefore, need checking.
■ 'The Last Hours', based on the latest research, is an *account* of what happened, but it is written in the present tense. It is useful source material for a recount, but all the detail is not needed. Pick out the main points.

Finally, using the 'Unsinkable' news cutting, model the process of note-making, showing how to focus on and record only the main relevant points.

Differentiated group activities

Briefly explain the tasks the children will undertake in the group work in Hours 1 and 2. They will be writing two different pieces (an historical recount and a diary extract) and for both will be using notes they have made from the information on photocopiable pages 49 and 50.

For the recount:
■ Decide which details can be left out. Make notes from the sources. Put the events in order. Decide where to fit in some of the facts.
■ Rewrite everything using the standard features of recount texts (see above).
■ Suggest that the historical recount be between one and two sides of A4.
■ Suggest that the children choose one or two of the illustrations to go with the published account.

For the diary entry:
■ Write diary entries from the point of view of a passenger on the *Titanic*.
Bring out the contrast between the luxury at the beginning of the voyage and the horror of the sinking.
■ Make use of the timings in 'The Last Hours' notes.
■ Go beyond the facts to suggest emotions and so on.
1*: Write an historical recount. This group should aim to write no more than two sides of A4, as one of the key skills is selection of detail. They should base their account on all the information on the photocopiable sheets.
2 & 3: Write diary entries.
4*: Write an historical recount. This group could aim for one side of A4 and base their account on '*Titanic* Disaster' and 'The Last Hours'. Encourage the children to cut down the 'The Last Hours' by deleting sections before they begin to draft their article. Emphasize that all verbs need to be in the past tense.

Conclusion

Select some children from Groups 1 and 4 to read out their historical recounts and some from Groups 2 and 3 to read out their diary entries. Discuss the differences between the two types of text.

Introduction

Re-read the two newspaper cuttings on photocopiable page 49.

Whole-class skills work

Investigate the use of verb tenses in the two newspaper cuttings as follows:
■ Use three different coloured highlighters for past, present and future tenses and mark each verb in the appropriate colour.
■ Use a fourth colour to mark auxiliary verbs. Explain that auxiliary verbs are 'helper' verbs. They help to form different kinds of past, present and future tenses. Look out particularly for 'is' + main verb in the present tense, 'was' + main verb, and 'has' + main verb in the past tense, and 'will' or 'shall' + main verb in the future tense.
■ Explain why a particular tense is used at a particular point. The first cutting is written entirely in the present tense because it explains the safety features of the *Titanic* at the time she was built – the present. Most of the second article is in the past tense because it is describing what has already happened. However, paragraph 3 is in the present tense because it reports a wireless message with up-to-date (in the present) news. The last section is in the present tense because it is a statement that the White Star Line are making at the time the article is being written.

Differentiated group activities

1: Write diary entries from the point of view of a passenger on the *Titanic* (see Hour 1).
2 & 3*: Write a historical recount using all the information on the resource sheets and aiming at one to two sides of A4 in length.
4: Write diary entries from the point of view of a passenger. Help the children by suggesting that they read a small section of the photocopiable text, imagine what the situation would be like, then write a short diary entry without looking at the text again. This will help to avoid over-reliance on the photocopiable texts.

Conclusion

Select some children from Groups 2 and 3 to read out their historical recounts and some from Groups 1 and 4 to read out their diaries. Discuss the differences and recap on the features of recount.

Introduction

Show a video clip from one of the films or documentaries about the *Titanic*. Discuss whether the film glamorizes the disaster in any way. Does it distort the facts? Compare with the 'factual' sources on the photocopiable sheets. In addition (or if a video clip is not available) extend the discussion using the following ideas:
■ The sinking of the *Titanic* has fascinated people since the day it happened because of the contrast between the magnificence of the ship and the horror of its end, and also because it shows man's arrogance – revealed by calling the ship 'unsinkable' – brought low by the forces of nature.
■ One of the greatest poets of the time, Thomas Hardy, wrote a poem about it, and there have since been several books and films. The most well-known book is *A Night to Remember* by Walter Lord (1955, Bantam Books) which was made into a black and white film. See also *Exploring the Titanic* by Robert D Ballard (1993, Scholastic). Interest in the *Titanic* was revived when the wreck was found and extensively photographed in 1985. This culminated in the 1998 film 'Titanic'.
■ Many other ships have sunk with great loss of life, for example the *Lusitania* disaster had many similarities with the *Titanic* and almost as many people died. Why are we not equally interested in this?
(The *Lusitania* was a British passenger liner. It was torpedoed by a German submarine on 7 May 1915, with the loss of 1198 lives.)

Whole-class skills work

Introduce the children to the vocabulary of camera techniques by teaching these terms:
■ **Close-up**: a shot showing head and shoulders of actors. This is useful for dialogue, or showing emotions.
■ **Mid-shot**: this will show a group of figures or a small scene such as a room. It is the most useful shot of all, and is used for dialogue, action and so on.
■ **Long shot**: sometimes called an 'establishing shot'. This gives the whole picture, for

example it can show the whole of the *Titanic*, so that the audience knows that the next scene, a mid-shot, is on board the *Titanic*.

■ **Pan**: the camera swings horizontally from one side of a scene to another, often following the action.

■ **Tilt**: the camera swings up or down the scene.

■ **Zoom**: moving in to a close-up, or out from a close-up to a mid- or long-shot.

Run a short sequence of the film or video again, and ask the children to a) identify the different types of shots, and b) to say why the director chose them, and what effect they have. Discuss whether these techniques have parallels in writing – for example, the close-up shot is like a detailed description of a character's physical appearance; the long shot is like a general description of a setting and so on.

Differentiated group activities

1–4*: Allow the children to choose one of the following activities. Note that they are listed in approximate order of difficulty to help you guide the children into appropriately challenging choices:

■ Write your own story based on the *Titanic* disaster. Try to find a different angle, for example the *Titanic* is somehow saved.

■ Imagine you are a *Titanic* survivor in old age. Write the chapter of your autobiography that deals with the *Titanic* incident.

■ Write your own newspaper front page using the information on the photocopiable pages.

■ Design a storyboard for another film on the *Titanic*. Try to find a different angle.

■ Design a poster advertising the *Titanic's* maiden voyage.

Conclusion

Try to arrange for one example of each of the different forms covered in the group activities to be read out or shown. Discuss how they enable the disaster to be seen differently.

FOLLOW-UP (1 HOUR)

See page 51 which provides a grid plan for a 1-hour follow-up unit based on a simplified version of 'The Convergence of the Twain', a poem by Thomas Hardy about the *Titanic*. The poem is on photocopiable page 52.

TITANIC NEWSPAPER CUTTINGS

'UNSINKABLE'

Mr Franklin, vice-president of the International Mercantile Marine, which controls the White Star Line, issued in New York yesterday the following statement:-

'We are perfectly satisfied that the *Titanic* is unsinkable. We are absolutely certain that she is able to withstand any damage. She may be down by the head, but would float indefinitely in that condition.'

The *Titanic* is described as unsinkable owing to the strength with which she is constructed and to the fact that she is fitted with fifteen transverse water-tight bulkheads. This means that the vessel is divided into fifteen separate compartments, each of which can be rendered water-tight at a moment's notice by the closing of the water-tight doors.

Any two of these compartments can be simultaneously flooded without in any way imperilling the safety of the ship.

The largest water-tight compartments are those containing the reciprocating and turbine engines, which are 69 feet and 57 feet long respectively. The foremost compartments, which would be the first to be flooded in the event of a collision, are smaller.

These transverse bulkheads extend from the ship's double bottom to the upper deck in the fore part of the ship, so even were the bow to sink to the level of the upper deck (beneath the promenade decks) there would be no danger of the after compartments being flooded. The only real danger is that the bulkheads should collapse owing to the pressure of the water or that serious leakage should be caused all over the ship owing to the shock of the collisions having displaced numerous bolts and rivets.

The *Titanic* is especially strongly built, owing to her size and great length. The doors in the foremost bulkheads would in the natural course be kept closed when at sea. Each door is held in the open position by a friction clutch, which can be instantly released by means of a powerful electric magnet controlled from the captain's bridge, so that the captain can instantly close all the doors by simply moving an electric switch.

As a further precaution, floats are provided beneath the floor level, which, in the event of water entering the compartment, automatically lift and thereby close the doors.

TITANIC DISASTER

SUNK AFTER COLLISION WITH AN ICEBERG

LOSS OF LIFE

WIRELESS CALLS FOR AID

The White Star liner *Titanic* (46 382 tons), which left Southampton on Wednesday on her maiden voyage to New York, came into collision with an iceberg at a point about 41.46 North and 50.14 West off the North American coast at 10.25pm on Sunday night American time. The vessel was badly damaged and wireless messages were sent out for help. A number of other liners in the neighbourhood hastened to her assistance, but she sank yesterday morning as will be seen from the following message received as we are going to press:-

NEW YORK, April 13, 3.45pm
The following despatch has been received here from Cape Raes:

'The steamer *Olympic* reports that the steamer *Carpathia* reached the *Titanic*'s position at daybreak, but found boats and wreckage only. She reported that the *Titanic* foundered. About 2.20am in lat. 41deg. 10min. long. 50deg. 14min.'

The message adds: 'All the Titanic's boats are accounted for. About 675 souls have been saved of the crew and passengers. The latter are nearly all women and children. The Leyland liner *California* is remaining and searching the vicinity of the disaster. The *Carpathia* is returning to New York with the survivors.' – *Reuter.*

NEW YORK, April 13, 8.20pm
The following statement has been given out by the White Star officials:-

'Captain Haddock of the *Olympic*, sends a wireless message that the *Titanic* sank at 2.20am on Monday after all the passengers and crew had been lowered into lifeboats and transferred to the *Virginian*. The steamer *Carpathia*, with several hundred passengers from the *Titanic*, is now on her way to New York.' – *Reuter.*

The White Star officials now admit that many lives have been lost. – *Reuter.*

THE *TITANIC*

SOME FACTS

■ Launched on 31 May, 1911, the *Titanic* cost £1,500,000, and was said to be the last word in luxury. It was also said to be 'unsinkable' because it had a double-bottomed hull and 16 watertight compartments and could still float with any four flooded.

■ The *Titanic* had a top speed of 23 knots.

■ The *Titanic* was the first ocean liner to have a swimming pool and gym.

■ The liner was 882ft (269 metres) long. If placed upright, the *Titanic* would be as high as an 11-storey building.

■ The liner had 20 lifeboats – enough for 1,178 people.

■ On her maiden voyage, which began on 10 April 1912, she carried 3,511 passengers and crew.

■ The iceberg caused a 295ft (90 metres) gash in its hull which ripped open five of the watertight compartments.

■ The *Titanic* sank two and a half hours later, with the loss of 1,513 lives.

■ The wreckage of the *Titanic* was found in 1985, about 497 miles (800 kilometres) south-west of Newfoundland.

THE *TITANIC* – **THE LAST HOURS**

11.40pm: The *Titanic* is moving at 22½ knots. Suddenly, lookouts see an iceberg dead ahead about 500 yards (457 metres) away. They immediately sound the warning bell and telephone down to the bridge: 'Iceberg right ahead'. Murdoch calls 'hard-a-starboard' to helmsman and orders 'full astern'. The helmsman spins wheel as far as it will go and after several seconds the *Titanic* begins to veer to port, but the iceberg strikes starboard side of the ship.

12.00am: Water pours into number 1, 2, and 3 compartments, and boiler room no. 6. Thomas Andrews, the ship's designer, calculates the ship can stay afloat from one to one-and-a-half hours only, because if more than four compartments are flooded, the water will spill into the next compartment and the next and so on. The *Titanic's* bow begins to sink. Captain Smith orders the ship's wireless operator to send out a distress call. The *Titanic's* estimated position is: 41° 46' N, 50° 14' W.

12.25am: The order is given to start loading the lifeboats with women and children. The *Carpathia*, about 58 miles (93 kilometres) away, receives the distress call and immediately heads full speed to rescue.

1.15am: The water reaches the *Titanic's* name on the bow and she now lists to port. The tilt of the deck grows steeper. The lifeboats, which at first left half-empty, are now being more fully loaded.

2.17am: Captain Smith tells crew members, 'It's every man for himself', and returns to the bridge to await the end. The *Titanic's* bow goes underwater. The ship's band stops playing. Many passengers and crew jump overboard. The *Titanic's* forward funnel collapses crushing a number of swimming passengers.

2.18am: A huge roar is heard as all moveable objects inside the *Titanic* crash toward the submerged bow. The ship's lights blink once and then go out.
Many survivors witness the ship break in two.
  The bow half sinks.

2.20am: The *Titanic's* broken-off stern section settles back into the water, righting itself for a few moments. Slowly, it fills with water and again tilts its stern high into the air before slowly sinking into the sea.
  Over 1,500 lives are lost in the 'greatest maritime disaster in history'.

THE CONVERGENCE OF THE TWAIN: FOLLOW-UP

OBJECTIVES

UNIT	SPELLING/VOCABULARY	GRAMMAR/ PUNCTUATION	COMPREHENSION/ COMPOSITION
READING POETRY 'The Convergence of the Twain' by Thomas Hardy.	Develop vocabulary from reading.	Explore the grammar of poetry.	Read a poem by a significant poet and identify what is distinctive about content and format.

ORGANIZATION (1 HOUR)

	INTRODUCTION	WHOLE-CLASS SKILLS WORK	DIFFERENTIATED GROUP ACTIVITIES	CONCLUSION
HOUR 1	Read and re-read the Hardy poem on photocopiable page 52. Discuss the meaning of each verse.	Analyse the verse form and rhyme scheme. Discuss any difficult vocabulary.	1–4*: Using two different coloured highlighter pens, highlight everything in the poem that describes the beauty and majesty of the *Titanic* in one colour and everything that describes the horror of her fate in another.	Discuss the contrast in the poem which the marking up has brought out. If video clips from the *Titanic* are available, show how the director has used shots of the wreck cross-faded to shots of the *Titanic* in its glory, to achieve the same effect.

THE CONVERGENCE OF THE TWAIN

Lines on the Loss of the *Titanic*

In the solitude of the sea
Away from human vanity
And the pride that planned her, lies she.

Steel chambers which were the pyres
Of her mighty fires
Are turned by tides to rhythmic lyres.

Over the mirrors which
Reflected once the rich
Slimy sea worms crawl and twitch.

Jewels that were designed
To please a rich girl's mind
Lie in the mud, their sparkles black and blind.

Strange fishes swimming near
Gaze at the gilded gear
And ask, why all these riches here?

* * *

As the smart ship grew
In size and grace and hue
In silent distance grew the iceberg too.

So different were they
That no mortal thought this way
That they would meet one day

Or that the way they went
By tides and currents sent
Made them two halves of one great event.

Till the Spinner of the Years
Said 'Now', and each one hears.
The meeting comes and jars two hemispheres.

*Simplified version of Thomas Hardy's
'The Convergence of the Twain'*

ESTABLISHING ROOTS

OBJECTIVES

UNIT	SPELLING/VOCABULARY	GRAMMAR/PUNCTUATION	COMPREHENSION/ COMPOSITION
REFERENCE AND RESEARCH SKILLS Dictionary work: Identify roots, derivation, spelling patterns.	Widen vocabulary and develop awareness of spelling patterns. Identify word roots and name prefixes and suffixes in specific examples.	Sort words with the same root and use them appropriately in sentences.	Compile own collections of words with the same root.

ORGANIZATION (1 HOUR)

	INTRODUCTION	WHOLE-CLASS SKILLS WORK	DIFFERENTIATED GROUP ACTIVITIES	CONCLUSION
HOUR 1	Discuss origin of the root word *cent*.	Look at words derived from *cent* and distinguish these from words derived from *centre*. Consider the position of the root within different words. Revise the terms *prefix* and *suffix*.	1*: Complete parts A–C of the photocopiable sheet. 2 & 3: Complete parts A & B of the photocopiable sheet. 4*: Complete parts A & B of the photocopiable sheet with teacher support.	Representatives from each group share their work with the class.

RESOURCES

Board or flip chart, conventional dictionaries, at least one etymological dictionary, photocopiable page 55 (Exploring Root Words), writing materials.

PREPARATION

Make enough copies of photocopiable page 55 for one between two. Write the root word *cent* on the flip chart or board, together with the following words derived from it:

century	centurion	centimetre	centilitre
centigrade	centenary	centenarian	centipede

Introduction

Introduce the idea that there are groups or 'families' of words derived from the same root word. Tell the children that a 'root word' is a word to which we can add beginnings (prefixes) or endings (suffixes) to make other words. For example, in the words 'unclear', 'clearly' and 'cleared', the root word is *clear*. Explain that *cent* is a root word. Ask the class what they think *cent* on its own means (hundredth of a dollar; 'one hundred' in French). Tell the children that the word *cent* originally came from the Latin word *centum*, meaning 'hundred'. When the Romans conquered Britain and Gaul (France), many Latin words passed into the English and French languages and formed the roots of words that are in common use today.

Whole-class skills work

Read out the prepared list of words (see 'Preparation') that have sprung from the root *cent*. Ask the children to tell you what each of these words means. If they don't know, ask them to look up the meanings in their dictionaries. Point out the significance of the 'hundred' in each definition. Ask whether they think that *cent* always means 'one hundred' or 'hundredth' when it is part of a word. For example, does the *cent* in the word 'centre' mean 'one hundred'?

Explain that *centre* is itself a root word (from the Latin *centrum*, meaning the centre of a circle). Can the children discover any words that are formed from this root? Scribe appropriate examples on the chart or board, such as *central, centred, centring, centric, concentric, centrifugal*.

Talk about the way in which the -e ending of the root word is omitted in nearly all the words in this list. Who can spot the one exception ('centred')? Discuss and scribe other examples of words in which the root word's ending is slightly altered (for example *write – written, writing; please – pleasant, unpleasant; happy – happiness, happily, unhappily* and so on).

Now talk about the position of root words in the words that are formed from them. Who has noticed that in the examples 'concentric' and 'unpleasant', the root is in the middle of the word? Ask individuals to come out and underline the roots of these words. Emphasize that the root of a word may be found at the beginning, in the middle, or at the end of it. In 'unhappy', for example, it is at the end.

Remind the class that the part of a word that goes before the base or root word is called a 'prefix' and the part that goes after it is called a 'suffix'. Test the children orally to check that these concepts have been grasped. Ask individuals to point out the roots, prefixes and suffixes in quickly-scribed examples such as *unfair, fairly, unfairness; printer, reprint, misprinted.*

Differentiated group activities

The children should work in pairs in their ability groups. Give each pair a copy of photocopiable page 55.
1*: Complete all parts (A–C) of the photocopiable sheet.
2 & 3: Complete parts A and B.
4*: Complete parts A and B with teacher support.

Conclusion

Go over the answers to part B. Ask some of the children from each group to read out their responses to parts A and C. Have they discovered all the options? Have they grasped the concepts of root, prefix and suffix?

EXPLORING ROOT WORDS

PART A

■ How many words can you find with these **root words**? Write them below. Use a dictionary to help you.

act   line

■ Now look at the words you have written. Underline **prefixes** in ink and **suffixes** in pencil.

PART B

■ Choose from the list of words below to complete the sentences:

signify	sign	resigned	signal	signature	significant

1. When I _____ my name at the end of a letter, I write

my _____.

2. The starter gives a _____ to _____ that the

race has begun.

3. It was a _____ day for the team when their top player

_____.

■ What is the **root** word?

PART C

■ Use the prefixes and suffixes listed below to make as many words as you can from these roots:

prefixes:	please part take appear	suffixes:
de-		-ure
dis-		-ed
mis-		-ant
un-		-ance
over-		-ing
under-		-ly

THE FIRST MEN ON MERCURY

OBJECTIVES

UNIT	SPELLING/VOCABULARY	GRAMMAR/PUNCTUATION	COMPREHENSION/ COMPOSITION
READING POETRY 'The First Men on Mercury' by Edwin Morgan.	Investigate irregular plurals (plurals by vowel change) eg *man/men*.	Understand the difference between direct and reported speech. Revise the setting out and punctuation of dialogue.	Read and understand the poem.

ORGANIZATION (3 HOURS)

	INTRODUCTION	WHOLE-CLASS SKILLS WORK	DIFFERENTIATED GROUP ACTIVITIES	CONCLUSION
HOUR 1	Read the poem on photocopiable page 60 and help pupils with the pronunciation of the nonsense words. Briefly discuss the situation in the poem.	Understand the difference between direct and reported speech.	1*: Guided reading and discussion of poem. 2 & 3: Write a sequel to the poem. 4*: Guided reading and discussion of poem.	Group 4 gives a choral presentation of the poem to the class. Group 2 presents its sequel.
HOUR 2	Group 1 gives a choral presentation of the poem to the class.	Investigate irregular plurals (plurals by vowel change), eg 'men' in the title of the poem.	1: Write a sequel to the poem. 2 & 3*: Guided reading and discussion of poem. 4: Write a sequel to the poem.	Group 3 gives its choral presentation of the poem to the class. Group 1 presents its sequel.
HOUR 3	Re-read the poem to the class, focusing on the way it consists entirely of dialogue. Discuss what would be needed to set out the poem as a passage of dialogue in a story.	Revise the setting out and punctuation of dialogue and introduce the skill of adding a phrase of description to the reporting clause.	1–4*: All groups work on turning the poem into a prose dialogue or story.	Selected pupils read examples of their stories.

RESOURCES

Board or flip chart, photocopiable page 60 ('The First Men on Mercury'), OHP and acetate (optional), writing materials.

PREPARATION

Make enough copies of the poem on photocopiable page 60 for one per child. If possible, prepare the poem as an OHT, or make an A3 enlargement.

Introduction

Display 'The First Men on Mercury' (photocopiable page 60) on the OHP or as an A3 enlargement. The poem is best suited to reading in pairs or small groups. However, you will need to begin by reading it to the children to help them with the pronunciation of the nonsense words. Briefly discuss the children's first impressions of the poem – do they understand the overall 'gist'? What has happened to the earthmen's language by the end of the poem?

Whole-class skills work

Explain to the children that they are going to look at the difference between direct and reported speech. Remind them that direct speech is when words are actually spoken rather than reported. Direct speech is easy to identify in text because speech marks are used before and after the words spoken (apart from in playscripts), for example *"It's time to get up for school, Josie," said her mother.* Reported (or indirect) speech is where the writer reports what has been said but does not actually quote it, for example *Josie's mother told her that it was time to get up for school.*

Now provide an example of the same sentence written as both direct and reported speech on the board or flip chart so that the children can see the difference. What changes do they notice apart from the speech marks? Guide them towards recognizing these differences between direct and reported speech:

■ verbs – change of tense from present to past, for example *"It's time to get up..."*; *...it was time to get up*

■ change of person – usually from 1st or 2nd person to 3rd person, for example *'I'm telling you to be quiet.'*; *She told her to be quiet.*

Explain that other changes are simply common-sense changes to ensure that the meaning is clear, for example *She told Sarah to be quiet.*

Now reinforce the children's understanding by asking them to play the Reporting Game:

■ Work in groups of three.

■ Child 1 tells Child 2 briefly about something he or she did earlier in the week, for example *"I went to see a film"*. Child 2 writes this down as direct speech, using speech marks and a reporting clause: *"I went to see a film," said Samantha.*

■ Child 2 then tells Child 3 what has been said using indirect speech, beginning with the reporting clause *He/she said that....*

■ Child 3 writes down the indirect speech.

■ Children compare the two written versions, then swap roles and repeat the process.

Differentiated group activities

Give each child a copy of 'The First Men on Mercury' poem on photocopiable page 60.
1*: Guided reading of the poem. The following questions can be used as a starting point for discussion:

■ What kind of a poem is it? Does it rhyme? Can you detect a regular rhythm? (The poem is free verse.)

■ What situation is described in the poem?

■ What do the earthmen say to the Mercurians?

■ What do the Mercurians reply? (There are just enough recognizable words or parts of words to deduce this!)

■ What happens at the end of the poem?

■ Why will the earthmen remember Mercury?

The group then prepares the poem for a choral presentation.

2 & 3: Write a sequel to the poem in which the earthmen return to earth and try to tell others what they have seen. (Remind the children that the earthmen's language changes to 'Mercurian' towards the end of the poem.) Prepare a choral presentation of the sequel.

4*: Guided reading of the poem. Spend some time working on the pronunciation of the 'Mercurian' nonsense words. The children should be shown how to break these words up into syllables, and to apply regular English pronunciations. Then discuss the poem using the above questions as a starting point, adapting them as necessary. The children finish by preparing the poem (or part of it) for a choral presentation.

Conclusion

Group 4 gives its choral presentation of the poem to the class. Group 2 gives a presentation of its sequel. The rest of the class briefly discuss how successful or effective they think the sequel is.

Introduction
Group 1 gives a choral presentation of the poem to the class (as prepared in Hour 1). The rest of the class briefly evaluate the choral reading, for example how clear it was to follow, how expressive it was and so on.

Whole-class skills work
Together, revise the rules for the pluralization of nouns:
- add -s to most words
- add -es to most words ending in -s, -sh, -ch
- change -f to -ves (but note exceptions: *dwarfs, chiefs, griefs, proofs, roofs, beliefs*)
- when -y is preceded by a consonant (for example 'sky'), change to -ies; when -y is preceded by a vowel (for example 'toy'), add -s.

Next, investigate irregular plurals, focusing on words that become plural through a vowel change – 'men' in the title of the poem is one example. Can the children think of any other examples?

The following list provides a good starting point of familiar words:

SINGULAR	PLURAL
foot	feet
goose	geese
louse	lice
man	men
mouse	mice
tooth	teeth
woman	women
oasis	oases

You may wish to include discussion of nouns such as 'sheep' and 'fish' which use the same form for both singular and plural.

Differentiated group activities
1: Write a sequel to the poem, as described for Groups 2 and 3 in Hour 1. Prepare a choral presentation of the sequel.
2 & 3*: Guided reading and discussion of the poem, as described for Group 1 in Hour 1. Finish by preparing a choral presentation of the poem.
4: Write a sequel to the poem (see Hour 1), but keep the text brief and simple.

Conclusion
Group 3 gives a choral presentation of the poem to the class. Group 1 gives a presentation of its sequel. The class briefly evaluate both presentations.

Introduction
Re-read 'The First Men on Mercury' to the class, focusing on the fact that it consists entirely of dialogue. Ask the children what they would need to do to set the poem out as a passage of dialogue in a story. What punctuation would be needed? As well as adding speech marks, what else would need to be included? Guide the children to the idea that reporting clauses would be necessary to complete the transition to prose.

Whole-class skills work
Now ask the children to help you turn the first three speeches in the poem into dialogue. Invite their suggestions and write them up on the board or flip chart. The result might be something like the following:

"We come in peace from the third planet. Would you take us to your leader?" asked Arthur, nervously.
"Bawr stretter! Bawr. Bawr. Stretterhawl?" chirped the Mercurians.
"This is a little plastic model of the solar system…is this clear?" inquired Henry with an anxious frown.

Refer to the text on the board to revise previous work on dialogue in order of difficulty as follows:

■ Speech marks are placed before and after the words spoken.
■ Sentences spoken begin with a capital letter.
■ Examine the positioning of punctuation between speech marks. In the above example, Arthur speaks two sentences. The final punctuation (a question mark) comes *before* the second speech marks.
■ Look at the setting out of dialogue, noting that each new speaker starts a new indented line.
■ A synonym of 'said' is used to show how the Mercurian spoke.
■ A synonym of 'asked' is used in the third speech to reflect a question.
■ An adverb is added to the reporting clause to show how Arthur spoke.
   Finally, introduce the new skill of adding a phrase of description to the reporting clause, as in Henry's speech in the above sample text. Ask the children for their own suggestions and add a descriptive phrase to the appropriate part of the text on the board.

Differentiated group activities

All groups focus on transforming 'The First Men on Mercury' poem into a prose dialogue or story text at the levels suggested below. The children should consolidate their skills at the appropriate level, and then add one more skill from the list explored in the whole-class activity above. The teacher supports each group as necessary.
1*: Turn the poem into a complete story, including the following:
■ a description of the setting and characters
■ correct punctuation and setting out of all the dialogue (remind the children that the whole poem is dialogue)
■ some explanation of what is happening.
2 & 3*: Write out a version of the dialogue including correct layout, punctuation and reporting clauses, together with some description, for example details about the Mercurians.
4*: Write out a short section of the poem as dialogue with correct punctuation and layout, including simple reporting clauses. Emphasize that it is better to do a small part of the poem well rather than finishing the whole poem.

Conclusion

Selected children read examples of their stories, with the class providing constructive feedback and ideas for improvement.

THE FIRST MEN ON MERCURY

– We come in peace from the third planet.
Would you take us to your leader?

– Bawr stretter! Bawr. Bawr. Stretterhawl?

– This is a little plastic model
of the solar system, with working parts.
You are here and we are there and we
are now here with you, is this clear?

– Gawl horrop. Bawr. Abawrhannahanna!

– Where we come from is blue and white
with brown, you see we call the brown
here 'land', the blue is 'sea', and the white
is 'clouds' over land and sea, we live
on the surface of the brown land,
all round is sea and clouds. We are 'men'.
Men come –

– Glawp men! Gawrbenner menko. Menhawl?

– Men come in peace from the third planet
which we call 'earth'. We are earthmen.
Take us earthmen to you leader.

– Thmen? Them? Bawr. Bawrhossop.
Yuleeda tan hanna. Harrabost yuleeda.

– I am the yuleeda. You see my hands,

we carry no benner, we come in peace.
The spaceways are all stretterhawn.

– Glawn peacemen all horrobhanna tantko!
Tan come at'mstrossop. Glawp yuleeda!

– Atoms are peacegawl in our harraban.
Menbat worrabost from tan hannahanna.

– ou men we know bawrhossoptant. Bawr.
We know yuleeda. Go strawg backspetter wuick.

– We cantantabawr, tantingko backspetter now!

– Banghapper now! Yes, third planet back.
Yuleeda will go back blue, white, brown
nowhanna! There is no more talk.

– Gawl han fasthapper?

– No. You must go back to your planet.
Go back in peace, take what you have gained
but quickly.

– Stretterworra gawl, gawl'

– Of course, but nothing is ever the same,
now is it? You'll remember Mercury.

Edwin Morgan

SHADES OF MEANING

OBJECTIVES

UNIT	SPELLING/VOCABULARY	GRAMMAR/PUNCTUATION	COMPREHENSION/ COMPOSITION
WRITING POETRY 'It Can't Be – Can It?' by Chris Webster.	Explore synonyms of key words in the poem. Explain the differences between various synonyms.	Analyse the verse form.	Read and understand poem. Choose words with exactly the right shade of meaning when writing poem.

ORGANIZATION (2 HOURS)

	INTRODUCTION	WHOLE CLASS SKILLS WORK	DIFFERENTIATED GROUP ACTIVITIES	CONCLUSION
HOUR 1	Introduce the photocopiable poem 'It Can't Be Can It?' on page 64.	Revise the use of a thesaurus. Explore synonyms of a common, everyday word. Write definitions of six of these synonyms to explore their shades of meaning.	1: Complete the synonyms exercise on photocopiable page 65, using alternative synonyms to those in the list if they wish. Write another verse for the poem, choosing key words carefully. 2 & 3: As for Group 1, but keep to the list provided. 4*: Complete the photocopiable exercise with teacher support.	Selected pupils from Groups 2 and 3 read their continuations of the poem. The class briefly evaluates them.
HOUR 2	Display the original version of 'It Can't Be Can It?' Re-read, and compare with the pupils' version from Hour 1. Discuss whether any of the revised versions are an improvement on the original.	Analyse the rhythm and rhyme pattern of the second verse of the poem.	All groups do a reverse version of the synonym exercise in Hour 1, creating their own lists of synonyms. 1: Compile lists of synonyms for at least eight key words. Rewrite the poem. 2 & 3*: As above, but with teacher support. 4: Focus on the main exercise. Rewrite one verse.	Selected pupils read out their revised versions of the verses. The class discusses the effect of substituted synonyms.

RESOURCES

Thesauruses, photocopiable pages 64 ('It Can't Be – Can It?') and 65 (Shades of Meaning), a selection of poetry anthologies containing short, simple poems suitable for work on synonyms, board or flip chart, OHP and acetate (optional), writing materials.

PREPARATION

Prepare an OHT of the poem on photocopiable page 64, or enlarge it to A3 size. Make enough copies of the poem for one between two children. Make enough copies of photocopiable page 65 (Shades of Meaning) for one between two children. Write three lists of words (taken from a thesaurus) on the board or flip chart as follows:

1. spook	2. strolls	3. dark
spectre	walks	black
spirit	creeps	sad
ghost	flits	sombre
shade	glides	gloomy

Introduction

Display the poem 'It Can't Be – Can It?' as an OHT or A3 enlargement. Explain to the children that they are going to use the poem as part of an exercise in choosing words which have exactly the right meaning. (Explain the phrase 'shades of meaning'.) This will help to show them the process that writers go through as they search for the best words to achieve the desired effect in their writing.

Read the poem and briefly discuss its theme (ghosts) and atmosphere – is it humorous or eerie? Ask the children how the poet builds up the eerie atmosphere. Guide them to look closely at the poet's choice of words and how these contribute to the overall effect. Explain that a careful choice of words is important to achieve a successful effect in writing. Demonstrate this by focusing on the first line of the first verse and asking the children to pick out three key words ('phantom', 'floats', 'ghostly'). Now show them the prepared lists of words written on the board or flip chart (see Preparation), saying that these alternatives have been taken from a thesaurus. Revise the term *synonym*, explaining that the words in the list are similar in meaning to the selected key words in the poem. Then briefly go through each list, guiding the discussion along the lines below to ensure that a good model for further work is provided.

The first key word to be replaced with a synonym is 'phantom':

■ 'spook' – a humorous word for ghost; humour would destroy the atmosphere of the poem
■ 'spectre' and 'spirit' – not often used these days
■ 'ghost' and 'shade' – 'shade' could be confused with 'shadow', so 'ghost' is probably the better choice.

The next word is a verb describing the ghost's movement:

■ 'strolls' – inappropriate, as it would be humorous in this context and spoil the atmosphere
■ 'walks' and 'creeps' – these verbs are not appropriate as they are more suited to human movement
■ 'flits' and 'glides' – both appropriate to describe ghostly movement, but 'glides' alliterates with (or begins with the same sound as) 'ghost' so is the better choice.

The next word 'ghostly' is an adjective and needs to describe the noun ('gloom') appropriately. Direct synonyms of 'ghostly' are not very promising, so we need to be more flexible and think of other ways to describe gloom:

■ 'dark' and 'black' – these are rather plain!
■ 'sad' – this doesn't really fit the context
■ 'gloomy' – too repetitive alongside 'gloomy'
■ 'sombre' – a really powerful adjective which is in keeping with the poem's atmosphere, so this is the best choice.

So, the first line now reads: *A ghost glides through the sombre gloom.* Point out that when a word comes at the end of a line, the writer needs to choose it especially carefully to make sure there is a possibility of rhyme. Finish off by trying out some bad choices for fun, and to make the point that careful choice of words is worth the effort, for example *A spook strolls through the black gloom; A shade creeps through the dark gloom.*

Whole-class skills work

Revise the use of a thesaurus. Ask the children to look up a simple, everyday word such as 'book'. They will be surprised at the number of synonyms they find. Emphasize that the key skill is to be able to distinguish between the different shades of meaning, just as they did when exploring synonyms for the first line of the photocopiable poem. Explain that dictionaries do not usually attempt to define these finer distinctions, so we have to tease them out carefully, paying attention to their appropriateness to the context.

Next, ask the children to pick out six synonyms for 'book' (or other word) and together, write a definition for each one that everyone agrees on. The children will see that although a dictionary can help, it will only give them the basic meaning, so they still have to rely on their own knowledge of how a word is used to define it accurately.

Differentiated group activities

All the children work in pairs within their ability groups to discuss the synonyms listed on photocopiable page 65 (Shades of Meaning) before deciding on a final version of the poem. Each child should produce his or her own copy of the poem to allow individual choices to be made after paired discussion.

1: Complete the exercise on the photocopiable sheet, but the children should be encouraged to look up and choose alternative synonyms from a thesaurus if they wish, rather than limiting themselves solely to the list. They then write another verse for the poem, choosing key words carefully to sustain the atmosphere.

2 & 3: Do the exercise on the photocopiable sheet, choosing from the list of synonyms provided. Follow by writing another verse for the poem, using the thesaurus to help choose the best words.

4*: Complete the exercise on the photocopiable sheet with teacher support.

Conclusion

Ask selected children from Groups 2 and 3 to read their continuations of the poem and briefly evaluate the results.

Introduction

Re-read the original version of the photocopiable poem. Then share several of the children's own versions written in Hour 1. Look at how effective the synonyms are in each case – how well do the words in the children's version fit in with the original poem? (Focus on the shades of meaning here.) Discuss what difficulties the children encountered when choosing alternative words. Are any of the revised versions better than the original? The children should begin to realize that it is very difficult to improve on a skilled poet's work, and this is evidence of the rigour and power of poetry as a form.

Whole-class skills work

Display the original poem as an OHT or A3 enlargement. Explain to the children that you are going to analyse the rhythm and rhyme pattern of the poem, focusing on the second verse. Remind them that the rhythm of a poem comes from the pattern of stressed and unstressed syllables. Slowly read each line aloud and use diagonal strokes to mark the stressed syllables. Recap on how letters of the alphabet can be used to show a poem's rhyme pattern. The first two lines are analysed below as an example:

```
       /        /      /       /
As the phantom flits by outside your room (a)
      /       /        /        /
A ghostly glimmering fills the gloom      (a)
```

Differentiated group activities

This activity is a reversal of the task in Hour 1. Instead of choosing one word from a given list of synonyms, the children use a thesaurus to create their own list of synonyms for selected key words in the photocopiable poem. (They should avoid repeating the synonyms listed in the photocopiable exercise!)

1: Find at least four synonyms for each key word they select from the poem. (Choose a minimum of eight key words – these can be the same as for Hour 1 if necessary.) The children should then rewrite the poem, choosing from their list of synonyms. This time, however, they can opt to change the mood of the poem with their final selection of words.

2 & 3*: As for Group 1, but with teacher support.

4: This group should focus on the main exercise, choosing four to five key words to replace in a single verse only. However, they should try to retain the mood of the original verse in their revised version.

Conclusion

The children share their new versions of the poem or single verse. Discuss whether any of their word choices have significantly changed the mood of the poem to reinforce the effect of different shades of meaning in words selected.

IT CAN'T BE – CAN IT?

A phantom floats through the ghostly gloom
Of your empty hall and living room,
And who can tell what he's trying to find,
Wailing with the sound of rushing wind.
It can't be a ghost, you say to yourself
Looking over the window sill –
But the world outside is silent and still.

As the phantom flits by outside your room,
A ghostly glimmering fills the gloom
And filters through your half-closed door,
Filling your mind with doubts once more;
It can't be a ghost, you say to yourself,
Going outside to turn out the light –
But the passageway is black as night.

Chris Webster

SHADES OF MEANING

■ Rewrite the first verse of 'It Can't Be – Can It?' by choosing synonyms for the words in bold type. You can choose from the synonyms given, or use a thesaurus to find your own. Choose your words carefully so that they all work together to build up the atmosphere. Finish off by adding another verse.

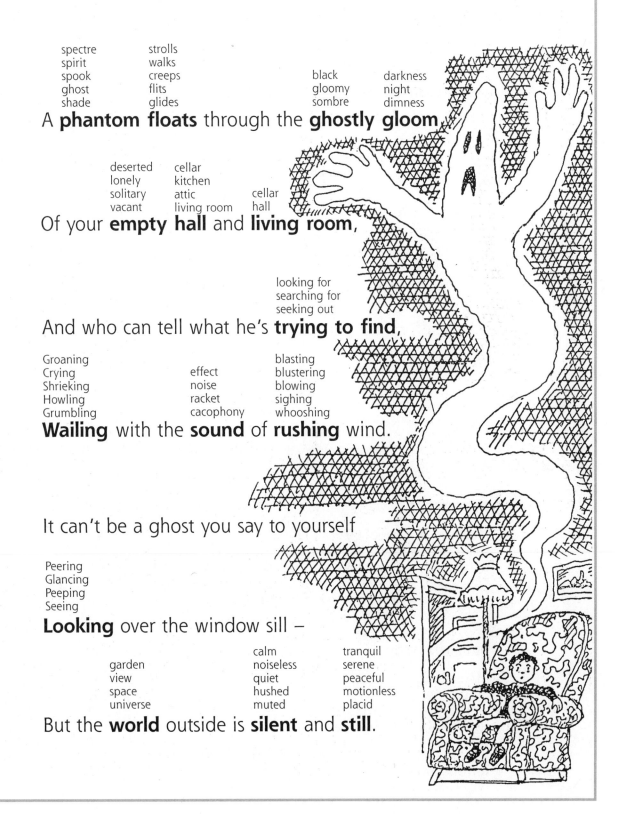

spectre	strolls		
spirit	walks		
spook	creeps	black	darkness
ghost	flits	gloomy	night
shade	glides	sombre	dimness

A **phantom floats** through the **ghostly gloom**,

deserted	cellar	
lonely	kitchen	
solitary	attic	cellar
vacant	living room	hall

Of your **empty hall** and **living room**,

looking for
searching for
seeking out

And who can tell what he's **trying to find**,

Groaning		blasting
Crying	effect	blustering
Shrieking	noise	blowing
Howling	racket	sighing
Grumbling	cacophony	whooshing

Wailing with the **sound** of **rushing** wind.

It can't be a ghost you say to yourself

Peering
Glancing
Peeping
Seeing

Looking over the window sill –

	calm	tranquil
garden	noiseless	serene
view	quiet	peaceful
space	hushed	motionless
universe	muted	placid

But the **world** outside is **silent** and **still**.

JURASSIC CLASSROOM

OBJECTIVES

UNIT	SPELLING/VOCABULARY	GRAMMAR/PUNCTUATION	COMPREHENSION/ COMPOSITION
READING PLAYS 'Jurassic Classroom'.	Understand and use vocabulary related to drama conventions.	Mark up a text to support reading aloud. Identify statements, questions, orders and exclamations.	Understand the conventions of playscripts. Use appropriate gesture and expression to communicate character/action. Make notes.

ORGANIZATION (3 HOURS)

	INTRODUCTION	WHOLE-CLASS SKILLS WORK	DIFFERENTIATED GROUP ACTIVITIES	CONCLUSION
HOUR 1	Introduce the photocopiable play 'Jurassic Classroom' (pages 69–72), discussing how the script works, including conventions such as stage directions.	Discuss the importance of expression in reading. Identify statements, questions, orders and exclamations. Read examples of each sentence type from the play using the correct intonation.	1–4*: Read the play in mixed-ability groups of five or six.	Selected groups read different parts of the play. The rest of the class evaluates the readings.
HOUR 2	Investigate using gesture and facial expression to enhance the performance. Explain the term 'blocking'.	Look at the 'blocking' process and ways of making blocking notes on the playscript.	1–4*: In mixed-ability groups, pupils discuss ideas and plan their blocking on paper. They then try out their blocking and rehearse the play, paying attention to gesture and expression.	Two different groups present their blocked version of the play. The rest of the class evaluates.
HOUR 3	Revise improvisation.	Carry out a 'hot-seating' activity, with children in role answering questions.	1–4*: Each mixed-ability group chooses a 'what if...' scenario based on the play.	Groups who have not yet performed to the class present their improvisations. The rest of the class evaluates.

RESOURCES

Photocopiable pages 69–72 ('Jurassic Classroom'), OHP and acetate (optional), a large space (drama studio or hall, if available, otherwise, a classroom with tables pushed out of the way), writing materials, the following props (optional – but will help to bring the play to life): four exercise books, a history text book, a piece of amber (violin rosin or a lump of yellow Plasticine will do), some stones for the fossil display, a tattered jacket, some crisps, a bucket.

PREPARATION

Make enough copies of the play on photocopiable pages 69–72 for one per child and if, possible, prepare OHTs of the script. Alternatively, enlarge each sheet to A3 size. Prepare a performance area at the front of the drama studio, hall or classroom. Collect the props together if these are to be included as part of the drama activity.

Introduction

Display the photocopiable playscript as OHTs or A3 enlargements, and go through it with the children, discussing how it works. Point out that scene descriptions and stage directions (which are in italics in brackets) should not normally be read out. Ask the children to pay particular attention to the way in which the characters describe what is happening to Ryan when they are peering through the gap in the classroom door. Without the special effects available for film, this is the only way that such scenes can be handled on the stage. Done well, they are very effective. After all, the best special effect of all is the imagination!

Whole-class skills work

Remind the children of the importance of expression in reading, particularly in plays. Revise the four types of sentence (statements, questions, orders and exclamations) and how these should be expressed:

- Statements end with a full stop and a *falling* intonation (tone of voice).
- Questions end with a question mark and a *rising* intonation.
- Orders end with a full stop or exclamation mark and have a *level, 'clipped'* intonation.
- Exclamations end with an exclamation mark and have and have a *high, rising* intonation.

Now ask the children to identify some examples of each type of sentence in the playscript and practise reading them with the correct intonation.

Differentiated group activities

1–4*: Provide each child with a copy of the playscript. Note that all groupings for this unit are mixed-ability groups of five. If a group of six is necessary because of total numbers, the sixth person should be a narrator and read all the text appearing in italics.

The first task is to allocate the parts. Tell the children not to try to match the gender of the characters (for example, Ryan can be a boy or girl). Groups should then read the play a number of times, concentrating on developing realistic expression. Encourage the children to mark their text with reminders to aid their expression. They could also underline or highlight their part just as real actors do. During the session, the teacher gives organizational support to all groups.

Conclusion

One group should be chosen to read Scene 1, with Scene 2 divided among two other groups (the second group reading Scene 2 picks up from the stage direction *'Trudy and Robert go off stage left'*). A further group can round off by reading the very short final scene. The rest of the class should evaluate the readings by commenting on how true to life the readers' expression was, and giving suggestions for improvement.

Introduction

Start by talking about how the characters will be conveyed in the play. Emphasize that although the words are an important way of revealing a character's personality, gestures and facial expressions are also essential. (Remind the children that these things are all they have to make the audience believe in the dinosaur transformation scene!)

Encourage them to look closely at the stage directions for the different characters, saying that these give valuable pointers to suitable actions or expressions. Briefly go through several of the stage directions in Scene 1, for example line 2: *'(loudly and proudly)'*. How might the characters look at this point – smiling or frowning, looking up at their teacher or down at their feet? Ask the children to practise some facial expressions that convey pride. What about line 13 *'(confused)'*? How do we look when we are in this state of mind? Again, encourage the children to try out some appropriate expressions and gestures.

Now tell the children that they are going to plan out the movements of the characters for the 'Jurassic Classroom' play and remind them that this process is called 'blocking'. Explain that when movements are being planned, the position of the audience must be kept in mind to ensure that they have a clear view of everything that happens and that the actors are facing the audience as much as possible.

First, arrange the front of the classroom as a simple performance area (see 'Preparation'). Though only one group will be able to rehearse in it at a time, all groups should plan with that space in mind.

Whole-class skills work

Work through the process of blocking by asking the children to brainstorm ideas for the actors' movements in the first part of Scene 1. Remind them that they must think carefully about what the characters are saying and to whom, so that their movements are realistic. They should then use notes and/or symbols (for example, move →; **X** to Ryan) to show the movements on their script.

Differentiated group activities

1–4*: Each mixed-ability group should plan its ideas and make notes on paper before beginning to try them out in the space allocated. All groups try out their blocking, and then rehearse the whole play a number of times. They should be encouraged to pay careful attention to expression and gesture. The teacher gives support where required.

Conclusion

Ask two different groups to present their version of the fully blocked play in the performance area. The other children should be encouraged to evaluate the blocking: can they see what is happening? Do the movements help to put across the meaning of the words? Can all the actors be heard clearly? Did the actors' expressions and gestures convince the audience that the action was really happening?

Introduction

Revise the term 'improvisation': it means 'making it up as you go along'. Remind the children that it is a technique much used by actors for practice, and also in performance as a way of creating true-to-life dialogue.

Whole-class skills work

In groups, practise improvisation by 'hot seating' different characters in the play. Each child then takes it in turn to ask one of the characters a question, for example:
■ (To Ryan) *How do you feel now that you are a dinosaur?*
■ (To Mrs Scratchit) *Why are you so cross with Mr Beetham? It wasn't his fault.*
 Prompt them where necessary, reminding them that improvisation requires careful listening since partners have to respond realistically to what each one says. Finish by discussing how convincing the characters' responses are to the questions. Are they in keeping with what we already know about the character?

Differentiated group activities

1–4*: Each mixed-ability group chooses from one of the following 'What if...' scenarios to practise their improvisation skills. Their comprehension of the plot and characters, as well as a whole range of speaking, listening and drama skills will be demonstrated in how well they do this, and so differentiation will be by outcome. The teacher supports each group as necessary.
What if:
■ Mr Beetham's trick failed to turn Ryan back into a human again?
■ Mrs Scratchit found out what happened before Ryan could be turned back?
■ All the other children eat pieces of fossil and turn into dinosaurs?
■ Mrs Scratchit eats a fossil and turns into a T rex?
■ Mr Beetham doesn't get his early retirement?

Conclusion

Groups who have not performed before present their improvisations to the class, followed by a brief evaluation discussion.

FURTHER IDEAS

■ Each group could work out its own complete version of the play and prepare to present it without scripts.
■ Turn the play into a short story. This would make a valuable exercise in punctuating and setting out dialogue.
■ The next unit, 'Writing Plays: Washing-up Woes', is an ideal follow-up to this unit.

JURASSIC CLASSROOM

CAST: Mr Beetham (the class teacher); The Improvers Group: Ryan, Robert, Tracy, Trudy.

SCENE 1: *Mr Beetham's classroom.*

Mr Beetham:	I hope you all did your homework last night.
Ro, Tra, Tru:	*(Loudly and proudly)* Yes, Sir!
Ryan:	*(Quietly)* No, Sir.
Mr Beetham:	Good, good. Hand it in then. I'll mark it at break time. *(He ticks off the work as it is handed in.)* Ryan, where is yours?
Ryan:	Er...the dog ate it, Sir.

(Mr Beetham frowns.)

Tracy:	*(Whispering)* You used that excuse last week!
Ryan:	Er, no. I mean...my little sister was sick on it, Sir.
Trudy:	*(Whispering)* You haven't got a little sister!
Mr Beetham:	I didn't know you had a little sister, Ryan!
Robert:	*(Whispering)* Say you meant my little sister was sick on it.
Tracy:	*(Whispering)* No, no, just say you did it but forgot to bring it.
Ryan:	*(Confused)* Er...er...Robert's little sister did it and I forgot to be sick on it...I mean...
Mr Beetham:	I've heard enough of your excuses, Ryan, you can stay in at break and do it then. Now, I want you all to do these sums on the board.

(The class work quietly while Mr Beetham marks homework. After a few moments, the Improvers Group starts to chat.)

Robert:	Hey, did you see that dinosaur film on telly last night?
Trudy:	I think dinosaurs are dead boring.
Tracy:	Yeah, I prefer romance.
Robert:	What d'ya mean?
Tracy:	Y'know, falling in love and kissing.
Ryan:	Yuk, just the thought of it makes me sick.
Robert:	Anyway, there was some kissing in this film.
Trudy:	*(Looking interested)* Yeah?
Robert:	Yeah. This guy was just kissing this girl when...
Ryan:	*(Interrupting)*...a T rex bit his head off. It was great.
Robert:	And then the rex ate her too!
Tra and Tru:	*(Shuddering)* Ugh
Ryan:	*(Thoughtfully)* I wish I was a T rex.
Tracy:	Don't be daft – you're ugly enough already!
Ryan:	Shurrup, you!
Robert:	What do you want to be a T rex for?
Ryan:	*(His voice getting louder)* 'Cause I'd get my own back on old Beetham. I'd..
Mr Beetham:	QUIET! And get on with your work!

(The Improvers Group work quietly for a few moments. Then a bell sounds.)
(Ryan tries to sneak out.)

JURASSIC CLASSROOM 2

Mr Beetham: Trudy, collect in the work. Thank you. Off you go.

(Ryan tries to sneak out.)

Mr Beetham: Not you, Ryan! Here, History Block Units. Read this, and answer these
                   questions.
Ryan: *(Miserably)* Yes, Sir.
Mr Beetham: I'm going to the staffroom to put my feet up...I mean, to mark the
                   homework, so don't you go fiddling around with my displays. Those fossils
                   at the back are valuable, especially that fly in amber.

*(Ryan pretends to work as Mr Beetham leaves the room. As soon as the door is closed, Ryan jumps
up and goes to look at the display. The scene ends as Ryan picks up the piece of amber.)*

SCENE 2: *The corridor outside the classroom. The door is slightly open and The Improvers Group
are peering in with amazed expressions on their faces. The bell goes and Mr Beetham enters.*
Mr Beetham: Inside now, all of you. We've got work to do!
Tracy: Please, Sir...we daren't!
Mr Beetham: Nonsense, girl! Why not?
Trudy: There's a...a...
Mr Beetham: Stand aside! I'll have no more of this nonsense!

*(Mr Beetham pushes the pupils aside and strides boldly into the classroom. A mighty roar is heard
followed by lots of banging and scuffling. Minutes later, Mr Beetham stumbles out of the classroom,
his clothes in tatters.)*

Mr Beetham: Why didn't you tell me there was a monster in there!
Tracy: We did try, Sir!
Robert: Anyway, its not a monster, it's a Triceratops!
Mr Beetham: A What-a-tops?
Robert: A Triceratops, Sir. A Triceratops is a dinosaur!
Mr Beetham: Heaven help us!
Tracy: Shall we call the police, Sir?

(Mr Beetham nods.)

Trudy: And the fire brigade?

(Mr Beetham nods.)

Tracy: And the army?

(Mr Beetham nods.)

Trudy: And Mrs Scratchit, the headmistress?
Mr Beetham: *(Shaking his head vigorously)* No, no...on second thoughts we'd better try
                   to sort this out ourselves.
Robert: Anyway, Sir, there's nothing to be afraid of.

JURASSIC CLASSROOM 3

Mr Beetham:	Nonsense, boy! She'll stop my early retirement!
Robert:	No Sir, I mean the Triceratops! Triceratops are vegetarian, Sir.
Mr Beetham:	Why did it attack me then?
Robert:	*(after thinking for a moment)* Sir, can I have a word in private?

(Mr Beetham nods and Robert leads him a little way from the others.)

Mr Beetham:	Well?
Robert:	Sir, it might look like a Triceratops, but really it's Ryan.
Mr Beetham:	What?
Robert:	Sir, last night, Ryan and I watched a film where they clone dinosaurs from the blood of Jurassic flies preserved in amber.
Mr Beetham:	Well?
Robert:	I think Ryan must have eaten the fly from your display.
Mr Beetham:	And you think it's changed him into a dinosaur?
Robert:	I can't think of any other explanation.
Mr Beetham:	What can we do?
Robert:	We could try to make him sick to get it out of his system.

(They go back to the girls. Mr Beetham, feeling a little better now, tries to take command.)

Mr Beetham:	We must try to make the Triceratops sick. I suggest that we try to get it to drink salt water.
Tracy:	Why?
Trudy:	What if it's not thirsty?
Tracy:	I know, let's throw it some crisps. They'll make it thirsty.
Trudy:	It'll need quite a few.
Mr Beetham:	There's a hundred packets in the school tuck shop. Trudy, here's the money, you get the crisps. Robert, go to the kitchen and get a bucket of salty water.

(Trudy and Robert go off stage left and come on again moments later with crisps and water. Trudy throws the crisps through the door and Robert pushes the bucket in. They all watch through a small gap.)

Trudy:	It's eating the crisps – and the packets – all in one go!
Tracy:	Yeah, but only the salt and vinegar ones!
Robert:	They're it's favourite flavour.
Tra and Tru:	*(Looking curiously at Robert)* How do you know?
Mr Beetham:	It's drinking the water!
Robert:	It seems to be enjoying it!
Tracy:	I thought it was supposed to be sick.
Trudy:	It didn't work. Any more bright ideas?

(Robert scratches his head thoughtfully.)

Robert:	Listen, girls, I've just had an idea. I want you to shout something at the Triceratops.

JURASSIC CLASSROOM 4

(He whispers something in their ears.)

Tra and Tru:	What? That's daft! Anyway we might get hurt!
Robert:	Just shout it! You don't have to go in there!
Tra and Tru:	*(Shouting through the gap in the door)* WE'RE COMING IN AND WE'RE GOING TO GIVE YOU A REALLY SOPPY, SLOBBERY, WET KISS!
Mr Beetham:	It's heaving! It's going to be...No, it's managed to fight it off.
Tra and Tru:	*(Arms folded)* Thought it was a daft idea!

(They all look at each other trying to think what to do next.)

Mr Beetham:	Listen! I think I've got it. I've thought of something that really will make it sick!

(Mr Beetham hisses through the gap in the door.)

Mr Beetham:	Now Ryan, I know it's you. And I'm very cross at all the trouble you've caused. So cross, that I'm going to give you three hours of homework every night for the rest of your life!

(A terrible roaring comes from the classroom followed by a disgusting vomiting sound. Everyone watches what happens through the gap in the door.)

Tracy:	Urrgghh! It's throwing up all over the place!
Trudy:	It's all yellow and green and it stinks!
Tracy:	Never mind that – it's working!
Trudy:	The Triceratops is shrinking and its face is shrivelling up like a prune!
Tracy:	It's even uglier now!
Trudy:	Blimey, it's *Ryan!*
Tracy:	I always thought he was a beast!
Robert:	He's still being sick.
Mr Beetham:	Just a minute. I think I can help. *(He shouts through the door)* ON SECOND THOUGHTS, I'LL LET YOU OFF.
Tracy:	He's looking better already!

(Ryan stumbles out into the corridor looking sick, pale and untidy.)

Robert:	Phew – thank goodness you're okay!
Mr Beetham:	Thank goodness Mrs Scratchit didn't find out!

SCENE 3: *Back in the classroom.*

Mr Beetham	Now for this afternoon's lessons we're going to do some history.
Ryan:	Oh no!
Mr Beetham:	Don't worry, Ryan, this time you'll be top of the class.
Ryan:	What do you mean, Sir?
Mr Beetham:	We're going to do a topic on dinosaurs!

(The Improvers Group all cheer.)

WASHING-UP WOES

OBJECTIVES

UNIT	SPELLING/VOCABULARY	GRAMMAR/PUNCTUATION	COMPREHENSION/COMPOSITION
WRITING PLAYS 'Washing-up woes'.	Recognize (and use in own writing) idiomatic phrases, clichés and expressions. Understand when they are appropriate to use in speech and writing.	Understand the difference between the punctuation and setting out of dialogue in a story and in a play.	Write a playscript using layout conventions correctly. Write convincing dialogue. Write production notes for a playscript.

ORGANIZATION (3 HOURS)

	INTRODUCTION	WHOLE-CLASS SKILLS WORK	DIFFERENTIATED GROUP ACTIVITIES	CONCLUSION
HOUR 1	Read the photocopiable play 'Washing-up Woes' (pages 76 and 77). Briefly summarize the main theme.	Introduce the terms 'idiom' and 'cliché'. Discuss examples and explore/check meanings using a dictionary. Discuss appropriate usage of these expressions.	1–4*: Prepare a performance of the play in mixed-ability groups of four.	A selected group presents its performance of the play. The rest of the class evaluates it.
HOUR 2	A selected group presents its performance as prepared in Hour 1. The issues raised in the play are discussed.	Explore the difference between the punctuation and setting out of dialogue in a story with dialogue in a play.	1–4*: In mixed-ability groups of four, pupils choose from several improvisations to prepare a performance.	Selected groups present two different improvisations.
HOUR 3	Selected groups present the other improvisations not performed in Hour 2.	Examine in detail the conventions used in a playscript	1–4*: All mixed-ability groups write a scripted version of the play, based on their own improvisations in Hour 2. They revise the scripts to make the dialogue as realistic as possible.	Selected groups perform their improvisations. The rest of the class evaluates the realism of the dialgoue.

RESOURCES

Photocopiable pages 76 and 77 ('Washing-up Woes'), a short extract containing dialogue taken from a story book, board or flip chart, OHP and acetate (optional), dictionaries (suitable for exploring idioms), writing materials.

PREPARATION

Make enough copies of the photocopiable play ('Washing-up Woes') on pages 76 and 77 for one per child. If possible, prepare an OHT of the play, or an A3 enlargement. Choose a short extract containing dialogue from a story book and make an OHT or A3 enlargement of this.

Introduction

Display the 'Washing-up Woes' playscript (pages 76 and 77) as an OHT or A3 enlargement, and read it through. Ask the children to briefly summarize the play's main theme.

Whole-class skills work

Introduce the terms 'idiom' and 'cliché'. Do the children know the meaning of these? Explain that a cliché is an over-used expression or opinion, for example 'green with envy', 'birds of a feather...' and so on. Tell the children that an idiom is a phrase like 'over the top' or 'under the weather'. We can't take idioms literally – instead we must rely on our existing knowledge of such phrases to understand their meaning. Emphasize that these kind of expressions are a familiar part of our everyday language, and including them as part of dialogue in writing can lend a realistic touch if done well.

Now look at the photocopiable play again and ask the children to pick out some examples of idioms and clichés (for example, *It's given up the ghost'*; *'It's clapped out'*; *'... cost a pretty penny'* and so on). Discuss the meanings of these phrases, then check a few examples by looking them up in the dictionary. Which ones have the children heard in use before? How many more expressions can the children think of themselves? List some examples on the board or flip chart.

Briefly discuss how we use these kind of phrases, focusing on a few of the above examples. When would it be appropriate to include these in our speech or writing? Present some different contexts (for example talking to a friend; talking to an important guest visiting the school; writing a letter to a family member; writing a letter to the House of Commons) and decide on when it would be acceptable to use these phrases and when we would need to avoid them.

Differentiated group activities

1–4*: The children work in mixed-ability groups of four to prepare a performance of the photocopiable play. Less confident children can play the role of Trev, who has the fewest lines. The teacher provides support as appropriate.

Conclusion

A selected group presents its performance of the play. The children briefly discuss the quality of the presentation. How might it have been improved?

Introduction

Another group presents its performance of the play, and this is followed by a discussion of the issues it raises:
- Are the rest of the family being unfair to Mum?
- Is Dad right to expect to do less since his shifts are longer?
- Do you think he is right about his job being harder?
- What impression do you get of the two children? Should they do more to help?

Whole-class skills work

Tell the children that they are going to explore the difference between the punctuation and setting out of dialogue in a story and dialogue in a play. Display a short extract containing dialogue from a story book (see 'Preparation') on an OHP and ask the children to compare this with their copy of the photocopiable playscript. What do they notice? Point out that in the story dialogue, speech marks are used, but in playscripts these are always omitted. However, both the story text and playscript allow a new line each time for new speakers. (Looking at the layout of the dialogue in the playscript can help children to grasp the need for a new line for each new speaker in stories.)

Discuss other differences between the prose and playscripts, including the general layout of the text, the way that description is handled and so on. Then, using this knowledge, work together on the following exercises.
- Turn a short section of the playscript into story format.
- Turn the story extract into a playscript.

Differentiated group activities

1–4*: Children work in mixed-ability groups of four. They choose one of the following improvisations based on 'Washing-up Woes' to prepare a performance of:
- What would happen if Mum decided to make the rest of the family take an equal share?
- What would happen if Dad brought a new dishwasher home next day?
- What would happen if Trevor got 0 out of 10 in a maths test next day?
- What would happen if Trish got a very bad school report?

Conclusion

Groups perform two different improvisations. This is followed by a discussion of the issues involved.

Introduction

Selected groups perform the other improvisations not presented in Hour 2.

Whole-class skills work

Display 'Washing-up Woes' as an OHT or A3 enlargement. Read through the play, then examine the conventions used in playscripts. Remind the children of the key features of the script's layout:

■ Title.
■ Cast list (usually in order of appearance).
■ Character names are followed by a colon.
■ Scenes are numbered.
■ Description of the set required usually follows a scene.
■ Stage directions are placed in brackets.

Differentiated group activities

1–4*: All groups write a script of their version of the play, based on their improvisations in Hour 2. They should pay careful attention to the correct layout, using the conventions discussed in the skills session. The scripts should then be tried out and revised to try to make the dialogue as realistic as possible. The teacher supports each group as appropriate.

Conclusion

Some of the completed playscripts are read out. The rest of the class evaluate how far the writers have managed to preserve the natural rhythm of real-life dialogue.

FURTHER IDEAS

Each group could write production notes for its script. These could include:
■ detailed guidance on any props that are needed
■ a detailed description of the scenery
■ suggestions about the movement of characters
■ suggestions about sound effects and lighting.

WASHING-UP WOES

CAST: Mum (a harassed working mum), Trish (the teenage daughter), Trev (her cheeky ten-year-old brother), Dad (works shifts).

SCENE 1: *The Trubbs are a typical modern family. Dad is a train driver, while Mum works in a high street bank – which can cause problems when it comes to dealing with the terrible twosome, Trish and Trevor. The scene is the kitchen in their typical, modern semi-detached house.*

Mum:	Trish!
Trish:	*(From offstage)* Yes, Mum?
Mum:	Trish, will you do the drying up?
Trish:	What's wrong with the dishwasher?
Mum:	It's given up the ghost.
Trish:	Aw, Mum! Why can't Trev do it?
Mum:	Trevor!
Trev:	*(From offstage)* Yes, Mum?
Mum:	Come and help with the drying up.
Trev:	I would, but I'm tied up with my homework.
Trish:	No he isn't. He's not up to it. He's telling stories.
Trev:	Yes I am – I've turned over a new leaf.
Trish:	*(Hearing the front door open)* Here's Dad. He'll sort it out!

(Dad enters. Trish and Trev rush in to greet him.)

Dad:	Hello, love. Hi, kids!
Tr & Tr:	Hi, Dad!
Mum:	Can you help me with the drying up? We're up a creek without a paddle.
Dad:	What's wrong with the dishwasher?
Mum:	It's clapped out.
Dad:	Clapped out? Cost me a pretty penny that dishwasher!
Mum:	*(Sarcastically)* Oh yes, that second-hand dishwasher for which you forked out all of £10!
Dad:	You should be more careful with it. It's a bad workman that blames his tools!
Mum:	*(Exasperated)* Oh, it never rains but it pours! Are you going to help with the drying up, or not?
Dad:	Look, love, I've been sat in that cab since 6.30 this morning, and I need to wind down. Ask one of the kids. *(Trish and Trev pretend to look busy).*
Mum:	*(Getting angry)* I just have and they won't lift a finger. Nobody ever helps! I slave all day behind that counter,

WASHING-UP WOES

and I come home and slave all evening looking after you lot! You've got me burning the candle at both ends!

Dad: *(Trying to calm her)* OK. OK. Don't lose your head. We'll get a new dishwasher, then.

Mum: That's not the point! I'm fed up with being everybody's dogsbody. You've all got to pull your weight!

Dad: *(Feeling threatened)* Yes, but my shifts *are* longer than yours – and it's harder work, driving a train! You can't expect me to help around the house as well!

Mum: *(Angrily)* Oh yes I can! It's not exactly a bed of roses in that bank, but I have it all to do when I get home!

Dad: *(Trying to shift the blame)* It's those kids I blame!

Trish: That's out of order. School is a real grind. We work hard too!

Dad: When I was a lad I had to work hard at school *and* I had chores to do when I got home.

Trev: Yeah, yeah, but times have changed, Dad.

Trish: Yeah, there are machines to help, now: hoovers and washing machines and dishwa...

Mum: *(Hissing angrily)* Precisely – and the dishes have still not been done!

Trev: *(Pointing to the sink)* Don't worry, Mum! Look, they've drip-dried while we've been arguing... er, talking – all's well that ends well, eh!

CRIPPEN HANGED

OBJECTIVES

UNIT	SPELLING/VOCABULARY	GRAMMAR/PUNCTUATION	COMPREHENSION/ COMPOSITION
READING NON-FICTION 'Crippen Hanged'.	Investigate unfamiliar vocabulary. Develop of knowledge of prefixes.	Revise simple present and simple past tense. Know past tense of irregular verbs. Identify the past tense in recounts.	Understand a crime report and explore the issues raised.

ORGANIZATION (2 HOURS)

	INTRODUCTION	WHOLE-CLASS SKILLS WORK	DIFFERENTIATED GROUPS ACTIVITIES	CONCLUSION
HOUR 1	Explain that the 'Crippen Hanged' newspaper article on photocopiable pages 81 and 82 describes a crime which actually happened nearly 100 years ago. Read the article.	Investigate prefixes.	1*: Guided reading/ discussion. 2 & 3: Write 'Wanted' posters for suspects. 4*: Guided reading/ discussion.	Pupils from Groups 2 & 3 display their 'Wanted' posters. The rest of the class evaluates them by checking to see if any important information has been missed out.
HOUR 2	Re-read the 'Crippen Hanged' article.	Revise simple present and simple past tense. Investigate past tense of irregular verbs. Investigate use of tense in the text.	1: Write an article to protest about hanging. 2 & 3*: Guided reading/ discussion. 4: Design a 'Wanted' poster for Crippen.	Pupils from Group 4 display their 'Wanted' posters for Crippen. The rest of the class checks to make sure that all important information has been included.

RESOURCES

Photocopiable pages 81 and 82 ('Crippen Hanged'), board or flip chart, OHP and acetate (optional), a set of dictionaries, writing materials.

PREPARATION

Make enough copies of the photocopiable newspaper article (pages 81 and 82) for one per child. If possible, prepare an OHT of the article, or enlarge to A3 size. Prepare another OHT of the list of prefixes covered in Hour 1 (see 'Whole-class skills work') or write the list on the board or flip chart.

Introduction

Display the 'Crippen Hanged' newspaper article as an OHT or A3 enlargement. Introduce it by explaining that the article describes a crime which actually happened nearly 100 years ago, and that its solution was a superb example of detective work. Then read the article.

Discuss briefly the meaning of the difficult vocabulary used in the text, particularly the journalistic, legal and medical terms, for example:

exclusive	artiste	narcotic
drowsiness	unconsciousness	abdominal
condolence	post-mortem	

Whole-class skills work

Display the prefixes shown below on an OHT or written on the board or flip chart (see 'Preparation'). Briefly revise the term 'prefix' and discuss the meanings of those on the list. Explore the 'Crippen Hanged' article and ask the children to point out as many words as they can with these prefixes (examples from the text are shown in brackets):

ab-	from	(*abdominal, about*)
ad-	to	(*address*)
ante-	before	
anti-	against	
bi-	two	
con-	with	(*consolation, condolence*)
de-	down	(*description, decided*)
in-	in	
ex-	out	(*exclusive, expensive, explained, examination*)
hyper-	above	
inter-	between	
poly-	many	
post-	after	(*post-mortem*)
pro-	forwards	(*prodded*)
re-	back	(*report, returned, remains, remained*)
sub-	below	
super-	beyond	
syn-	together	
tele-	far away	
tri-	three	
uni-	one	

Now ask the children to use a dictionary to find at least two examples of words containing the other prefixes not included in the 'Crippen Hanged' text. Write each example next to the appropriate prefix and discuss the meaning of each word.

Differentiated group activities

1*: Guided reading and discussion of the 'Crippen Hanged' newspaper article. The following questions and suggestions for discussion can be used as a starting point:
■ Begin by examining the text as a whole. What kind of text is it? Who is speaking in the main body of the text?
■ Ask questions to test basic factual recall and understanding, for example, Why was Dr Crippen hanged? What was his wife's name? How did he murder his wife? and so on.
■ Look at the three police descriptions. How do they differ from character descriptions in stories?
■ What was it that first made Chief Inspector Dew suspicious?
■ How did he follow up his suspicions, and what did he find?
■ How did medical experts know that the remains were those of Crippen's second wife?
■ How did Crippen try to cover his escape to Quebec?
   Ask questions exploring the issues raised by the text, for example, Why did Crippen murder his wife? Could he have solved his domestic problems in another way? Was it right to hang him for the crime? (Discuss this last question in particular detail to prepare for the article this group will write in the second hour.)
2 & 3: Design a 'Wanted' poster for Crippen and another for Ethel le Neve. The posters should include:
■ a brief statement of the crime of which they are accused
■ a brief description (summarize or abridge the description in the article)
■ a sketched reconstruction of the appearance of the accused.
4*: Guided reading and discussion. Spend some time re-reading parts of the text with the children to ensure that they understand some of the more difficult vocabulary. Then discuss the text as for Group 1, but with greater emphasis on the simpler questions, adapting them as appropriate.

Conclusion

Children from Groups 2 and 3 display their 'Wanted' posters. The rest of the class should evaluate them by checking to see if any important information has been missed out.

Introduction

Re-read the 'Crippen Hanged' article with the class. Revise the meanings of any difficult words.

Whole-class skills work

Display the 'Crippen Hanged' text as an OHT or A3 enlargement. Start by revising the simple present tense and the simple past tense. Build on previous work on the latter by focusing on irregular verbs. Explain that the simple past tense is formed in two ways:

■ with an -*ed* suffix (regular verbs), for example 'live/lived'
■ by vowel change (irregular verbs), for example 'run/ran'.

Now ask the children to find some examples of irregular verbs in the 'Crippen Hanged' text. Choose an example, such as 'give/gave', and conjugate it as shown below:

	SINGULAR	PLURAL
1st person	I gave	We gave
2nd person	You gave	You gave
3rd person	He/she/it gave	They gave

Make a list of present/past pairs of irregular verbs used in the text (for example *run/ran, find/found, go/went, fall/fell, write/wrote, tell/told, become/became*).

Finally, investigate the use of tenses in 'Crippen Hanged'. Which sentences are in the present tense and which are in the past? Discuss how the beginning of the news article is in the past tense because it is retelling events that have happened; this is followed by Chief Inspector Dew giving a *recount* of his experiences. Explain that news stories and police reports are both examples of *recounted texts*. However, the descriptions of suspects are in the present tense – they would have been written when all three suspects were still living.

Differentiated group activities

1: Write an article for the *Newgate Gazette* in which you argue that hanging Dr Crippen was too severe a punishment and that life imprisonment would have been fairer.
2 & 3*: Guided reading and discussion, as for Group 1 in Hour 1.
4: Design a 'Wanted' poster for Crippen, along the lines of that described for Groups 2 and 3 in Hour 1.

Conclusion

Children from Group 4 display their 'Wanted' posters for Crippen, with the rest of the class checking to make sure that the important information has been included.

FURTHER IDEA

Many true stories are turned into novels, films or musicals. For example, the life of another famous Victorian murderer, Sweeney Todd, recently became the subject of a musical. The children could take the facts of the Crippen story and turn them into a short novel (or chapter from a novel) or a play.

𝔑𝔢𝔴𝔤𝔞𝔱𝔢 𝔊𝔞𝔷𝔢𝔱𝔱𝔢

24 November 1910   *1d*

CRIPPEN HANGED

Dr Crippen was hanged yesterday in Pentonville prison for the murder of his wife, Belle Elmore.

Chief Inspector Walter Dew of Scotland Yard gave this exclusive report on the crime to the Newgate Gazette.

Hawley Harvey Crippen was born in Coldwater, Michigan, in 1862. He had medical training, but never qualified as a doctor. The police description issued before his arrest runs as follows:

Hawley Harvey Crippen is a short (5ft 3ins) man with thinning hair, a long straggly, sandy moustache, and large grey eyes behind gold-rimmed glasses. He is courteous and quietly spoken. He is known to his friends as 'Peter'. His address is 39 Hilldrop Crescent.

His first wife died in 1890. His second wife was a music hall artiste called Belle Elmore. Her description is as follows:

Belle Elmore is short and stout, with dark eyes and hair. She wears colourful and expensive clothes and a great deal of jewellery. She seems like a plump bird of paradise. She speaks in a clear voice with a sharp American twang. She is a Roman Catholic and treasurer of the Music-Hall Ladies Guild.

Crippen and Belle Elmore did not get on too well. She went in and out just as she liked and this led to frequent rows. However, Crippen found consolation when he fell in love with his typist, Ethel le Neve. It seems that Crippen and Ethel wanted to get married, and so Crippen planned to murder his wife. This is the police description of Ethel written just before the arrest:

CRIPPEN. AND BELLE ELMORE IN HAPPIER DAYS

Ethel le Neve is 5ft 5 ins, pale-faced, with light brown hair, large grey-blue eyes. Nice looking, pleasant lady-like appearance. Quiet, subdued manner, talks quietly, looks intently when in conversation.

On 17 January 1910, Crippen ordered five grains of hyoscine (a narcotic poison) from a New Oxford Street chemist, Lewis and Burrows. He signed the poisons register.

On 31 January, the Crippens gave a small dinner party and it was after this, in the early hours of the morning that Crippen put the poison in Belle's drink. Taken in sweet tea or coffee, the hyoscine would have caused drowsiness, followed by unconsciousness, paralysis and death.

THE CHEMISTS WHERE CRIPPEN BOUGHT THE POISON

On the 12 March, Miss le Neve moved permanently into 39 Hilldrop Crescent. Crippen told friends that Belle had died while on an unexpected trip to America to visit a sick relative. He posted a notice of her death in *The Era* on 26 March. He dealt calmly with mourning friends, calls and letters of condolence until, about three months later, there were no further calls and it must have seemed that he was safe.

However, on 9 August, Mr and Mrs Nash, who were friends of Belle, returned from America. When they went to visit Belle, Crippen explained that she had died. They asked several questions, but were not satisfied with Crippen's answers, so Mr Nash told a friend of his at Scotland Yard.

That was when I was put on the case. I visited Crippen and questioned him closely, but could find nothing wrong with his answers. However, one thing seemed odd to me: Mrs Crippen had left behind most of her gorgeous gowns.

I decided to pay another visit on the 11 July, and was astonished to hear that Crippen had arranged to wind up his business affairs and had sent out the office boy to buy some clothing suitable for a boy. Crippen was away on a trip to Belgium so I could not question him about this, but I had his house searched again and again. At last, after prodding the coal-cellar floor with a poker, we found some loose bricks. Underneath were human remains. The report on the post-mortem examination stated that they were the remains of a stout female who bleached her hair and had had an abdominal operation. There were also traces of the poison, hyoscine: they had found all that remained of Belle Elmore.

On 16 July, a warrant was issued for the arrest of Crippen and Ethel le Neve. They were identified on 20 July on the *SS Montrose*, when the captain became suspicious about two of his passengers: a man and his young son, John. John's trousers were very tight about the hips and secured with safety pins. His manners at table were 'lady-like'. John turned out to be Ethel in disguise. When the ship was near Quebec, I went out to it in a pilot boat and arrested and charged him. That was the finest moment of my career.

CRIPPEN AND ETHEL LE NEVE WERE ARRESTED ABOARD
THE SS MONTROSE

POLICE REPORT

OBJECTIVES

UNIT	SPELLING/VOCABULARY	GRAMMAR/PUNCTUATION	COMPREHENSION/ COMPOSITION
WRITING NON-FICTION Police report.	Check spellings.	Understand the need for agreement of subject and verb.	Recognize the features of recounted texts. Write a report in the appropriate style.

ORGANIZATION (1 HOUR)

INTRODUCTION	WHOLE-CLASS SKILLS WORK	DIFFERENTIATED GROUP ACTIVITIES	CONCLUSION
Read the 'Crippen Hanged' newspaper article from previous unit and discuss the features of the report genre.	Check agreement of subject and verb.	1–4*: Fill in the Police Report form.	Selected pupils read out the narrative sections of their reports. The rest of the class evaluate them by checking that all the important details are included.

RESOURCES

Photocopiable pages 85 ('Police Report') and 81 and 82 ('Crippen Hanged') from the previous unit, board or flip chart, OHP and acetate (optional), writing materials.

PREPARATION

Make enough copies of the Police Report form on photocopiable page 85 for one per child. Make OHTs of the 'Crippen Hanged' story from the previous unit if you have not already done so, or provide individual copies for each child.

Introduction

Start by briefly recapping the main events of the 'Crippen Hanged' news story from the previous unit. Explain to the children that they are going to complete a police report based on the Crippen case, so they will need to listen very carefully for appropriate details in the reading. Follow this with a shared reading of 'Crippen Hanged', displaying it on an OHP if possible.

Remind the children that 'Crippen Hanged' is a news report which also includes an account by Chief Inspector Walter Dew of his experiences. The text is an example of a *recount*. Discuss the features of recounted texts:

- usually an introduction is included
- text is written in chronological sequence
- there may be some supporting illustrations
- the style of the text, such as degree of formality
- the use of connectives, for example first..., next..., then... and so on.

How many of these features does the 'Crippen Hanged' text include? Discuss: the brief introduction informing readers that the Chief Inspector's account follows; the chronological sequence used in the Chief Inspector's account; the relatively formal style and technical language, for example *'Taken in sweet tea or coffee, the hyoscine...paralysis and death'*; the use of dates to sequence the events.

Although most of the text is written in the past tense, the descriptions of Crippen, Belle Elmore and Ethel le Neve (taken from a police report at the time) are in the present tense. This is because they were written while these people were alive as a means of helping the public to identify them.

Whole-class skills work

Use the 'Crippen Hanged' text as a basis for focusing on the correct agreement of subject and verb. Point out to the children that a common error is to use 'was' instead of 'were' with a plural subject. Explain how the verb changes to agree with the subject, for example, He *was* arrested/They *were* arrested. Write down the following phrases on the board or flip chart and invite individuals to come up and rewrite them in the plural (using 'they'):

- He was in love.
- He was hoping to get married.
- He was sure he was safe.
- He was away in Belgium.
- He was identified on the *SS Montrose*.
- He was charged with the crime.

Differentiated group activities

The children will each need a copy of the Police Report form on photocopiable page 85 and a copy of the 'Crippen Hanged' news article on pages 81 and 82 from the previous unit.

1–4*: The children should imagine that they are Chief Inspector Dew and fill in the form using information about Crippen from the news article. Emphasize that for the 'Narrative' section of the sheet, they should not copy out whole passages but instead, list key dates and facts from the article. Particular emphasis should be given to evidence (for example the post-mortem) and they will need to refer to the text closely for this to ensure the accuracy of their facts.

Children in Group 4 should be encouraged to look for the dates in the text to help them write the events in the correct sequence.

Conclusion

Selected children read out the narrative sections of their reports. The rest of the class evaluates these by checking that all the important details are included.

POLICE REPORT

Report Number: **Date:**

Details of Person Reporting the Crime:
Name:
Date of Birth:
Address:

Details of Victim(s):
Name:
Date of Birth:
Address:

Details of Suspect(s):
Age:
Height:
Weight:
Build:
Eye colour:
Hair colour:
Hair style:
Other details:

Narrative (describe what happened):

Reporting Officer's signature

NOTE-TAKING

OBJECTIVES

UNIT	SPELLING/VOCABULARY	GRAMMAR/PUNCTUATION	COMPREHENSION/COMPOSITION
REFERENCE AND RESEARCH SKILLS Note-taking.	Use simple abbreviations.	Formulate questions and note relevant information.	Discuss the purpose and some of the methods of taking notes. Take notes in different formats.

ORGANIZATION (1 HOUR)

	INTRODUCTION	WHOLE-CLASS SKILLS WORK	DIFFERENTIATED GROUP ACTIVITIES	CONCLUSION
HOUR 1	Set up an imaginary interview scenario. Formulate questions and demonstrate the need to record replies through note-taking.	Discuss purposes of note-taking. Talk about the different sources of information for note-taking. Demonstrate different forms of notes, eg timeline, flow chart, topic web and diagram.	All groups make notes from a five-minute interview. 1: Devise a time-line linked to a current topic. 2 & 3*: Draw a flow chart, with teacher support. 4: Label a diagram prepared by the teacher.	Report back to the class and discuss the efficiency of their note-taking and how much using abbreviations helped them.

RESOURCES

Board or flip chart, a selection of information materials on science and history topics that the class is currently studying, OHP and acetate or A3 paper, writing materials (including notepads and pencils).

PREPARATION

Prepare for display on large posters or OHP a sample of each of the formats below for note-taking. (To help the children's understanding, these should be based on information familiar to them through topic work already covered.)

- A timeline.
- A flow chart.
- A topic web.
- A labelled diagram.

Finally, prepare copies of a topic-related diagram for the children in Group 4 to label after the main group activity.

Introduction

Tell the children that as part of the group activities, they are going to role play journalists interviewing pupils about the things they do outside school hours. Explain that they will be equipped only with notepads and pencils, and will have to work to a strict time limit, with exactly five minutes to write down what their interviewee says. Emphasize that, as they will have no tape recorders, they will need to take notes effectively so that they can remember what was said later when they come to write up their reports.

Discuss how the children will go about their interviews. What questions will they ask? Give the class two or three minutes to brainstorm some ideas, then record them on the board or flip chart in note form, pointing out how you are shortening some of the words to speed up your writing. For example you might put: *'How oft watch TV?' 'What are yr fav progs?'* Decide on five questions which all children are likely to respond to.

Whole-class skills work

Now go on to talk about other situations in which people might take notes to help them remember what someone said, for example students at lectures; adults at meetings; the police at the scene of a crime; judges and barristers in court; children recording what a teacher tells them about a topic and so on. Say that talk is an important source of information and scribe on the board or flip chart the words: *'Talk is impt source of info.'* Repeat that it saves time when you are writing quick notes if you abbreviate some of the words, and use as few words as possible.

Next, ask for suggestions of other sources of information that could be used to take notes from. List these in abbreviated form on the board or flip chart. Other sources of info are: *pics, info bks, CD-ROMS, radio progs, encycs, photos, vids* and so on.

Move on to explain that the form of note-taking can be varied according to the purpose. Using the samples you have prepared on posters or OHP (see 'Preparation'), explain how each in its way gives a quick overview of its subject. The **timeline** makes it easy to see what happened when. It is a useful way of placing objects or events in time (or *chronological*) order, for example in a history topic. The **flow chart** with its arrows is a good way of shortening an explanation of how to make or do something or of noting the different aspects of a process, for example in science. A **topic web** helps when making notes about different aspects of the same subject. Putting labels on a quickly-sketched **diagram** helps to recall the look of an object and what goes where.

Differentiated group activities

Within their ability groups, the children work in pairs to complete the interviewing activity, using the list of questions written up during the introduction. They should note their partner's responses to the questions as quickly and briefly as possible, using abbreviations wherever they can. After five minutes, interviewers and interviewees switch roles so that everyone has a turn at note-taking. It is possible that some children will not have time to cover all the questions. Once the children have finished the interviews, they should carry out the following activities (these may need to be followed up outside the Literacy Hour):

1: Use a variety of information sources to prepare notes in the form of a timeline (with clear date limits) on a topic chosen by the teacher (for example Inventions in Victorian Times; The Life of Tutankhamun and so on).

2 & 3*: Work with the teacher to make notes for a flow chart linked to a current topic, for example in science.

4: Label a topic-related diagram previously prepared by the teacher (see 'Preparation').

Conclusion

Ask some of the children to report back to the class on the note-taking they did for their interviews. What abbreviations did they use? Did efficient note-taking help them to cope with the time limit? What problems did they encounter and how did they resolve them?

ALLITERATION

OBJECTIVES

UNIT	SPELLING/VOCABULARY	GRAMMAR/PUNCTUATION	COMPREHENSION/COMPOSITION
WORD PLAY Alliteration: 'Shrewd Simon Short' by Alvin Schwartz.	Be aware of the use of adverbs to qualify verbs.	Understand the use of punctuation as an aid to the reader.	Explore the use of alliteration.

ORGANIZATION (1 HOUR)

	INTRODUCTION	WHOLE-CLASS SKILLS WORK	DIFFERENTIATED GROUP ACTIVITIES	CONCLUSION
HOUR 1	Introduce alliteration by discussing tongue-twisters.	Investigate the use of alliteration in a humorous story, 'Shrewd Simon Short', on photocopiable page 90.	1: Work with a partner to produce a piece of alliterative writing. 2*: Work on adverbs. 3*: Prepare a reading of the photocopiable story for presentation. 4: Design an alliterative shop sign.	Pupils share the process and outcome of their activities. Recap on what alliteration is.

RESOURCES

Photocopiable page 90 ('Shrewd Simon Short'), board or flip chart, OHP and acetate (optional), dictionaries, writing and drawing materials.

PREPARATION

Make enough copies of photocopiable page 90 ('Shrewd Simon Short') for one between two children. If possible, also prepare the sheet as an OHT or enlarge to at least A3. Practise the tongue-twister 'Peter Piper' and then practise reading aloud the story 'Shrewd Simon Short' before you present it in the introductory session.

Introduction

Ask the children if they know what a 'tongue-twister' is. Why is it called a tongue-twister? Do they know any tongue-twisters? Ask volunteers to recite those that they know. A good example to read to the children is 'Peter Piper':

Peter Piper picked a peck of pickled pepper.
A peck of pickled pepper Peter Piper picked.
If Peter Piper picked a peck of pickled pepper,
Where is the peck of pickled pepper Peter Piper picked?

Explain the term 'alliteration' as the repetition of the same sound at the beginning of a group of consecutive or closely connected words. What is the initial sound that is repeated in the words of 'Peter Piper'? Discuss what effect the alliteration has on this verse, such as it makes it humorous! Discuss what other effects can be achieved with alliteration – for example 'slithery snake' mimics the hiss of a snake, while 'He clasps the crag with crooked hands' provides a musical, rhythmic pattern in poetry.

Make a list of the tongue-twisters that the children know and identify the repeated initial sound for each. Give the children a few minutes to make up some short examples of their own.

Whole-class skills work

Tell the children that they are now going to look at a collection of alliterative sentences that form a story. Introduce 'Shrewd Simon Short' on photocopiable page 90. Give out one copy of the story between two, and display it on an OHP if possible. Read the story slowly, then ask the children to discuss what it is about. Ask them to tell you sentences or phrases which appeal to them. Are there any unusual words? Why have these words been used? Encourage the children to explain the meanings of unusual vocabulary, for example 'self-same', 'serenade', 'sauntered' and so on using a dictionary to help them where necessary.

Refer back to the term 'alliteration'. What letters do the children think might be easy to use alliteratively? Can they think of any that would be difficult or impossible to use (for example *u*, *x*, *z*)?

Return to the story and ask for volunteers to read a few sentences each. Tell the children that you had to practise it carefully before reading it to them. Can they suggest some important considerations when reading an alliterative story? These could include pace, clarity and the importance of taking note of punctuation.

Differentiated group activities

1: Working with a partner, the children choose a suitable letter and write a short alliterative piece based around it.
2*: Remind the children what an adverb is. Make a list of those in the photocopiable story. Choose another letter and make an alliterative list of adverbs.
3*: Guided re-reading of the photocopiable story as a group, with the children taking on roles of individual characters and narrator. Prepare the piece to share with the class.
4: Design 'Simon's Squeaking Shop Sign', using words from the story to put on the sign.

Conclusion

Ask selected children from Groups 2 and 4 to share their adverb collections and shop signs. Choose one alliterative passage from Group 1 to read aloud. Did the children find it difficult? What did they learn from writing it? Ask Group 3 to perform their story.

SHREWD SIMON SHORT

Shrewd Simon Short sewed shoes. Seventeen summers saw Simon's small, shabby shop still standing, saw Simon's self-same squeaking sign still swinging swiftly, specifying:

Simon's spouse, Sally Short, sewed sheets, stitched shirts, stuffed sofas. Simon's stout sturdy sons – Stephen, Samuel, Saul, Silas – sold sundries. Stephen sold silks, satins, shawls. Samuel sold saddles, stirrups. Saul sold silver spoons, specialities. Silas sold Sally Short's stuffed sofas.

Simon's second son, Samuel, saw Sophia Sophronia Spriggs somewhere. Sweet, sensible, smart Sophia Sophronia Spriggs. Sam soon showed strange symptoms. Surprisingly, Sam sighted sorrowfully, sang several serenades slyly, sought Sophia Spriggs' society, seldom stood selling saddles.

Simon stormed, scowled severely, said, 'Sam seems so silly singing such senseless songs.'

'Soft,' said sweet Sally. 'Sam's smitten. Sam's spied some sweetheart.'

'Smitten!' snarled Simon. 'Scatterbrained simpleton! Sentimental, silly schoolboy!'

Sally sighed sadly. Summoning Sam, she spoke sympathizingly. 'Sam,' said she, 'Sire* seems singularly snappish. So, Sonny, stop strolling streets so soberly, stop singing sly serenades. Sell saddles sensibly, Sam. See Sophia Sophronia Spriggs speedily.'

'So soon?' said Sam, startled.

'So soon, surely,' said Sally, smilingly, 'specially since Sire shows such spirit.' So Sam, somewhat scared, sauntered slowly storeward, shaking stupendously. 'Sophia Sophronia Spriggs...Sam Short's spouse...sounds splendid,' said Sam softly.

Sam soon spied Sophia starching shirts, singing softly. Seeing Sam, she stopped, saluting Sam smilingly.

Sam stuttered shockingly. 'Sp-sp-splendid s-s-summer s-s-season, So-So-Sophia.'

'Somewhat sultry,' suggested Sophia.

'S-s-sartin,' said Sam.

'Still selling saddles, Sam?' said Sophia.

Silence, seventeen seconds.

'Sire shot sixteen snipe Saturday, Sam,' said Sophia.

Silence, seventy-seven seconds.

'See sister Sue's sunflowers,' said Sophia socially, stopping such stiff silence.

Such sprightly sauciness stimulated Sam strangely. So, swiftly speaking, Sam said, 'Sue's sunflowers seem saying, "Sophia Sophronia Springs, Samuel Short stroll serenely, seek some sparkling streams, sing some sweet, soul-stirring strain. . . ."'

Sophia snickered, so Sam stopped. She stood silently several seconds.

Said Sam, 'Stop smiling, Sophia. Sam's seeking some sweet spouse!'

She still stood silently.

'Speak, Sophia, speak! Such silence speculates sorrow.'

'Seek Sire Spriggs, Sam,' said Sophia.

Sam sought Sire Spriggs.

Sire Spriggs said, 'Sartin.'

*An old-fashioned word for Father

THE FUN THEY HAD

OBJECTIVES

UNIT	SPELLING/VOCABULARY	GRAMMAR/PUNCTUATION	COMPREHENSION/ COMPOSITION
READING FICTION Science fiction short story: 'The Fun They Had' by Isaac Asimov.	Extend vocabulary from vocabulary in text. Investigate antonyms. Identify vocabulary that indicates in which culture the story was written.	Construct sentences in different ways.	Investigate key features of science fiction genre. Discuss appeal of science fiction.

ORGANIZATION (2 HOURS)

	INTRODUCTION	WHOLE-CLASS SKILLS WORK	DIFFERENTIATED GROUP ACTIVITIES	CONCLUSION
HOUR 1	Preview and then read story. Investigate key features of science fiction.	Experiment with constructing sentences in different ways.	1*: Guided reading and discussion. 2 & 3: Write a description of an 'electronic teacher'. 4*: Guided reading and discussion.	Share opinions on how well Asimov predicted the future. Discuss appeal of science fiction genre.
HOUR 2	Selected pupils read their descriptions of an 'electronic teacher'.	Investigate antonyms.	1: Write a description of an 'electronic teacher'. 2 & 3*: Guided reading/ discussion. 4: Write a description of an 'electronic teacher'.	Discuss own predictions for the schools of the future. Relate key features of science fiction to story.

RESOURCES

Photocopiable pages 95 and 96 ('The Fun They Had'), board or flip chart, OHP and acetate (optional), writing materials.

PREPARATION

Make enough copies of the story for one between two children. If possible, prepare the story as an OHT or enlarge to at least A3 size.

Introduction

Explain that the story you are about to read is a science fiction short story. Find out what the children already know about the genre. What stories have they read, or what films have they seen that they would consider to be science fiction?

Discuss the genre's general features, writing the key ones on the board or flip chart – for example:

Plot: The main events just might really happen because they are based on scientific facts that we know to be true.
Time: Set in the future.
Place: Usually a futuristic earth, or another place that scientists think could exist.
Characters: Fictional, but they behave in ways that are sensible from a scientific point of view.

Explain that the story 'The Fun They Had' was written in 1957 and is set 200 years into the future. Read the story.

Whole-class skills work

Experiment with constructing sentences in different ways. For example, brainstorm with the children all possible ways of rewriting the first sentence of the story.

Margie even wrote about it that night in her diary.
That night, Margie even wrote about it in her diary.
In her diary that night, Margie wrote about it.
Margie, that night, wrote about it in her diary.

Discuss the slight differences in emphasis. The first one emphasizes Margie. The second focuses on 'That night', as though it had been a special night of some kind. In the third sentence, the diary is emphasized. This would be appropriate in a story in which the diary played an important part.
 Ask the children to repeat this exercise with the following sentence from the story:

He smiled at Margie and gave her an apple, then took the teacher apart.

What changes in meaning occur when this sentence is reordered? Explain the importance to the children of re-reading their own writing to ensure that the meaning they want to convey is, in fact, conveyed in the best way.

Differentiated group activities

1*: Guided reading and discussion. The following questions can be used as a starting point:

- What do Margie and Tommy find surprising about books?
- In what way has the future come true long before Asimov predicted?
- What is sometimes used instead of books today?
- Which do you enjoy reading/using most?
- Why does the 'mechanical teacher' sound out-of-date to us?
- What does Margie think was good about the old schools?
- Which kind of teaching would you prefer?
- What do you think teaching in the future will be like?
- Which words and phrases tell us that Asimov was an American author?

2 & 3: Children should re-read the description of the 'mechanical teacher' and write a more up-to-date version – an 'electronic teacher'. Describe what would be possible with today's technology, for example CD-ROM, Internet and so on. Write a description so that it would fit into the story.
4*: Guided reading and discussion. Support children's basic comprehension of the text and encourage expressive reading aloud. Then use some of the above questions for discussion as appropriate.

Conclusion

Discuss how features of science fiction are reflected in the story. Share opinions on how well Asimov predicted the future. Discuss what the children feel is the appeal of this type of fiction.

Introduction

Ask selected children from Groups 2 and 3 to read their descriptions of an 'electronic teacher'.

Whole-class skills work

Focus this session on extending vocabulary by investigating antonyms.
 Review the term 'antonym' – a word that means the opposite of another word. Display the OHT or enlarged text of the story and ask the children to find opposites for all the words on the first page that have opposites: for example night – day; old – new; little – big; first – last. This should lead to an interesting discussion about words and what kind have opposites. Does the word 'today' have an opposite? If so, is it 'tonight', 'tomorrow', 'yesterday'? What is the opposite of a 'real book' – an 'unreal book' or a 'fake book'? What is the phrase 'real book' contrasted to in the story ('telebook')?

Differentiated group activities

1: Children should re-read the description of the 'mechanical teacher' and write a more up-to-date version – an 'electronic teacher' (see above).

2 & 3*: Guided reading and discussion. Ask some children to read aloud from the paragraph beginning 'Margie went into the schoolroom' to the end, concentrating on the timing and expression, particularly the last paragraph.

4: Children should re-read the description of the 'mechanical teacher' and write a more up-to-date version – an 'electronic teacher'. This can be a simple list of features and need not be in the style of the story.

Conclusion

Discuss children's own predictions for the schools of the future.

FURTHER IDEAS

■ Ask children to work in pairs to modernize the story so that it is a 1990s/2000s view of the future, 200 year hence.

■ Ask children to write their own school story set in the future.

THE FUN THEY HAD

Margie even wrote about it that night in her diary. On the page headed 17 May 2157, she wrote, 'Today Tommy found a real book!'

It was a very old book. Margie's grandfather once said that when he was a little boy *his* grandfather told him that there was a time when all stories were printed on paper.

They turned the pages, which were yellow and crinkly, and it was awfully funny to read words that stood still instead of moving the way they were supposed to – on a screen, you know. And then, when they turned back to the page before, it had the same words on it that it had had when they read it the first time.

'Gee,' said Tommy, 'what a waste. When you're through with the book, you just throw it away, I guess. Our television screen must have had a million books on it and it's good for plenty more. I wouldn't throw it away.'

'Same with mine,' said Margie. She was eleven and hadn't seen as many telebooks as Tommy had. He was thirteen.

She said, 'Where did you find it?'

'In my house.' He pointed without looking, because he was busy reading. 'In the attic.'

'What's it about?'

'School.'

Margie was scornful. 'School? What's there to write about school? I hate school.'

Margie always hated school, but now she hated it more than ever. The mechanical teacher had been giving her test after test in geography and she had been doing worse and worse until her mother had shaken her head sorrowfully and sent for the County Inspector.

He was a round little man with a red face and a whole box of tools with dials and wires. He smiled at Margie and gave her an apple, then took the teacher apart. Margie had hoped he wouldn't know how to put it together again, but he knew how all right, and, after an hour or so, there it was again, large and black and ugly, with a big screen on which all the lessons were shown and the questions were asked. That wasn't so bad. The part Margie hated most was the slot where she had to put homework and test papers. She always had to write them out in a punch code they made her learn when she was six years old, and the mechanical teacher calculated the mark in no time.

The Inspector had smiled after he was finished and patted Margie's head. He said to her mother, 'It's not the little girl's fault, Mrs Jones. I think the geography sector was geared a little too quick. Those things happen sometimes. I've slowed it up to an average ten-year level. Actually, the over-all pattern of her progress is quite satisfactory.' And he patted Margie's head again.

Margie was disappointed. She had been hoping they would take the teacher away altogether. They had once taken Tommy's teacher away for nearly a month because the history sector had blanked out completely.

So she said to Tommy, 'Why would anyone write about school?'

Tommy looked at her with very superior eyes. 'Because it's not our kind of school, stupid. This is the old kind of school that they had hundreds and hundreds of years ago.' He added loftily, pronouncing the word carefully, '*Centuries* ago.'

Margie was hurt. 'Well, I don't know what kind of school they had all that time ago.' She read the book over his shoulder for a while, then said, 'Anyway, they had a teacher.'

'Sure they had a teacher, but it wasn't a *regular* teacher. It was a man.'

'A man? How could a man be a teacher?'

'Well, he just told the boys and girls things and gave them homework and asked them questions.'

'A man isn't smart enough.'

'Sure he is. My father knows as much as my teacher.'

'He can't. A man can't know as much as a teacher.'

'He knows almost as much, I betcha.'

Margie wasn't prepared to dispute that. She said, 'I wouldn't want a strange man in my house to teach me.'

Tommy screamed with laughter. 'You don't know much, Margie. The teachers didn't live in the house. They had a special building and all the kids went there.'

'And all the kids learned the same thing?'

'Sure, if they were the same age.'

'But my mother says a teacher has to be adjusted to fit the mind of each boy and girl it teaches and that each kid has to be taught differently.'

'Just the same they didn't do it that way then. If you don't like it, you don't have to read the book.'

'I didn't say I didn't like it,' Margie said quickly. She wanted to read about those funny schools.

They weren't even half finished when Margie's mother called, 'Margie! School!'

Margie looked up. 'Not yet, Mamma.'

'Now!' said Mrs Jones. 'And it's probably time for Tommy, too.'

Margie said to Tommy, 'Can I read the book some more with you after school?'

'Maybe,' he said nonchalantly. He walked away whistling, the dusty old book tucked beneath his arm.

Margie went into the schoolroom. It was right next to her bedroom, and the mechanical teacher was on and waiting for her. It was always on at the same time every day except Saturday and Sunday, because her mother said little girls learned better if they learned at regular hours.

The screen was lit up, and it said: 'Today's arithmetic lesson is on the addition of proper fractions. Please insert yesterday's homework in the proper slot.'

Margie did so with a sigh. She was thinking about the old schools they had when her grandfather's grandfather was a little boy. All the kids from the whole neighbourhood came, laughing and shouting in the schoolyard, sitting together in the schoolroom, going home together at the end of the day. They learned the same things, so they could help one another on the homework and talk about it.

And the teachers were people . . .

The mechanical teacher was flashing on the screen: 'When we add fractions ½ and ¼ – '

Margie was thinking about how the kids must have loved it in the old days. She was thinking about the fun they had.

(Extract from 'The Fun They Had' by Isaac Asimov from Isaac Asimov: The Complete Stories, Vol 1 . Copyright 1993 Isaac Asimov. Published by Harper Collins.)

SCIENCE FICTION CARDS

OBJECTIVES

UNIT	SPELLING/VOCABULARY	GRAMMAR/PUNCTUATION	COMPREHENSION/ COMPOSITION
WRITING FICTION Science Fiction Cards.	Extend vocabulary from vocabulary in text.	Revise and extend writing of dialogue.	Apply skills of story writing learned in 'Harwell Hall' unit (Term 1) but with more imaginative content. Use a planning grid.

ORGANIZATION (3 HOURS)

	INTRODUCTION	WHOLE-CLASS SKILLS WORK	DIFFERENTIATED GROUP ACTIVITIES	CONCLUSION
HOUR 1	Introduce oral storytelling activity using Science Fiction Cards. Give tips for oral presentation.	Use the cards as a basis for revision of skills covered to date.	1–4: All groups play the Science Fiction Cards game and tell their orally-composed stories to each other. *The teacher works with Groups 1 & 4.	One pupil from each group is chosen to tell his/her oral story to the whole class.
HOUR 2	Display the Story Planner. Relate to stories previously read – 'Harwell Hall' (Term 1) and 'The Fun They Had' (previous unit).	Use the Story Planner to write a plan for the oral story.	1–4: Pupils in all groups begin to turn their oral story into a written story. *The teacher works with Groups 2 & 3.	Examples of promising beginnings are read out.
HOUR 3	Display 'The Fun They Had' and draw attention to the way dialogue is handled.	Revision and development of writing and punctuating speech.	1–4: Pupils in all groups finish the first draft of their stories. *The teacher works with Group 4.	Selected pupils read out their first draft.

RESOURCES

Photocopiable pages 100–103 (Science Fiction Cards), 104 (Story Planner), 95 and 96 ('The Fun They Had' from the previous unit), 35 and 36 ('Harwell Hall' from Term 1) and 105 (2020), sturdy card, lamination materials (optional), scissors, board or flip chart, OHP and acetate (optional), writing materials.

PREPARATION

Photocopiable pages 100–103 (Science Fiction Cards) should be printed onto card, laminated and cut into sets. One set per group of four or five children is needed. Prepare enough Story Planners (page 104) for one per child and enough copies of '2020' (page 105) for one between two children. If possible, prepare OHTs of the Story Planner and the stories 'Harwell Hall' (Term 1) and 'The Fun They Had' (previous unit) – or use the ones prepared earlier for those units. Prepare the chart given under Hour 1 of 'Whole-class skills work' as an OHT, or write it up on the board or flip chart.

Introduction

The main aim of this unit is to revise key writing skills introduced in the 'Harwell Hall' unit, particularly skills of planning and structuring stories. It also provides an ideal context for examining differences between spoken and written language.

Begin by arranging the class into groups of four to five children, broadly according to ability, but overlapping where necessary to create groups of the required size. Then model the oral storytelling activity using the set of cards prepared from pages 100–103. Demonstrate the procedure by taking one group of children through the following process while others watch:

■ Shuffle each set of cards (BEINGS, PLACES, MACHINES and SITUATIONS) separately and place the sets face down in the middle of the table.

■ The first player takes the top card from each set and places them face up in front of him/her.

■ The player must make up an oral story using all the cards (the teacher should do this during the demonstration session). The story should be told in the *1st person*. (Remind the children what a story in the 1st person means. In this case, it means that the storyteller (the child) is a key character in the story. He or she will tell the story from his or her point of view, using 'I'.)

■ Continue the game clockwise around the table.

■ When everyone has had a turn, decide whose was the best story.

■ The rest of the group should then help that person to prepare the story for presentation to the class or other groups.

Explain that by playing the game the children are preparing story structures with a beginning, middle and end, and that each story should have characters, a plot and setting.

Whole-class skills work

Use the oral story-telling activity as the basis for exploring the differences between spoken and written language. Brainstorm the differences, writing the children's ideas on the board or flip chart. Then display this chart (either on OHP or on the board or flip chart) and work with the children to complete it.

	When we tell the story	*When we write the story*
Questions Statements Exclamations Description Dialogue Expressing anger Expressing fear Expressing nervousness Whispering Shouting etc	Questions are shown by a rising tone of voice.	Use a question mark at the end of the sentence.

Differentiated group activities

1–4*: All groups play the Science Fiction Cards game and tell their orally-composed stories to each other. The teacher works with Groups 1 and 4.

Conclusion

Choose one child from each group to tell his/her oral story to the whole class. The rest of the class should listen carefully and positive comment should be invited. For example, ask the class: 'What did you like about that story?' Ask the class if they can repeat any unusual vocabulary that gave them clues that the stories were set in the future.

Introduction

Explain that the oral stories from Hour 1 are going to be developed into written stories, and that you wish to revise and extend the skills taught during the 'Harwell Hall' unit (Term 1). The first key skill is planning a story with an effective structure, such as a good beginning, middle and end. Display the Story Planner (photocopiable page 104) and go through the different sections reminding the children how it applied to 'Harwell Hall' and how it could apply to the Asimov short story studied in the previous unit, 'The Fun They Had'.

Whole-class skills work

Give a copy of the Story Planner to all children. Remind them of the 'Harwell Hall' story and explain that the boxes in the planner are to help them write a story with a similar structure. Children in Group 1 should be encouraged to adapt the structure freely, or to write a plan in a completely different way, if they wish. Children in Groups 2 and 3 should be encouraged to follow the basic structure, but write several paragraphs in each section. Children in Group 4 should follow the planner closely, writing one paragraph for each section. Explain to all the children that they can develop or change their oral stories in any way, and can borrow ideas from the stories they heard at the end of Hour 1. Remind the children of the ending of 'Harwell Hall'. What was it called? (An *anti-climax* ending.) Can the children adapt their science fiction stories to end in a similar way?

Differentiated group activities

1–4*: All groups begin to turn their oral story into a written story. The teacher works with Groups 2 and 3 with a particular focus on planning and structuring the story.

Conclusion

Good examples of beginnings written by children in Groups 2 and 3 should be read out to the class. Invite other children to say what they liked about them. Comment on effective features and encourage other children to use them. Children from the same groups (who will have heard the oral version of the story) could be invited to comment on the differences between the oral and written versions.

Introduction

In this hour, the children have the opportunity to finish and redraft their stories. Ask the children to give particular attention to structuring sentences. Choose one of the stories to show how sentences can be constructed in different ways. Read out a paragraph, then suggest ways of reordering the words and phrases to create sentences of different lengths and types. Ask the children to comment on the different effect created on the reader by the different types of sentence.

Whole-class skills work

Explain that when the children come to redraft their stories, they should experiment to achieve the most effective sentence construction. Display photocopiable page 105 (2020) and discuss different ways of combining the words and phrases into sentences of different kinds. Give pairs of children a copy of the sheet and allow them to work on it for a short while. Then come together again and discuss the outcomes.

Differentiated group activities

1–4*: Children in all groups should finish the first draft of their stories, discuss them with a partner and begin to redraft them with a particular focus on sentence construction. The teacher works with Group 4, who should restrict their focus for redrafting to one paragraph.

Conclusion

Invite the children to share the results of their focus on sentence construction by reading out some 'before' and 'after' examples. The hour should be rounded off with a good example of a complete story.

SCIENCE FICTION CARDS 1: BEINGS

BEINGS **ROBOT**	BEINGS **EARTHLING**	BEINGS **MARTIAN**
BEINGS **GALACTIC LORD**	BEINGS **INSECTONS**	BEINGS **BLOB**
BEINGS **SPACE BIRDS**	BEINGS **XARGIAN WARRIORS**	

SCIENCE FICTION CARDS 2: PLACES

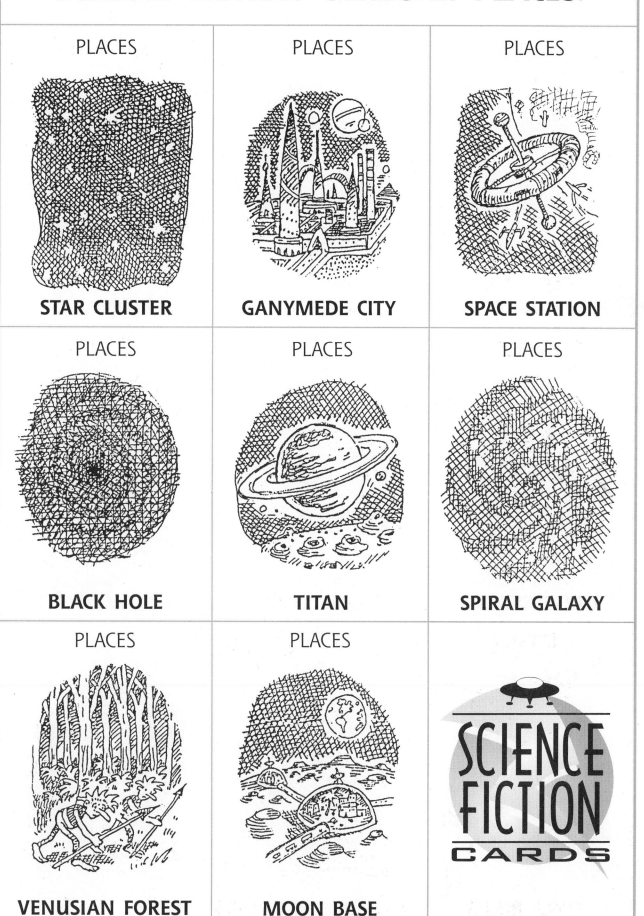

PLACES

STAR CLUSTER

PLACES

GANYMEDE CITY

PLACES

SPACE STATION

PLACES

BLACK HOLE

PLACES

TITAN

PLACES

SPIRAL GALAXY

PLACES

VENUSIAN FOREST

PLACES

MOON BASE

SCIENCE FICTION CARDS

SCIENCE FICTION CARDS 3: MACHINES

MACHINES

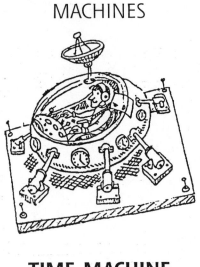

TIME MACHINE

MACHINES

SPACESHIP

MACHINES

TUNNELLER

MACHINES

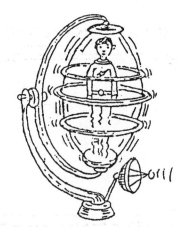

TELEPORTER

MACHINES

LASER CANON

MACHINES

ROBOT WARRIOR

MACHINES

FLYING SAUCER

MACHINES

SPACEPORT

SCIENCE FICTION CARDS

SCIENCE FICTION CARDS 4: SITUATIONS

SITUATIONS

STARSHIP MAIN COMPUTER

UNIDENTIFIED SPACECRAFT
IN SECTOR 9.

SITUATIONS

STARSHIP MAIN COMPUTER

!!!RED ALERT!!!
METEOR STRIKE!
HEAVY DAMAGE SUSTAINED.
RAPID AIR AND FUEL LOSS.

SITUATIONS

STARSHIP MAIN COMPUTER

POSITION UNKNOWN.
GRAVITATIONAL EFFECT OF
BLACK HOLE HAS PROJECTED
THE SHIP INTO AN
UNCHARTED SECTOR OF THE
GALAXY.

SITUATIONS

STARSHIP MAIN COMPUTER

APPROACHING PLANT KRELL.
PLANET STATUS REPORT:
TYPE: EARTH-LIKE
GRAVITY: 1.2G
ATMOSPHERE: BREATHABLE
LIFE: VEGETATION
NO INTELLIGENT BEINGS.

SITUATIONS

STARSHIP MAIN COMPUTER

REPORT FROM SICK BAY:
CREW MEMBER SICK WITH
HIGHLY INFECTIOUS SPACE
VIRUS.

SITUATIONS

STARSHIP MAIN COMPUTER

!!!RED ALERT!!!
ALIEN BEING DETECTED
ABOARD STARSHIP.

SITUATIONS

STARSHIP MAIN COMPUTER

MESSAGE FROM WARLORD OF
PLANET KRELL:
OUR BATTLEFLEET HAS YOU
IN ITS LASER SIGHTS. YOU
MUST SIGNAL YOUR TOTAL
SURRENDER IN 30 SECONDS.

SITUATIONS

STARSHIP MAIN COMPUTER

COMPUTER VIRUS DETECTED.
PREPARE FOR MANUAL
OPERATION OF SHIP.
PREPARE FOR MANUAL
CALCULATION OF
TRAJECTORY.
PREPARE
FO>>>>>>>>>>>>>>>>>>>

SCIENCE FICTION CARDS

STORY PLANNER

■ Look at this grid which outlines three different kinds of plots you may have read. When you plan your own story, you can combine any beginning, middle and end from the grid.

Beginning	Description of main character(s).	Description of place.	Dialogue.
Middle	Description of place. Setting out a problem. Attempts to solve the problem.	Description of main character(s). Setting out a problem. Dialogue about the problem. Attempts to solve the problem.	Description of a place or character(s). Description of a problem. Dialogue about the problem. Build up the suspense.
End	Problem solved.	A twist in the tale.	Anti-climax.

■ Use this grid to plan your own story.

Beginning

Middle

End

2020

■ Read the following words and phrases, then try combining them in different ways to make different kinds of sentences which tell a story. Try the following:

■ Combine the words and phrases into a series of long sentences.
■ Combine the words and phrases into a series of short sentences.
■ Experiment with changing the order of the sentences.
■ Experiment with changing the adjectives.
■ Write a short version by omitting some description.
■ Write a long version by adding description.

One morning in 2020

fine

sunny

robot dog

synthetic nylon fur

an electronic bark

programmed to behave like a real dog

called Larry

went for a walk

owner

Ben

a small boy

who loved animals

they met

an old man

slow

stooping

with

the most unusual

robot dog

he had ever seen

big

floppy

wet tongue

slavering lips

all at once he realized

it was a real dog!

100 LITERACY HOURS ■ YEAR 5 TERM 2

REDRAFTING SIMULATION

OBJECTIVES

UNIT	SPELLING/VOCABULARY	GRAMMAR/PUNCTUATION	COMPREHENSION/ COMPOSITION
REDRAFTING SIMULATION Two stories: 'Virtual Jurassic' and 'The Titan'.	Identify misspelled words in own writing	Revise use of apostrophes, questions marks, speech marks. Revise and extend use of conjunctions. Construct sentences in different ways. Use punctuation effectively to signpost meaning.	Review, edit and evaluate writing. Investigate how to redraft the content and format of writing.

ORGANIZATION (3 HOURS)

	INTRODUCTION	WHOLE-CLASS SKILLS WORK	DIFFERENTIATED GROUP ACTIVITIES	CONCLUSION
HOUR 1	Read and discuss the first story, 'Virtual Jurassic', on photocopiable page 109 before giving out pupil copies.	Revise and extend use of conjunctions to join sentences.	1–4: All pupils work within groups according to ability to redraft story. *The teacher works with Group 4.	Share selected redrafts, compare and evaluate.
HOUR 2	Read the second story, 'The Titan', on photocopiable page 109, with pupils following.	Identify the general kinds of punctuation errors. Revise possessive apostrophes in contractions, questions marks, speech marks and dialogue layout.	1–4*: All pupils work on punctuation exercise according to ability.	Share corrections and make a final class version on OHT.
HOUR 3	Read and discuss Redrafting Checklist (page 110).	Revise aspects of checklist not covered in previous two hours.	1–4*: All pupils work in pairs within groups to redraft a recently written story.	Compare and evaluate examples of stories 'before' and 'after' revision and discuss redrafting process.

RESOURCES

Photocopiable pages 109 (Two Stories) and 110 (Redrafting Checklist), board or flip chart, OHP and acetate (optional), writing materials, different coloured highlighter pens, drafts of stories children have recently written.

PREPARATION

Prepare enough copies of photocopiable page 109 (Two Stories) for each child, and enough copies of photocopiable page 110 (Redrafting Checklist) for one between two. If possible, make OHTs of these pages (or enlarge to at least A3 size).
    Prepare for Hour 3 by modifying the Redrafting Checklist on photocopiable page 110 to take into account the ideas suggested by children at the end of Hour 2, and the abilities of the children in the different groups. The Redrafting Checklist is a full version suitable for children in Group 1. Modifications can be simplified from this.

Introduction

Begin the session by explaining to the children that they are going to take part in a simulation in which they play the role of a teacher marking children's work and that this simulation will help them to redraft their own work. The focus for this session is on sentence construction.

Read through the first story ('Virtual Jurassic') on photocopiable page 109 without letting the children see the text. Ensure that your read emphasizes the continuous, unbroken and unpunctuated nature of this original text. Ask the children to comment on it. They should notice that it is written in a 'breathless rush', and they should be able to determine that this is probably because it is written as one continuous sentence with no punctuation. Discuss what the story is about, ensuring the children understand what a virtual reality game is.

Whole-class skills work

Determine with the class that in order to improve 'Virtual Jurassic', it is necessary to create sentences out of the long flow of words, joining related phrases and statements and then adding punctuation to signpost meaning.

Ask the children if they can remember what the grammatical term for a 'joining word' is (*connective* or *conjunction*). Write a few of the following list of conjunctions on the board or flip chart as a starting point and then ask the children to brainstorm others:

and	where	for
but	as	while
because	before	until
although	when	so

Then write these two sentences:

The divers could not raise the sunken ship.
They brought all the gold to the surface.

Ask the children to suggest how conjunctions can be used to join them together, for example:

■ The divers could not raise the sunken ship *so* they brought all the gold to the surface.
■ *Although* the divers could not raise the sunken ship, they brought all the gold to the surface.
■ The divers brought all the gold to the surface *because* they could not raise the sunken ship.

Discuss what subtle differences of meaning are achieved by the use of different conjunctions.

Finally, distribute copies of photocopiable page 110 (Redrafting Checklist) and explain to the children that, in their group work, they will be working on sentence construction with 'Virtual Jurassic'. Suggest the following method:

STEP 1: Underline or highlight the separate statements and write them down in list form (miss out all conjunctions and connectives).
STEP 2: Experiment with the best way of combining the statements into sentences using conjunctions. No sentence should contain more than three statements; most will contain only two.
STEP 3. Write out a final version.

Differentiated group activities

All children undertake the rewriting exercise as described above, and according to the instructions on the sheet.
1: Work independently.
2 & 3: Work in pairs.
4: Concentrate on the first part of the story only with support from the teacher.

Conclusion

Share, compare and evaluate different versions of the corrected story.

Introduction

Explain that the redrafting simulation continues. Ask individual children to read parts of the second story ('The Titan') in turn while the other children follow. At the end, comment on the lack of flow, intonation and expression and ask the children why the reading was so difficult. Identify the lack of punctuation as a problem. Highlight the need for good punctuation to clarify meaning and aid reading. Read the story again and ask the children to look out for the punctuation mistakes.

Whole-class skills work

Identify the types of punctuation mistakes in the story:
■ missing apostrophes in contractions
■ missing possessive apostrophes
■ missing question marks
■ missing speech marks
■ dialogue not set out properly.
  Briefly revise each of the above, writing examples on the board or flip chart to act as an aide-mémoire for children when undertaking the group activities.

Differentiated group activities

All children correct the punctuation mistakes in the second story ('The Titan').
1*: Rewrite the passage independently or in pairs, correcting it as they go.
2 & 3*: Highlight each type of mistake in turn with a different colour.
4*: Concentrate on the use of speech marks. Help them to do this by asking them to highlight or underline words actually spoken.

Conclusion

Go over the passage using the OHP or enlarge version, to confirm with the children where each of the mistakes are and how they should be corrected.
  Recap on the focus for improvement in each story, and then ask: 'What other qualities would a teacher look for in a good story?' As the children brainstorm ideas, jot them down on the board or flip chart.

Introduction

Remember to prepare for this hour by modifying the Redrafting Checklist as suggested in the 'Preparation' section above. Introduce the Redrafting Checklist and point out the parts which related to the work on the previous session.

Whole-class skills work

Briefly revise aspects of the checklist which were not covered in the previous two hours.
  Explain to the children how to use the checklist, as follows:
■ Work with a partner.
■ Go through the checklist first by yourself and make all the improvements you can.
■ Go through the checklist with your partner who should make additional suggestions and suggest further improvements.
■ Consult the teacher on any problems still remaining.
■ Redraft your work.
  This procedure can be written on the board or flip chart to remind the children as they work in their groups.

Differentiated group activities

1–4*: All children, working in pairs within groups, should use the Redrafting Checklist to redraft a recent story. Less able children will need support to help them identify areas for improvement in their partner's work and to make appropriate and helpful comments.

Conclusion

Ask selected children to reading examples of the following:
■ a section of their original story which was later revised
■ the comments made by a partner
■ the revised section of the story.
  Discuss which areas needed most improvement and which comments were most helpful.

TWO STORIES

Imagine you are a teacher helping the children of these stories to improve their writing.

- ■ Read each story through.
- ■ Give it a mark out of 10.
- ■ Write out a correct version.
- ■ Write a comment to explain to the pupil what he or she did wrong and how to avoid the same mistakes next time.

VIRTUAL JURASSIC

John put on the special headset and saw a Tyrannosaurus rex coming straight for him so he turned and ran and stumbled over a chair and then he remembered that he wasn't supposed to run but to push the joystick on the controller but it was too late now the Tyrannosaurus rex was on top of him its huge jaws opened and he saw the rows of teeth like rows of sharp bread knives and he screamed as the jaws closed on him though he felt nothing because it seemed so real then he took the headset off reset the game and started again this time he did better he moved the joystick and it seemed as though he was running from the Tyrannosaurus rex but the Tyrannosaurus rex was catching up so he flicked the joystick to the right and the Tyrannosaurus rex went straight past him so he was safe but then to his horror he saw he had walked into a pterodactyl's nest and the pterodactyl didn't look too pleased about it.

THE TITAN

Theyd been travelling all morning. First theyd taken a taxi to the railway station, then there was the long train journey to Southampton. Now at last they were ready to start the main part of their holiday. But Sarah didnt look too happy. She was staring at the ships name. Cant we fly to Italy she said. David squeezed Sarahs hand. Of course we cant he said were not going to Italy were going on a cruise. Cant we go on a different ship she said. Why, whats wrong with this one, asked David. I dont like the name of the ship. Why not. Well, look, its called The Titan. David looked at her in amazement. So what, he said. Well, it sounds a bit like.... I know, interrupted David, but thats nonsense. You've been watching too many films.

REDRAFTING CHECKLIST

■ Work through this checklist first by yourself, then with a partner.

PART 1: CONTENT
✓ Find descriptions of people and places. Is there enough detail to help the reader imagine what they looked like?

✓ Find the action in the story. Is it described in enough detail? Investigate synonyms for some of the verbs to find better alternatives. Could adverbs be added to good effect?

✓ Is the reader kept informed about how the characters feel?

✓ Find the nouns. Add adjectives where appropriate.

✓ Is there a place where a simile or metaphor would make description more vivid?

✓ Look at the dialogue. Would a synonym of 'said' be more effective? Would it be effective to add an adverb to the reporting clause?

PART 2: GRAMMAR, PUNCTUATION AND SPELLING
✓ Is the story written in sentences and paragraphs?

✓ Is sentence construction clear? Would it be better to break up a part of the story into statements and put it back together again using appropriate conjunctions?

✓ Have capital letters been used for beginning sentences, names, places, days, months and special occasions?

✓ Are speech marks used before and after words actually spoken?

✓ Does speech begin with a capital letter?

✓ Is there a comma, full stop, question mark or exclamation mark before final speech marks?

✓ Have apostrophes been used to show missing letters in contractions?

✓ Is 's used to show ownership?

✓ Check the spelling.

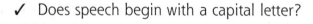

VENUS

OBJECTIVES

UNIT	SPELLING/VOCABULARY	GRAMMAR/PUNCTUATION	COMPREHENSION/COMPOSITION
READING NON-FICTION Information genre: 'Venus'.	Collect, define and spell correctly technical words from reading.	Combine sentences in different ways, while retaining meaning.	Read non-chronological information text. Prepare for reading by identifying what is already known. Identify features of information genre. Critically appraise information texts.

ORGANIZATION (3 HOURS)

	INTRODUCTION	WHOLE-CLASS SKILLS WORK	DIFFERENTIATED GROUP ACTIVITIES	CONCLUSION
HOUR 1	Establish previous knowledge. Shared reading of double-page spread on photocopiable pages.	Investigate features of layout and writing. Revise relevant vocabulary.	1*: Guided reading and discussion. 2 & 3: Reading Comprehension, parts A & B. 4*: Guided reading and discussion.	Discuss how the integration of texts and pictures works in information texts.
HOUR 2	Re-read 'Venus' with a focus on understanding information in table.	Experiment with combining sentences in different ways, while retaining meaning.	1: Reading Comprehension, all parts. 2 & 3*: Guided reading and discussion. 4*: Reading Comprehension, part A.	Discuss answers to Reading Comprehension.
HOUR 3	Examine a selection of information texts, identifying different formats and features.	Use a non-fiction Big Book to identify information retrieval devices. Model skimming and scanning techniques.	1–4*: Compare and evaluate information sources.	Share outcomes of group work. Discuss importance of critically appraising texts for purposes of research.

RESOURCES

Photocopiable pages 114 and 115 ('Venus'), 116 (Reading Comprehension) and 117 (Information Source Study), a selection of information and reference books about space (try to include some older, mainly text-based, books for the purposes of comparison and, if resources allow, CD-ROMs could be included), any appropriate non-fiction Big Book, board or flip chart, OHP and acetate (optional), writing materials.

PREPARATION

Make enough copies of the photocopiables pages for one each between two children. Ideally, pages 114 and 115 should be photocopied side-by-side on A3 to reflect the double-page spread layout. If possible, make OHTs of these two pages as well.

Introduction

Write the word 'Venus' as a heading on the board or flip chart. Establish what the children already know about the subject and write this up in note form underneath the heading. (Be prepared for children to suggest the Venus of Roman mythology as well as

Venus the planet!)

Now display the text of 'Venus' on the photocopiable pages (or distribute copies of the page) and share the reading of the text aloud. Establish what genre of writing it is (*non-fiction information*) and what it is about (*a comparison of the planets Venus and Earth*). Refer back to the notes on the board or flip chart to ascertain whether any of the 'facts' have been confirmed or contradicted.

Whole-class skills work

Discuss the layout of text and illustrations, and study the features of information genre, using this list as a starting point:

■ Use of layout to aid clarity. Revise vocabulary: *title, subtitle, illustration, diagram, caption, label, typeface, font, bold, italics, serif, sans-serif* (see diagram for an explanation of these terms), *body text, subtitle, columns, text boxes, table*.
■ Non-chronological text.
■ Use of simple present tense.
■ Use of impersonal style.
■ Use of examples and visual information to clarify ideas that may be new to the audience.

SERIF & SANS-SERIF TYPEFACES OR FONTS

Serif

Serif typefaces or fonts are slightly easier to read, because the serifs (small tails) add clarity to the shape of the letter and help the eye to read it more quickly.

Sans-Serif

Sans-serif ('sans' is French for 'without') typefaces or fonts have no tails and often give a more modern look.

Ask the children to find examples of some of the above vocabulary terms in the text. Ask them to identify the few instances in which the simple present tense is not used and to explain why.

Differentiated group activities

1*: Guided reading and discussion. Discussion should focus on the technical vocabulary and the relative merits of the three ways of conveying information: text, illustration and table.
2 & 3: Complete Reading Comprehension, parts A and B.
4*: Guided reading and discussion. This group will need particular help with reading and understanding of difficult and technical words.

Conclusion

Discuss how the different ways of presenting information – text, table and illustrations – work together.

Introduction

Re-read the 'Venus' article, with a particular focus on making sense of the 'Comparison Table'. Ensure that the children understand all the terms. Some of the more difficult terms can be explained as follows:

Rotational period: length of day.

Mass: quantity of matter (explain this simply by saying that a piece of Venus which is the same size as a piece of Earth weighs slightly less).

Escape velocity: The speed at which an object needs to travel to get away from the pull of the planet's gravity.

Whole-class skills work

Experiment with constructing sentences in different ways, for example two statements (slightly adapted for this exercise) in the first paragraph are:
- Venus was once believed to be a twin of Earth.
- Venus is the closest of the other planets to Earth.

These can be combined in several ways:
- Venus was once believed to be a twin of Earth since it is the closest of the other planets to Earth.
- As Venus is the closest of the other planets to Earth, it was once believed to be a twin of Earth.
- Because Venus is the closest of the other planets to Earth, it was once believed to be a twin of Earth.
- Venus is closest of the other planets to Earth and, therefore, it was once believed to be a twin of Earth.

Ask the children what kind of word is used to join the sentences (conjunction). Note that a conjunction can still do this, even when it is placed at the beginning of the first of two statements. Ask the children to discuss which sentence is best (such as which 'flows' the best, which gets the idea across most elegantly).

They can try it themselves with these statements:
- Venus is one of the easiest planets to see.
- Venus is the brightest object in the sky.

Differentiated group activities

1: Complete Reading Comprehension, all parts.

2 & 3*: Guided reading and discussion (see Hour 1).

4*: Complete Reading Comprehension, part A. Spend time re-reading the text with this group, concentrating on understanding of difficult vocabulary and extended sentences.

Conclusion

Discuss answers to the Reading Comprehension questions with the whole class.

HOUR 3

Introduction

Introduce the selection of reference books by showing the children the different types – older, text-based reference books; modern, highly-illustrated books, CD-ROMs and so on. Identify the different features of these sources and investigate their advantages and disadvantages in terms both of the information they provide and also of the accessibility of the information. For example, an older reference book with a comprehensive index may not have as up-to-date information as a more recently published one, but the information may be more accessible than a more modern book with just a table of contents and no index.

Whole-class skills work

Use a non-fiction Big Book to identify information retrieval devices. Demonstrate how to locate information by skimming to gain an overall sense of text, and scanning to locate specific information or look for particular features.

Differentiated group activities

1–4*: Explain to the children that they are going to work in pairs to compare and evaluate two different information books (and other media sources if available) from the collection available.

Give each pair a copy of photocopiable page 117 (Information Source Study) and ask them to choose two books to compare. If CD-ROMs are among the sources, they should compare two of these (do not mix the different media).

Children in Group 4 could be given a simplified version of the sheet.

Conclusion

Share ideas from the information source study, such as can generalizations be made about which books are most informative? Which are the most interesting? Which books are intended for which age groups and so on.

Finally, discuss the importance of critically appraising texts when researching for information.

VENUS

Venus – the twin of Earth?

Venus is the second planet from the sun. It was once believed to be a twin of Earth, as it is closest of the other planets to Earth in both diameter and distance. The thick, cloudy atmosphere led scientists to believe that it could be like Earth in the Carboniferous era. They imagined a planet covered with dense rain forests, and possibly with the same kind of life forms that inhabited Earth millions of years ago: amphibians, reptiles or even dinosaurs!

Unfortunately, the unmanned space probe, Mariner 5, showed Venus to be a 'pressure cooker' planet, choked by clouds of sulphuric acid. These clouds revolve around the planet giving the V-shaped patterns in its appearance. The atmosphere retains so much heat that the surface temperature is hot enough to melt lead. Venus is so hostile to life that it would bake you, crush you or dissolve you in seconds! So, far from being Earth's twin, Venus is very different, and a much less promising destination for a manned space flight than Mars.

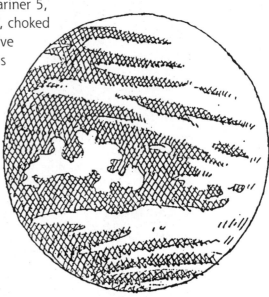

Venus is permanently covered in clouds.

The landscape of Venus

However, the American and Soviet space probes have taught us a great deal about the planet and, despite the thick clouds, the surface has been mapped. The main features are two huge uplands like our continents except they are not surrounded by water. These are called Aphrodite Terra and Ishtar Terra. The names are interesting, because they are the names of love-goddesses from different cultures. Venus was the Roman goddess of love, Aphrodite the Greek goddess of love, and Ishtar the Babylonian goddess of love.

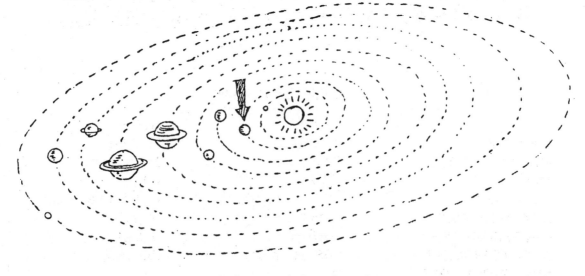

Venus is the second planet from the sun.

Looking for Venus

Venus is one of the easiest planets to see as it is the brightest object in the sky after the sun and moon – it can even cast a shadow! So, why not go out tonight and see it for yourself?

Don't waste your time looking at it through a telescope, though – all you will see are those thick white clouds of sulphuric acid!

Earth in the Carboniferous era.

DATA COMPARISON TABLE

	VENUS	EARTH
DIAMETER	12 104km	12 756km
ROTATIONAL PERIOD	243.02 days	23.94 hours
MASS	.815	1.00
ESCAPE VELOCITY	10.73km per second	11.31km per second
MAX TEMPERATURE	+480°C	+58°C
MIN TEMPERATURE	+470°C	–89°C
DISTANCE FROM SUN	108 million km	150 million km
NUMBER OF MOONS	0	1

READING COMPREHENSION

PART A

■ What did scientists think Venus was like before the Mariner 5 probe?

■ What were their reasons for believing this?

■ What did Mariner 5 show Venus was really like?

■ Why is Venus not a 'promising destination' for a manned flight?

■ What are the main features of the surface of Venus?

■ What is interesting about the names of these features?

■ Why is it not worth looking at Venus through a telescope?

PART B

■ Imagine you are an astronomer in the 1950s (before Mariner 5 showed us what Venus is really like). Write a description of what you think the first human explorers might find on the surface of the planet using the picture as a source of ideas.

■ Write a paragraph of description from the information given in the table. The first sentence is given below as an example:

'The diameter of Venus is 12 104km, which is only slightly smaller than Earth which has a diameter of 12 756km.'

PART C

■ Look at the information in the table. Do you think it would be possible for humans to land on the surface if they went in specially made vehicles, or do you think it would be impossible?

■ Examine the table. What are the similarities between Earth and Venus and what are the differences?

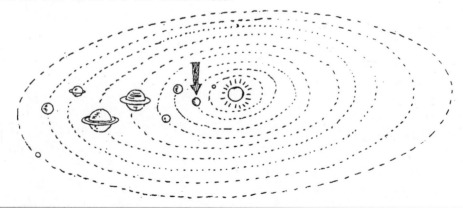

INFORMATION SOURCE STUDY

Find and compare two information books (or other information sources such as CD-ROMs) on the same subject. Look through them with a partner and use the questions below to help you review, compare and evaluate them.

TITLE OF BOOK/SOURCE		
AUTHOR		
PUBLISHER		
Which age range (audience) is the book aimed at? How can you tell?		
Is the text easy or hard to read? Are any difficult words explained?		
Does the book use: ■ pictures? ■ photographs? ■ bullet points? ■ diagrams?		
Do they help to make things clearer?		
How many pages have colour: none, some, or all?		
Do you like the choice of typefaces and the way the pages are laid out?		
Is it easy to find the information you want?		
Is there: ■ a contents page? ■ an index?		
SUMMARY What do you think of this book? Is it interesting and clear? Would you buy it?		
Which of these two books/sources is better? Why?		

WORDS IN WINDOWS

OBJECTIVES

UNIT	SPELLING/VOCABULARY	GRAMMAR/PUNCTUATION	COMPREHENSION/ COMPOSITION
WRITING NON-FICTION Information genre: Words in Windows.	Secure knowledge of information book related vocabulary.	Construct sentences from notes. Use conjunctions.	Plan and write non-chronological information text. Prepare for reading by identifying what is already known and what they need to find out. Make notes.

ORGANIZATION (2 HOURS)

	INTRODUCTION	WHOLE-CLASS SKILLS WORK	DIFFERENTIATED GROUP ACTIVITIES	CONCLUSION
HOUR 1	Read 'Venus' and discuss how features of layout help in accessing information.	Model the process of preparing for research: What do I already know? What do I want to know?	1–4*: Choose planet, carry out research and take notes. The teacher supports as needed.	Selected pupils present questions they asked and answers they found. Discuss: Why can't we find answers to some questions?
HOUR 2	Display 'Venus' spread and discuss the concept of 'windows of information'. Secure vocabulary.	Model how to construct sentences from notes. Revise and use conjunctions. Use 'Note-taking Guide' to structure information writing.	1–4*: All pupils prepare a rough draft of their article and plan a rough draft of the spread layout. Less able pupils are supported with a writing template.	Share examples of information spreads. Discuss what pupils found easy and difficult about the task.

RESOURCES

Photocopiable pages 121 (Note-taking Guide), 122 (Columns Template) and 114 and 115 ('Venus') from previous unit, a collection of information and reference books (and CD-ROMs if available) about space (as for the previous unit), board or flip chart, OHP and acetate (optional), writing materials.

PREPARATION

Although this unit is self-contained and can stand alone, the previous unit 'Venus' provides a valuable preliminary study. Prepare enough copies of photocopiable pages 121 (Note-taking Guide) and 114 and 115 ('Venus') for one between two children. If possible, prepare the photocopiable pages also as OHTs (or enlarge to at least A3 size). Prepare enough copies of photocopiable page 122 (Columns Template) as A3 enlargements for children who need extra support.

Introduction

Read or review (if recently read) the information text spread 'Venus' on the photocopiable pages from the previous unit. Discuss it, concentrating on how the information is conveyed through text and pictures and how the features of layout help to access the information. Explain to the class that in their group-work session, they will be producing a similar page but for a different planet.

The first stage in this process is to choose a planet and then research it using the collection of reference books and CD-ROMs.

Whole-class skills work

Model for the children the procedure of preparing for research by:
■ activating prior knowledge and jotting down a list of things they already know about the topic
■ setting up motivation for research by noting questions about the things they want (or need) to find out.

Write up on the board of flip chart a standard KWLW chart like the one below.

TOPIC:

K	W	L	W
List what you already **know** about the topic.	List questions about the topic that you **want to know** more about.	Using your questions as a guide, write what you have **learned**.	Write **where** you found the answers to your questions (book, title, page number).

Choose a topic about space that is not the planets – for example, the moon or constellations – and fill in the first two columns of the chart with the class as a demonstration.

Then revise the following information retrieval skills:
■ using contents and indexes
■ using titles and subheadings
■ skimming and scanning
■ note-taking (jot down key words, dates, facts, make rough sketches).

Differentiated group activities

1–4*: All children choose a planet and research it, using the books and other resources available. They should make notes and sketches in preparation for the writing session in the following hour. Children could work individually, in pairs or in small groups of 3 to 4, depending on ability and preference. Some children, particularly in Group 4, may need help in selecting texts and making notes. Give those children who are unsure how to make notes, a copy of photocopiable page 121 (Note-taking Guide).

Conclusion

Ask selected children to give oral presentations, saying what some of their questions were and what answers they found. Discuss whether they were able to find answers to all their questions. If not, what do they think the reasons might be (for example *inappropriate resources? inappropriate questions?*).

Introduction

Look at the 'Venus' article, and some selected double-page spreads from the collection of reference and information books. Display on OHP if possible. Relate the title of this unit which is called 'Words in Windows' to the layouts. Help the children to see that information is presented in 'windows' – such as boxes or columns to make the different sections easier to pick out. Ask them to talk about the layouts, making sure they are confident in the use of appropriate vocabulary – *title, illustration, diagram, caption, typeface, font, bold, italics, serif, sans-serif, body text, subtitle, columns, text boxes, bold, illustration, table.*

Whole-class skills work

Explain how to turn notes into an article as follows:
Step 1: Turn each note into a sentence, for example:

Mars is known as the red planet.
Mars is 34 million miles away.
Mars is named after the Roman god of War.
Mars has two moons.

Step 2: Study this list of conjunctions:

and	because	unless
but	before	until
after	if	when
although	in order that	whenever
as	since	where
as if	so that	wherever
as long as	than	while
as soon as	though	

Step 3: Experiment with different ways of combining the sentences using different conjunctions, for example:

Mars, known as the red planet, is 34 million miles away. It is named after the Roman god of war and has two moons.

Mars is named after the Roman god of war. It is 34 million miles away, has two moons and is known as the red planet.

Explain how the children could then use the structure outlined on the Note-taking Guide on photocopiable page 121 to sequence their information writing, for example:

PARA 1:   An introductory paragraph of key facts (see above).
PARA 2:   A description of the planet.
PARA 3:   A description of a diagram (which would be an explanation of something like the planet's orbit, or surface features).
PARA 4:   End with a sentence or two built around the interesting or unusual fact. This makes an effective way to end the text.

Differentiated group activities
1–4*: All children write a rough draft of their article and produce a rough version of its final layout. Less able children, particularly those in Group 4, could be given photocopiable page 122 (Columns Template) on which to write a rough version, leaving space for at least two illustrations.

Conclusion
Select some children to share their rough articles and layouts with the rest of the class. Discuss what the children found both easy and difficult about the task.

FURTHER IDEA

An additional hour could be provided for children to redraft and present their work, or they could be asked to finish it for homework.

 **NOTE-TAKING GUIDE**

TITLE OF TOPIC

TITLES OF BOOKS AND PAGE NUMBERS REFERRED TO

JOT DOWN 3 TO 6 KEY FACTS IN SINGLE WORDS OR SHORT PHRASES

FIND A PICTURE AND DESCRIBE IT IN WORDS

FIND A DIAGRAM AND DESCRIBE IT IN WORDS

FIND AN INTERESTING OR UNUSUAL FACT

COLUMNS TEMPLATE

— fold ————————————————————————————

WORDS IN WINDOWS

122

SKIMMING AND SCANNING

OBJECTIVES

UNIT	SPELLING/VOCABULARY	GRAMMAR/PUNCTUATION	COMPREHENSION/ COMPOSITION
REFERENCE AND RESEARCH SKILLS Skimming and scanning.	Identify key words and locate them in lists and texts.	Organize information into sentences and paragraphs.	Understand and use the processes of skimming for the main idea and scanning to locate specific information.

ORGANIZATION (1 HOUR)

	INTRODUCTION	WHOLE-CLASS SKILLS WORK	DIFFERENTIATED GROUP ACTIVITIES	CONCLUSION
HOUR 1	Knowing where to look – locate the key words in a set of questions. Discuss possible sources of answers.	Develop skill of scanning using different texts.	1–4: Skim different texts to find information. Make notes and collate facts. *The teacher works with Group 4.	Discussion on process and findings.

RESOURCES

Board or flip chart, OHP and acetate (optional), writing materials, dictionaries suitable for the ability range within the class, an assortment of different encyclopaedias (including CD-ROM versions) and information books (with contents pages and indexes) relevant to a topic that the class is currently studying.

PREPARATION

Check that the reference and information sources you collect contain information relevant to the questions that you decide to set for the 'Differentiated group activities' part of the hour.

Prepare an OHT of the following questions or write them up on the board or flip chart:

1. In what year did Queen Victoria ascend to the throne of England?
2. What animals are the prey of foxes?
3. What is the climate like in India?
4. How is chocolate manufactured?
5. Who invented the telephone?

Make an OHT or enlarged photocopy showing the index page of an information book containing an entry relevant to one of the questions above.

Decide on some topic-related subjects for the children to research during the 'Differentiated group activities'.

Introduction

Tell the children that the purpose of the lesson is to help them to find information quickly and easily. If they have to find something out from a text, the first step is to decide what they need to look up.

Show them Questions 1–5 and ask them to identify the key word in each question that they would use to look up the answer in the index of an encyclopaedia or information book. Check that the children understand which words are most likely to produce the information they require (such as *Victoria, foxes, India, chocolate* and *telephone*).

Whole-class skills work

Explain that what the children did when they located the key word or main idea in each question is called *skimming*. To *skim read* a text means to run your eyes over the words quickly to find what it is about. You are not expected to read every word when you *skim* a text.

If you already know exactly what to look for (as they do now), the process of looking it up is called *scanning*. *Scanning* is a bit like looking for your friends in the playground. It is the word that describes the process of finding the word you want in a dictionary, a telephone directory, an index, a list of contents or an encyclopaedia.

Use the OHT or enlarged photocopy to demonstrate the scanning process to the children by asking individual children to come up and point out various entries on the selected index page. Make sure that all the children understand that index entries are arranged in alphabetical order, and revise the process of using this if necessary. Give further practice in speedy scanning by asking children to work in pairs of similar ability and take turns to time one another as they look up various words in the dictionary. Can they improve on their own scanning times?

Differentiated group activities

1: Children should work individually using several different sources to look up and note down information on a topic or topics set by the teacher that is relevant to the current curriculum plan for the year group. They should try to stick to the subject set for them. Ask them to record this process in the following form:

Subject:

Sources of information:

Index entry/entries used:

Information found:

2 & 3: As above, but work in pairs to support one another.
4*: Work with teacher support to find out the answers to some of the questions that were used in the introductory activity.

Conclusion

Ask some of the children in Groups 1–3 to share the results of their investigations. Which did they find more difficult: skimming or scanning? Have they kept to the subject and succeeded in excluding irrelevant information? Give the children in Group 4 the opportunity to present the class with their answers to the original set of questions.

THE LADY OF SHALOTT

OBJECTIVES

UNIT	SPELLING/VOCABULARY	GRAMMAR/PUNCTUATION	COMPREHENSION/ COMPOSITION
READING POETRY Classical narrative poetry: 'The Lady of Shalott' by Alfred Lord Tennyson.	Identify and understand archaic words. Revise terms 'simile' and 'metaphor'. Introduce term 'figurative language'. Explore spelling patterns of rhyming words.	Explore grammar of poetry. Interpret punctuation appropriately when reading aloud.	Read a classical narrative poem and understand genre. Perform poem. Discuss imagery. Use structure of poem to write additional verses.

ORGANIZATION (4 HOURS)

	INTRODUCTION	WHOLE-CLASS SKILLS WORK	DIFFERENTIATED GROUP ACTIVITIES	CONCLUSION
HOUR 1	Shared reading of poem 'The Lady of Shalott', Parts I–III. Establish the story.	Use dictionaries to establish meaning of archaic words and phrases.	1*: Guided reading and discussion of Part I. 2 & 3: Write a description of Shalott for modern tourist brochure. 4*: As for Group 1 with emphasis on developing skills for reading poetry aloud.	Selected pupils from Groups 2 & 3 share their work. Class discuss and evaluate.
HOUR 2	Re-read Part II of poem.	Analyse verse form.	1: Write a short story about one of the characters mentioned in poem. 2 & 3*: Guided reading and discussion of Part II. 4: Make up a story about 'long-haired page'.	Selected pupils from Groups 1 & 4 share their stories. Class discuss and evaluate.
HOUR 3	Re-read Part III of poem.	Revise simile and metaphor and identify use in poem.	1*: Guided reading and discussion of Part III. 2 & 3: Write a description of Sir Lancelot in modern prose. 4*: Guided reading and discussion of Part III.	Selected pupils from Groups 2 & 3 share their descriptions. Class discuss and evaluate.
HOUR 4	Re-read Parts I–III of poem. Identify the structure of the narrative.	Examine the spelling patterns of the rhymes in the poem.	1–4*: All pupils write a continuation of poem, according to ability.	Selected pupils share their continuations. Read rest of poem and compare.

RESOURCES

Photocopiable pages 130–133 ('The Lady of Shalott'), dictionaries, board or flip chart, OHP and acetate (optional), writing materials.

PREPARATION

Make enough copies of the poem for one between two children. If possible, prepare it also as an OHT or enlarge on a photocopier to at least A3 size, with each Part on a different sheet. Practise reading the poem aloud.

Introduction

Explain that the class is going to read a narrative poem, and provide some brief background information as follows:

Alfred Lord Tennyson (1809–1892) was one of the great poets of the nineteenth century. Tennyson was appointed Poet Laureate in 1850. (This is an official court position appointed for life by the ruling English sovereign. The current Poet Laureate is Ted Hughes, with whose work the children may be familiar.) Tennyson was influenced by the English romantic poets, particularly John Keats, and his poetry is highly representative of the sensibilities and intellectual and moral values of the Victorian age in England.

A narrative poem is a poem which tells a story. This poem tells a story which is part of the legend of King Arthur and his Knights of the Round Table.

Distribute copies of Parts I–III only of the poem and, if possible, display it on OHP. Read Parts I–III. (You could read it yourself with the children following, or share the reading around the class with children reading a verse each.) Establish what the story is about and who the main characters are.

Whole-class skills work

Ask the children what they understand by the term 'diction'. Most probably they will relate the term to oral speech, such as 'good diction' is speech that is well pronounced and enunciated.

Explain that the term 'diction' can also refer to written language. A writer's diction is his choice of special words and phrases for a special purpose. In this case, Tennyson wants to create a medieval world, so he uses lots of archaic (old) words, for example:

wold (an Old English word for a piece of open, uncultivated country, down or moor land; often found in place names today, for example Stow-on-the-wold)
blow (to grow or blossom)
imbowers (encloses in a place with foliage)
flitteth (instead of 'flits' – this uses the old 3rd-person ending -eth)

Ask the children to identify other examples of Tennyson's use of archaic diction in the poem. Write these on the board or flip chart and ask the children to find their meaning in dictionaries, creating a class glossary for the poem which can be used throughout the study of the poem.

Differentiated group activities

1*: Guided reading and discussion. Focus on the description of the region around the island of Shalott, for example:

■ What kind of landscape is it?
■ What is the island of Shalott itself like?
■ Ask the children if they could sketch a rough map of the river, the island and the road to Camelot.
■ What can be seen at the casement of the window?
■ What can the reapers hear?
■ What impression do we have of the island of Shalott and its strange inhabitant?

2 & 3: Write a description of the area for a modern tourist brochure using modern language and style.
4*: Guided reading and discussion. Give guidance on the reading aloud of verse. For example, do not pause at the end of a line unless there is some form of punctuation. Read naturally, do not overemphasize the metre. Ask the children to read verses in turn. Help them to understand the archaic and other difficult vocabulary. Then use some of the questions above as the basis for discussion.

Conclusion

Select some children from Groups 2 and 3 to read out examples of their modern tourist brochures. Ask the rest of the class to evaluate how accurately they have transferred the physical details of the landscape and its 'ambiance' (the 'feel' of the place) in the new form.

Introduction
Re-read Part II of the poem.

Whole-class skills work
Revise how to analyse verse form with diagonal strokes for accented syllables (/) and letters of the alphabet for rhymes. Use the first verse of Part II, writing it up on the board, flip chart or OHP as follows:

```
  /        /        /         /
There she weaves by night and day          a
   /       /        /        /
A magic web with colours gay.              a
   /        /        /        /
She has heard a whisper say                a
     /       /       /       /
A curse is on her if she stay              a
      To look down to Camelot.             b
        /          /         /        /
She knows not what the curse may be,       c
      /      /          /    /
And so she weaveth steadily,               c
      /      /      /       /
And little other care hath she,            c
         /     /       /
      The Lady of Shalott.                 b
```

Explain this pattern of metre and rhyme to the children and ask them to experiment with it themselves by trying the following:

■ Write three lines of poetry ending with the same rhyme. Who can add a fourth?
■ Write a line of poetry with four main stresses. The best way to do this is to listen carefully to the metre of the poem and try to imitate it.
     Finally, discuss the challenge of telling a story using such a verse form!

Differentiated group activities
1: Choose one of the characters mentioned in the poem and write a short story about them. Who are they? What are they called? Where are they going? What will happen when they get there? And so on.
2 & 3*: Guided reading and discussion, using these questions as a starting point:
■ Why does the Lady of Shalott remain in her grey tower?
■ What does she do all day and night?
■ Why must she use a mirror to see the things that go on outside?
■ Who and what does she see in her mirror?
■ Is she happy?
4: Make up a story about the long-haired page. What is his name? Why is his hair long? Whose page (servant) is he? Why is he going to Camelot?

Conclusion
Select some children from Groups 1 and 4 to read out their stories. Ask the rest of the class to evaluate how well the stories fit the character, setting and period.

Introduction
Re-read Part III of the poem.

Whole-class skills work
Explain that one of the features of poetry is that it often uses 'figurative language' – word pictures to build sensory impressions and visual images. Figurative language is used in order to show a relationship between things that otherwise we would not associate or relate with each other. The literal, or actual, meaning of words or phrases in figurative language is not what is meant.

Revise the terms 'simile' and 'metaphor'. Similes and metaphors are examples of figurative language. They are comparisons which are used to make writing more vivid.

Similes are comparisons using the words 'like' or 'as', for example:

The lake shone like a mirror.
The sea was as smooth as glass.
His hands were as rough as sandpaper.
The man was as harmless as a dove.
The dog howled like the wind.
His face was a wrinkled as a prune.

Ask the children to explain how the comparison helps the reader to imagine the thing described more clearly.

Metaphors are comparisons that go further than similes. They appear to say two things *are* the same. Metaphors do not use the words 'like' or 'as'. For this reason they are more powerful, but harder to spot, for example:

In battle, King Henry was a lion, in peace, a lamb.
Ben was a great barrel of a man.
The thunder of traffic woke me up.
A blanket of snow covered the ground.
The sea is a hungry dog.
The car spluttered, coughed and died.

Ask the children to explain what is being compared to what in the above metaphors.

Finally, ask the children if they can find an example of each in Part III of the poem (similes: 'The gemmy bridle glittered free,/Like to some branch of stars we see'; 'Burned like one burning flame together; metaphor: Some bearded meteor). Discuss what is being compared to what, and how effective they are.

Differentiated group activities

1*: Guided reading and discussion. Discuss how Tennyson creates a dramatic entrance for Sir Lancelot. List words and phrases that make him stand out from the other characters described.
2 & 3: Write a description of Sir Lancelot in modern prose (ordinary writing) style.
4*: Guided reading and discussion. Re-read the poem with a particular emphasis on reading poetry correctly and understanding difficult vocabulary, then discuss Sir Lancelot's 'entrance' as above.

Conclusion

Ask selected children in Groups 2 and 3 to read their descriptions of Sir Lancelot. The rest of the class should listen carefully and then comment on whether they include in their prose pieces all the important information given in the poem.

Introduction

Re-read Parts I–III of the poem. Remind the children that this is a narrative poem that tells a story and that most stories have a beginning, middle and end. What is the beginning of this story? What is the middle? Explain that at the end of the whole poem the curse takes effect and the Lady of Shalott dies. What do they think happens in between that leads to her death? Explain that in their group activities they are going to write a continuation to the poem that answers that question. Discuss what they think are the main aspects of plot they must bear in mind when writing their continuations – for example:

■ At the beginning of Part II we are told that 'a curse is on her', and at the end of Part II we are told that she is 'half sick of shadows (sick of seeing the world only through her mirror).
■ There are many characters introduced in Part II.
■ Sir Lancelot makes a dramatic entry in Part III and makes a big impression on the Lady of Shalott

Whole-class skills work

Use the rhyme pattern of the poem to explore spelling patterns of rhyming words. Look, for example, at the rhyming words in the first four lines of the poem: *lie, rye, sky* and *by*. How many ways are there to spell the *i* as in 'lie' sound? List other words that fit these spelling patterns. Can they think of another way to spell the same sound (for example – *igh* as in 'high')?

Discuss whether all the rhyming words in the poem rhyme exactly. Explain that poets often play with rhyme, sometimes using words that sound almost the same, or words that look almost the same. Identify some of these in the poem.

Differentiated group activities

All children write a continuation to the poem.
1: Try to write using Tennyson's verse form (or a simplified version of it with this rhyme pattern: *a a b a a b*).
2 & 3: Write in blank verse – lines of poetry with metre but without rhyme.
4: Write in prose (ordinary writing).
*The teacher gives support as appropriate.

Conclusion

Select children from all groups to share examples of their continuations. Then read the rest of the poem to the class and compare it with their continuations. (NB The rest of the poem – Part IV – can be found on photocopiable page 133.)

THE LADY OF SHALOTT

PART I

On either side the river lie
Long the fields of barley and of rye,
That clothe the wold and meet the sky;
And thro' the field the road runs by
    To many tower'd Camelot;
And up and down the people go,
Gazing where the lilies blow
Round an island there below,
    The island of Shalott.

Willows whiten, aspens quiver,
Little breezes dusk and shiver
Thro' the wave that runs for ever
By the island in the river
    Flowing down to Camelot.
Four grey walls, and four grey towers,
Overlook a space of flowers,
And the silent isle imbowers
    The Lady of Shalott.

By the margin, willow-veil'd,
Slide the heavy barges trail'd
By slow horses; and unhail'd
The shallop flitteth silken-sail'd
    Skimming down to Camelot:
But who hath seen her wave her hand?
Or at the casement seen her stand?
Or is she known in all the land,
    The Lady of Shalott?

Only reapers, reaping early
In among the bearded barley,
Hear a song that echoes cheerly
From the river winding clearly,
    Down to tower'd Camelot:
And by the moon the reaper weary,
Piling sheaves in uplands airy,
Listening, whispers "'Tis the fairy
    Lady of Shalott."

PART II

There she weaves by night and day
A magic web with colours gay.
She has heard a whisper say,
A curse is on her if she stay
    To look down to Camelot.
She knows not what the curse may be,
And so she weaveth steadily,
And little other care hath she,
    The Lady of Shalott.

And moving thro' a mirror clear
That hangs before her all the year,
Shadows of the world appear.
There she sees the highway near
    Winding down to Camelot:
There the river eddy whirls,
And there the surly village-churls,
And the red cloaks of market girls,
    Pass onward from Shalott.

Sometimes a troop of damsels glad,
An abbot on an ambling pad,
Sometimes a curly shepherd-lad,
Or long-hair'd page in crimson clad,
    Goes by to tower'd Camelot;
And sometimes thro' the mirror blue
The knights come riding two and two:
She hath no loyal knight and true,
    The Lady of Shalott.

But in her web she still delights
To weave the mirror's magic sights,
For often thro' the silent nights
A funeral, with plumes and lights,
    And music, went to Camelot:
Or when the moon was overhead,
Came two young lovers lately wed;
'I am half sick of shadows' said
    The Lady of Shalott.

PART III

A bow-shot from her bower-eaves,
He rode between the barley-sheaves,
The sun came dazzling thro' the leaves,
And flamed upon the brazen greaves
    Of bold Sir Lancelot.
A red-cross knight for ever kneel'd
To a lady in a shield,
That sparkled on the yellow field,
Beside remote Shalott.

The gemmy bridle glitter'd free,
Like to some branch of stars we see
Hung in the golden Galaxy.
The bridle bells rang merrily
    As he rode down to Camelot:
And from his blazon'd baldric slung
A mighty silver bugle hung,
And as he rode his armour rung,
    Beside remote Shalott.

All in the blue unclouded weather
Thick-jewell'd shone the saddle-leather,
The helmet and the helmet-feather
Burn'd like one burning flame together,
    As he rode down to Camelot.
As often thro' the purple night,
Below the starry clusters bright,
Some bearded meteor, trailing light,
    Moves over still Shalott.

His broad clear brow in sunlight glow'd;
On burnish'd hooves his war-horse trode;
From underneath his helmet flow'd
His coal black curls as on he rode,
    As he rode down to Camelot.
From the bank and from the river
He flash'd into the crystal mirror,
Tirra lirra, by the river
    Sang Sir Lancelot.

She left the web, she left the loom,
She made three paces thro' the room,
She saw the water-lily bloom,
She saw the helmet and the plume,
    She look'd down to Camelot.
Out flew the web and floated wide;
The mirror crack'd from side to side;
"The curse is come upon me," cried
    The Lady of Shalott.

PART IV

In the stormy eat-wind training,
The pale yellow woods were waning,
The broad stream in his banks complaining,
Heavily the low sky raining
    Over tower'd Camelot;
Down she came and found a boat
Beneath a willow left afloat,
And round the about the prow she wrote
    The Lady of Shalott.

And down the river's dim expanse –
Like some bold seer in a trance,
Seeing all his own mischance –
With a glassy countenance
    Did she look to Camelot.
And at the closing of the day
She loosed the chain, and down she lay;
The broad stream bore her far away,
    The Lady of Shalott.

Lying, robed in snowy white
That loosely flew to left and right –
The leaves upon her falling light –
Thro' the noises of the night
    She floated down to Camelot:
And as the boat-head wound along
The willowy hills and fields among,
They heard her singing her last song.
    The Lady of Shalott.

Heard a carol, mournful holy,
Chanted loudly, chanted lowly,
Till her blood was frozen slowly,
And her eyes were darken'd wholly,
    Turn'd to tower'd Camelot.
For ere she reach'd upon the tide
The first house by the water-side,
Singing in her song she died
    The Lady of Shalott.

Under tower and balcony,
By farden-wall and gallery,
A gleaming shape she floated by,
Dead-pale between the houses high,
    Silent into Camelot.
Out upon the wharfs they came,
Knight and burgher, lord and dame.
And round the prow they read her name,
    The Lady of Shalott.

Who is this? and what is here?
And in the lighted palace near
Died the sound of royal cheer;
And they cross'd themselves for fear,
    All the knights at Camelot.
But Lancelot mused a little space;
He said, "She has a lovely face;
God in his mercy lend her grace,
    The Lady of Shalott."

Alfred Lord Tennyson

THE SPANISH ARMADA

OBJECTIVES

UNIT	SPELLING/VOCABULARY	GRAMMAR/PUNCTUATION	COMPREHENSION/COMPOSITION
WRITING POETRY Ballad: 'The Spanish Armada' *Anonymous*.	Investigate interesting and unusual words, including archaic ones.	Understand the grammar of poetry. Use punctuation to help convey meaning when reading aloud.	Read ballad and understand distinctive features. Retell story in a different format. Use structure of ballad read to write own ballad.

ORGANIZATION (2 HOURS)

	INTRODUCTION	WHOLE-CLASS SKILLS WORK	DIFFERENTIATED GROUP ACTIVITIES	CONCLUSION
HOUR 1	Give historical background. Read poem. Discuss the ballad format and features.	Identify and investigate interesting and unusual words, including archaic ones.	1*: Rewrite story as a reference book page. 2 & 3: Rewrite story as a front-page newspaper article. 4: Retell story as a film storyboard.	Share examples of the different versions of the story and discuss differences in form and style.
HOUR 2	Re-read poem aloud as a class.	Analyse the verse form of the poem.	1–4*: All groups write a collaborative ballad about an historical event. *The teacher supports Groups 3 & 4.	Each group presents its ballad. Evaluate and then discuss how to publish a class book of ballads.

RESOURCES

Photocopiable pages 136 ('The Spanish Armada'), 137 (Storyboard) and 138 (Spanish Armada Clip Art), board or flip chart, OHP and acetate (optional), dictionaries, writing materials, scissors, adhesive.

PREPARATION

Make enough copies of the poem (photocopiable page 136) for one between two children. If possible, prepare also as an OHT or enlarged version. Make copies for all children of the Clip Art sheet (photocopiable page 138) and enough copies of the Storyboard sheet (photocopiable page 137) for Group 4.

Introduction

The defeat of the Spanish Armada in 1588 is one of the most momentous events in British history. This anonymous ballad is a celebration of that victory. Illustrations on the Clip Art photocopiable sheet are adapted from a range of original materials designed to celebrate the victory.

Distribute copies of the poem and, if possible, display it on OHP or as an enlarged version. Before reading the poem, tell the children that it is a ballad, and explain that a ballad is a songlike poem that tells a story. It is usually written in short, regular verses with a consistent rhyme scheme. Ask them to listen out for these features as you read the poem.

After reading, identify the characteristic ballad features and establish the narrative that is told.

Whole-class skills work

Investigate interesting and unusual words, particularly the archaic words that place the poem in its historical context – for example:

hight = was called
wight = person
victualled = provisioned (such as with food)
pease = peas
fraught = provided
three score = 60

Ask the children to identify others and to suggest their meanings by context before looking them up in the dictionary.

Differentiated group activities

1*: Re-present the information in the ballad as a modern reference book page. Choose appropriate illustrations from the Clip Art sheet to support and extend their text.
2 & 3: Design a newspaper front page about the event using a selection from the Clip Art sheet as illustrations.
4*: Use photocopiable page 137 to retell the story of the Armada as a storyboard. Explain that a storyboard is usually used as a plan for a film. The main scenes are described in one or two sentences and illustrated with pictures. The children could use a combination of clip art and their own drawing for the illustrations.

Conclusion

Select children from each of the groups to share with the rest of the class their versions of the story. Discuss the differences in form and style.

Introduction

Re-read the ballad with the children sharing in the reading. This could be done by a group of children taking a verse each and the whole class reciting the last line of each verse. Encourage them to keep together, to bring out the rhythm of the poem and to vary the pace, volume and pitch of their voices to suit the meaning of the lines. Point out the use of commas in the poem and demonstrate how pausing at these points helps to convey meaning.

Whole-class skills work

Discuss the verse form of the ballad and analyse its rhythm, meter and rhyme scheme. Highlight the following features:
■ four stressed syllables in each line
■ lines 2 and 4 rhyme
■ lines 1 and 3 have internal rhyme (rhyme within a line)
■ sometimes rhymes are approximate (words that have approximate sound similarities, as in *young* and *strong*)
■ each verse ends with a refrain (repetition of previous line)

Differentiated group activities

1–4: Children in all groups work together to write a ballad collaboratively. The ballad should describe an historical event and be modelled on the verse form of 'The Spanish Armada'. If children are not sure what to write about, refer to recent history topics. They should write the story first in note form and divide it into sections for the verses. Children in Group 1 could then each write a verse while children in Group 2 could work in pairs on a verse. Finally, all the verses are edited together.
    *Children in Groups 3 and 4 should write one or two verses collaboratively with teacher support.

Conclusion

Ask each group to present its collaborative ballad (or ballad verses) and the rest of the class to evaluate it achievements. Discuss as a class how the poems could be 'published', perhaps as a class book.

THE SPANISH ARMADA

Some years of late, in eighty-eight
As I do well remember,
It was, some say, the tenth of May,
And, some say, in September,
And, some say, in September.

The Spanish train launch'd forth amain,
With many a fine bravado,
Their (as they thought, but it proved not)
Invincible Armado,
Invincible Armado.

There was a little man, that dwelt in Spain,
Who shot well in a gun-a,
Don Pedro hight, as black a wight
As the Knight of the Sun-a,
As the Knight of the Sun-a.

King Philip made him Admiral,
And bid him not to stay-a,
But to destroy both man and boy,
And so to come away-a,
And so to come away-a.

Their navy was well-victualled
With biscuit, pease, and bacon;
They brought two ships, well fraught with whips,
But I think they were mistaken,
But I think they were mistaken.

Their men were young, munition strong,
And, to do us more harm-a,
They thought it meet to join the fleet,
All with the Prince of Parma,
All with the Prince of Parma.

They coasted round about our land,
And so came in by Dover;
But we had men set on them then
And threw the rascals over,
And threw the rascals over.

The Queen was then at Tilbury,
What more could we desire-a?
And Sir Francis Drake, for her sweet sake,
Did set them all on fire-a,
Did set them all on fire-a.

Then, straight, they fled, by sea and land,
That one man killed three score-a;
And had not they all run away,
In truth he had killed more-a,
In truth he had killed more-a.

Then let them neither brag nor boast,
But if they come agen-a,
Let them take heed, they do not speed
As they did, you know when-a,
As they did, you know when-a.

Anonymous

136

STORYBOARD

SPANISH ARMADA CLIP ART

King Philip of Spain

Sir Frances Drake

Map of Spain and England

The Spanish Fleet sets sail – 20 May 1588

The Spanish Fleet: 130 ships, 19 290 soldiers, 8359 sailors, 2080 slaves, 2630 guns

Drake finishes his game of bowls

More than half the Spanish fleet is sunk

Most of the rest are shipwrecked on the way home

THE LAIDLEY WORM

OBJECTIVES

UNIT	SPELLING/VOCABULARY	GRAMMAR/PUNCTUATION	COMPREHENSION/ COMPOSITION
READING FICTION Traditional story: 'The Laidley Worm of Spindlestone Heugh'.	Look up difficult and archaic words in a dictionary. Investigate spelling of words with -ful suffix. Investigate doubling consonants when adding endings.	Revise different kinds of nouns. Recognize archaic syntax.	Read a traditional story in its earliest written version. Investigate different versions of the same story.

ORGANIZATION (3 HOURS)

	INTRODUCTION	WHOLE-CLASS SKILLS WORK	DIFFERENTIATED GROUP ACTIVITIES	CONCLUSION
HOUR 1	Give some background explanation and then read the story up to the 'choice' point.	Explore the archaic elements in the text.	1*: Guided reading and discussion. 2 & 3: Reading Comprehension, parts A & B. 4*: Guided reading and discussion. Prepare text for reading aloud.	Identify characteristic features of traditional stories. (Be sure NOT to discuss the story endings – in order to keep some element of mystery for Groups 2 & 3!)
HOUR 2	Group 4 re-reads the text to the class (up to the 'choice' point).	Explore spelling patterns of consonants, eg doubling consonant when adding endings and words with suffix -ful.	1: Reading Comprehension, all parts. 2 & 3*: Guided reading and discussion. 4: Reading Comprehension, part A.	Discuss the two endings with the whole class. Which ending fits best and why?
HOUR 3	Read a version of the 'St George and the Dragon' story and compare.	Revise the different kinds of nouns.	1–3*: Write versions of the story in modern narrative style. 4: Reassemble story from cut-up version.	Selected pupils from Groups 1–3 read out sections of their stories.

RESOURCES

Photocopiable page 142 ('The Laidley Worm of Spindlestone Heugh'), 143 (Alternative Endings to 'The Laidley Worm') and 144 (Reading Comprehension), large map of Britain, dictionaries, a version of the 'St George and the Dragon' story.

PREPARATION

Make enough copies of all the photocopiable pages for one between two children. Cut the copies of photocopiable page 143 in half so that the two endings of the story are available separately. In addition make enough copies of the story (with the 'Kiss' ending) and cut up into paragraphs for children in Group 4 to reassemble in Hour 3. Locate Bamburgh and Spindlestone for yourself on the map (on the east coast of Scotland, south of Berwick-upon-Tweed, opposite Farne Islands).

Introduction

Begin with some background explanation. Tell the children that they are going to read an ancient legend in the form in which it was written down in the eighteenth century (except for the ending which has been adapted to make the alternative endings possible). Spindlestone Heugh is a real place just outside Bamburgh in Scotland. Locate it on a map. 'Laidley' is an Old English word for 'loathsome' or 'horrible', and 'worm' is an Old English word for 'dragon'. We still use the word today, of course, but its meaning has shrunk a little!

Read the first part of the story to the class. Discuss the archaic vocabulary and sentence construction. Ask the children: *Which words are little used today? Which phrases sound odd or different? Are any spellings different? What do they notice about the use of capital letters?*

Whole-class skills work

Investigate the archaic language. The following ideas can be used as starting points:
■ Make a list of archaic and difficult words and identify their meanings, first by trying context, and then using dictionaries.
■ Copy out old-fashioned sounding phrases, and write a modern English version underneath them.
■ Rewrite the third paragraph using modern conventions for use of capital letters.

Differentiated group activities

1*: Guided reading and discussion. Base this on the first page to begin with. Ask questions to test basic understanding, and then ask questions which help children decide which ending to choose, for example:
■ Should we not always show pity and be merciful as a matter of principle?
■ How does the tale of the 'crocodyle' affect Childewynd's decision? Is the tale true?
■ Is there any link between the Woman of the wild Land-in-the-West, her witchcraft and the dragon? (Be careful how you ask this question – it could give too much away!)
Finally, read the ending chosen by the children – both endings if different children choose different endings.
2 & 3: Work on the Reading Comprehension sheet, parts A and B.
4*: Guided reading and discussion. Help children with the reading of difficult words and phrases and, in discussion, be sure to ask the third question above (see under Group 1) which contains the strongest clue. Ask this group to prepare a reading aloud of the story, perhaps each child taking a paragraph in turn.

Conclusion

Be sure NOT to discuss how the story ends – try to keep some element of mystery for Groups 2 and 3! Instead, explore the traditional elements in the story. Ask the children what kinds of people, creatures, situations and other characteristic features do we find in this story that appear in many other traditional folk and 'fairy' tales? (*King, princess, knight – 'childe' is Middle English for 'knight' – a witch, a dragon, a spell, a romantic rescue – with a kiss, a toad and a 'Once upon a time…' opening.*)

Introduction

Ask Group 4 to re-read the story to the class (first page only) as prepared in their group work of the previous hour.

Whole-class skills work

Write the following words from the story on the board or flip chart:
    beautiful
    hopeful
    peaceful

Establish that they mean:
    full of beauty
    full of hope
    full of peace

Discuss what happens to the word 'full' when you add it as a suffix to another word. Ask the children to formulate the spelling rule: when you add 'full' to the end of a word, drop the last 'l'.

Note that when the additional suffix '-ly' is added, the 'l' appears double again, for example joyful + ly = joyfully.

Ask the children to find the phrase 'full of tears' in the story and turn it into 'tearful'. Ask them to think of other examples.

Move on to discussing words which double the final consonant when adding a suffix if the consonant is preceded by a short vowel. Examples from the story are: 'stunning', 'hugging', 'saddened' and 'wrapped'.

Differentiated group activities
1: Work on the Reading Comprehension sheet, all parts.
2 & 3*: Guided reading and discussion – see above.
4: Work on Reading Comprehension sheet, part A.

Conclusion
Now that all the children have had a chance to explore the ending for themselves, discuss it with the whole class. Discuss which ending fits best and why.

Introduction
Read a version of the 'St George and the Dragon' story and compare it with 'The Laidley Worm of Spindlestone Heugh'. Identify similarities and differences.

Whole-class skills work
Revise different kinds of noun:
■ A **common** noun is the name of a person place or thing. Examples from the text: *worm, child, maiden, castle*.
■ A **proper** noun is the name of a particular person or place. Proper nouns begin with a capital letter. A good test for a proper noun is that it cannot usually be made plural, for example there is only one Northumbria. Examples from the text: *Margaret, Spindlestone Heugh, Bamburgh*.
■ **Collective** nouns describe a group or collection of people and things, for example *herd, swarm, class*. Examples from the text: *court, flocks, crew*.
■ **Abstract** nouns describe qualities rather than things, for example *love, goodness, friendship*. Examples from the text: *honour, beauty, fame, mercy*.

Ask the children to find the examples from the text given above (and any more they can find). (Remind them that they will have to ignore the capitalization in the text as it follows different rules to those in use today.)

Differentiated group activities
1: Rewrite the story as a modern narrative and with dialogue.
2 & 3*: As above, but keeping to the purely narrative structure of the original.
4: Give this group a copy of the story (with the 'Kiss' ending) cut up for them to reassemble.

Conclusion
Selected children from Groups 1 to 3 read out completed sections of their stories. Make sure that if they wish to do so, children are given additional time to finish their stories.

THE LAIDLEY WORM OF SPINDLESTONE HEUGH

nce upon a time there was a king in Northumbria, whose wife died leaving him with one child, a good and beautiful Maiden of eighteen named Margaret, beloved alike by Court and People.

Soon afterwards, a stunning dark Woman of the wild Land-in-the-West fascinated the King. So they married and he brought her to the Castle of Bamburgh where a great feast was spread in honour of their Homecoming.

Margaret ran to meet them at the Gate. The Queen greeted her with Smiles and Kisses, hugging her closely. But she was really jealous of her Beauty and soon determined to be rid of so dangerous a rival.

One day therefore she invited her to come and see some Jewels in a private Chamber, and no one being near, used her Witchcraft to cast a SPELL on the Maiden. No one saw her again after that day. And the saddened King grieved mightily.

At about that time, another terrible thing happened in Northumbria. A strange beast made its Lair upon the Crags, and from thence roamed abroad, blasting the Trees with its Breath and devouring the flocks for Miles around, and soon was known as The LAIDLEY WORM of Spindlestone Heugh.

Its fame spread far and at last reached a young knight, CHILDEWYND, who determined to free the Peasants from so onerous a Plague. So he set Sail, hopeful of success, and the Wind being fair soon reached Bamburgh.

Now the Queen being on the Watchtower saw the Ship afar and knowing why it came hastily sent a Man of war to destroy it. But Childewynd's crew was victorious and sunk the queen's boat with all on board.

The LAIDLEY Worm stood raging on the Cliffs and by its terrible Breath drove them out to Sea again. Finding no means of landing the Ship was run for Budle Bay and the Crew safely gained the Shore.

Childewynd then left his Men and followed the now retreating Beast: he overtook it among the Crags of Spindlestone and had raised his sword to strike when with Eyes full of Tears it piteously cried out.

It pleaded for mercy, saying that it was the victim of a spell, and that only a kiss would restore it to human form.

But Childewynd was no fool. He had heard tales of a beast called CROCODYLE which shed false tears to lure its prey. Perhaps this worm was another such beast that when he stooped to kiss it, it would devour him.

* * * *

If you think Childewynd should kiss the beast, read the ending marked 'Kiss'.
If you think Childewynd should kill the beast, read the ending marked 'Kill'.

ALTERNATIVE ENDINGS TO 'THE LAIDLEY WORM'

Kiss

The KNIGHT stooped down and kissed the loathsome Worm; its scales turned dim; it withered, dried, burst into flame and the princess MARGARET rose from the Ashes, more beautiful than ever before.

Childewynd wrapped her in his Cloak, placed her on Horseback and together they made their way to Bamburgh. Their coming was already spread abroad and the People ran joyfully to meet them.

The King was glad to see his DAUGHTER but the QUEEN was sore afraid and kept her chamber. There CHILDEWYND sought her and by her own Arts turned her into a speckled TOAD.

CHILDEWYND and MARGARET married and on the death of the KING they sat together on the Throne surrounded by their Children and ruled over a peaceful and contented People.

Kill

The KNIGHT plunged his sword into the creature's breast; its red blood spouted; its scales turned dim; it withered, dried, and began to change into human form. It was the princess MARGARET. The witch's spell was broken. But it was too late. The blood gushed from the wound that the sword had made.

Alas, said the Princess, if you had kissed me when I was that loathsome creature, you could have won my hand in marriage and ruled my father's kingdom. Now you must flee for your life before he hears what you have done.

So Childewynd fled and was never heard of again. The poor old KING died of sorrow when he heard the news; and the dark woman of the wild Land-in-the-West ruled Northumbria in his place and brought untold evil, pain and suffering to its unfortunate people.

READING COMPREHENSION

PART A

■ What kind of person was Margaret?

■ What kind of a person was the Woman of the wild Land-in-the-West?

■ What did the Woman of the wild Land-in-the-West do to Margaret?

■ What other terrible event happened at about the same time?

■ What did the Woman of the wild Land-in-the-West do when she saw Childwynd's boat approaching?

■ What happened when Childwynd raised his sword to strike the worm?

■ What other creature did Childwynd think of when he was trying to decide whether to kill the worm?

■ What did the old tales say about the crocodile?

PART B

■ The wild Land-in-the-West sounds like a fascinating place, but it is not described in the story? How do you see it in your imagination?

■ The Woman of the wild Land-in-the-West is not described very clearly. How would you describe her?

■ Using your imagination, write short descriptions of Childwynd and the worm.

PART C

■ Write about your response to the story. Did you enjoy it? Would you have enjoyed it more if it had been written in a modern style or did you enjoy the old-fashioned style?

WRITE A 'CHOICE' STORY

OBJECTIVES

UNIT	SPELLING/VOCABULARY	GRAMMAR/PUNCTUATION	COMPREHENSION/ COMPOSITION
WRITING FICTION Write a 'choice' story.	Investigate hard and soft 'c' spellings. Use known spellings as basis for spelling words with similar patterns.	Develop grammatical awareness through redrafting process.	Write own story based on traditional tale and using structure identified in reading.

ORGANIZATION (2 HOURS)

	INTRODUCTION	WHOLE-CLASS SKILLS WORK	DIFFERENTIATED GROUP ACTIVITIES	CONCLUSION
HOUR 1	Read (or-read) 'The Laidley Worm of Spindlestone Heugh' from previous unit. Discuss its structure with two endings.	Investigate hare and soft 'c' spellings.	1–4: All pupils plan their story. *The teacher supports Groups 1 & 4.	Pupils share draft stories with partners. One or two can be read to whole class.
HOUR 2	Share more first drafts of story with discussion on ideas for improvement and redrafting.	Revise key skills on Redrafting Checklist.	1–4: All pupils work in pairs to redraft stories. *The teacher supports Groups 2 & 3.	Selected pupils share their first drafts and redrafts and explain how they went about improving their stories.

RESOURCES

Photocopiable page 142 ('The Laidley Worm of Spindlestone Heugh' from previous unit), and 110 (Redrafting Checklist from the 'Redrafting Simulation' unit), board or flip chart, OHP and acetate (optional), writing materials.

PREPARATION

Make enough copies of all the photocopiable pages for one between two children. If possible, also prepare them as OHTs or enlarged versions for the whole-class sessions.

Write the following list of words from the story on the board or flip chart: *princess, mercy, once, court, fascinated, castle, come, crew, cliffs, scales, peaceful.*

Introduction

Read 'The Laidley Worm of Spindlestone Heugh' (or re-read if previous unit has been done) and discuss it with a focus on the choice of endings, and the clues which help the reader to make the right choice. Explain to the class that, in their group work, they are going to write a similar 'choice' story based on a traditional folktale.

Help the children with the planning of their 'choice' stories by drawing the following planning grid on the board or flip chart:

BEGINNING		
MIDDLE		
END	Ending 1	Ending 2

Make notes on how the story will develop in each box. When both endings have been drafted, go back and see what clues to the correct ending can be placed in the first box. Point out that the clues should not be too obvious!

Whole-class skills work

Use words from the story to investigate spelling words with hard and soft 'c'. Reveal the list of 'c' words on the board or flip chart. Read them out and ask children what they notice about the sound of the 'c' in each word. Then ask children to place them under the correct heading: hard 'c' or soft 'c'. Investigate the spellings and work with the children to see if they can formulate the rule: When 'c' sounds like an 's' (soft 'c'), it is usually followed by 'e', 'i' or 'y'. Brainstorm other 'c' words and place them under the correct heading. Some examples are: soft 'c' – *celery, cinema, mice, cider, ceiling*; hard 'c' – *corn, cucumber, accuse, claw*. The children may also come up with words that contain both: *bicycle, accident, circus*.

Differentiated group activities

1–4*: All children work on planning their choice stories, using the writing plan above and a traditional story of their choice. Children can work individually or in pairs or small groups depending on ability. More able children, in Group 1 and some of Group 2, could be encouraged to develop their stories to another one or two levels of choice. If less able children are having difficulty getting started, suggest a traditional story on which they can base their writing.

Conclusion

Children can read the first draft of their choice stories to each other, asking their partners (or partner pairs or groups) to try to make the right choice. One or two could be selected for whole-class presentation and evaluated on how effectively clues have been planted.

Introduction

Hear more presentations of the first draft of the 'choice' stories. This should be followed by discussion on how the stories could be further improved and developed.

Whole-class skills work

Distribute copies of photocopiable page 110 (Redrafting Checklist). Revise the key skills that you feel need support and remind the children how to use the checklist in pairs.

Differentiated group activities

1–4*: All children work in pairs within groups to redraft their 'choice' stories and begin making a neat presentation (which can be finished off for homework).

Conclusion

Select children from each group to read their redrafted stories. They should also read extracts from their first drafts and explain how they went about improving them.

FURTHER IDEA

Develop the 'choice' idea further and ask the children to write an adventure game.

THE MECHANICAL TELEVISION

OBJECTIVES

UNIT	SPELLING/VOCABULARY	GRAMMAR/PUNCTUATION	COMPREHENSION/ COMPOSITION
READING NON-FICTION Explanatory and recount texts: 'The Mechanical Television'.	Develop subject-specific vocabulary. Make a glossary for technical words.	Revise verb tenses.	Prepare for reading by establishing prior knowledge. Read a text that combines explanatory and recount genres and investigate and note features. Formulate questions for further research.

ORGANIZATION (2 HOURS)

	INTRODUCTION	WHOLE-CLASS SKILLS WORK	DIFFERENTIATED GROUP ACTIVITIES	CONCLUSION
HOUR 1	Prepare for reading by establishing prior knowledge. Shared reading and discussion of 'The Mechanical Television'.	and explanatory features. Make a glossary of	discussion. 2 & 3: Reading Comprehension, part A. 4*: Guided reading and discussion. 1*: Reading	information text provided and what other questions pupils might wish to research in other sources. Share and discuss answers to
HOUR 2	'Read' the diagram and provide oral explanation. Then cross-check with text. Identify recount	technical words. 1*: Guided reading and	Comprehension, parts A & C. 2 & 3*: Guided reading and discussion. 4*: Reading Comprehension, part B. Discuss what new	Reading Comprehension answers.

RESOURCES

Photocopiable pages 149 and 150 ('The Mechanical Television') and 151 (Reading Comprehension), OHP and acetate (optional), dictionaries, writing materials.

PREPARATION

If possible, copy photocopiable pages 149 and 150 side by side onto A3 paper to make a double-page spread. This will help the children to easily cross-reference between text and diagram. If possible, prepare also as an OHT or enlarged version.

Introduction
Ask the children what they know about the history of television. Read 'The Mechanical Television' on page 149 and discuss how text, pictures and diagram work together.

Whole-class skills work
Explain that this text combines the features of recount and explanation genres (because it includes information about the history of television as well as how the mechanical television works). Recap on the key features of each genre as follows:

■ *Recount genre* is 'chronological' and usually contains connectives that relate to sequence in time. It is usually written in the past tense and includes a high number of names, facts and dates. Illustrations are often used.

■ *Explanation genre* has an impersonal style and is usually written in the present tense. It includes a high number of technical terms and connectives to link procedural sequences and cause and effect. Pictures and diagrams are often used to make the text clearer.

Ask the children to identify which part of the text is written in which genre by looking carefully for distinguishing features.

Differentiated group activities

1*: Guided reading and discussion. The following ideas can be used as a starting point for discussion:

■ Using the diagram, explain in your own words how the mechanical television works.

■ How would you describe the example of the picture on a Baird television?

■ Why is the Emitron television system better?

2 & 3: Work on the Reading Comprehension sheet, part A.

4*: Guided reading and discussion. Spend some time checking understanding of technical terms, then discuss the text using some of the ideas from part A of the Reading Comprehension sheet.

Conclusion

Discuss what new information the text provided and why the Emitron system was better than the Baird system. Ask the children what other questions might they wish to research in other sources – for example about more recent developments such as colour television and satellite television.

Introduction

Display the diagram only of the mechanical television (on OHP if available, or as an enlarged version), then ask for a volunteer to explain in his/her own words how it works. Ask the rest of the class to evaluate the explanation. Cross-check this by reading the explanatory section of the text.

Whole-class skills work

Identify the technical vocabulary in the text and make a class glossary to go with the text. Encourage the children to use a variety of strategies to determine meaning – for example context, known words with similar roots, prefixes or suffixes, dictionary.

Differentiated group activities

1: Work on Reading Comprehension sheet, parts A & C.

2 & 3*: Guided reading and discussion (see above).

4: Work on Reading Comprehension sheet, part B.

Conclusion

Ask selected children from each group to share their answers to the questions on the Reading Comprehension sheet. Discuss these as a class.

FURTHER IDEA

The children could research the questions they formulated in the concluding session of Hour 1.

THE MECHANICAL TELEVISION

The mechanical television was developed by a Scotsman, John Logie Baird (1888–1946). It was based on a German discovery known as Nipkov's disk. This broke down a picture into 'dots' by spinning a disk with a series of holes: a process known as scanning. The system was used for experimental television transmissions from September 1929. However, by 1934 it had been replaced by the Emitron system which scanned pictures electronically. This is the basis of the TV system in use today.

JOHN LOGIE BAIRD

The mechanical television camera works as follows:

The subject (1), a dummy's head in the diagram, is placed in front of the Nipkov disk (2). Light coming through the disk is broken in separate dots by the shutter (3). The light is then turned into electronic pulses by the photoelectric cell (4). A photoelectric cell is a device which is sensitive to light. When light falls on it, it produces a small current of electricity. This current is sent to the radio transmitter (5), which amplifies and transmits the pulses as radio waves through an aerial (6). At the end of the apparatus is an electric motor (7) which turns the Nipkov disk and the shutter. This has a control to set the speed of rotation so that the image can be synchronized with the receiver.

The mechanical television receiver is like the camera in reverse. The motor (8) must be adjusted so that it is running at the same speed as the motor on the camera (7). The electronic pulses are received by an aerial (9) and taken to a radio receiver and amplifier (10). The amplified pulse is sent to a light bulb (11) which flickers on and off as the pulse varies. The shutter (12) and the Nipkov disk (13) ensure that the light comes through at the correct place to build up the picture seen by the person watching (14).

To form an idea of the picture quality you need to know that modern television (UK PAL system) has 625 lines. The Emitron system had 405 lines. The number of lines on a mechanical television depends on the number of holes in the Nipkov disk. Baird's early televisions had 30 lines and the maximum he achieved was 240.

THE PICTURE SEEN BY VIEWERS OF JOHN LOGIE BAIRD

THE MECHANICAL TELEVISION

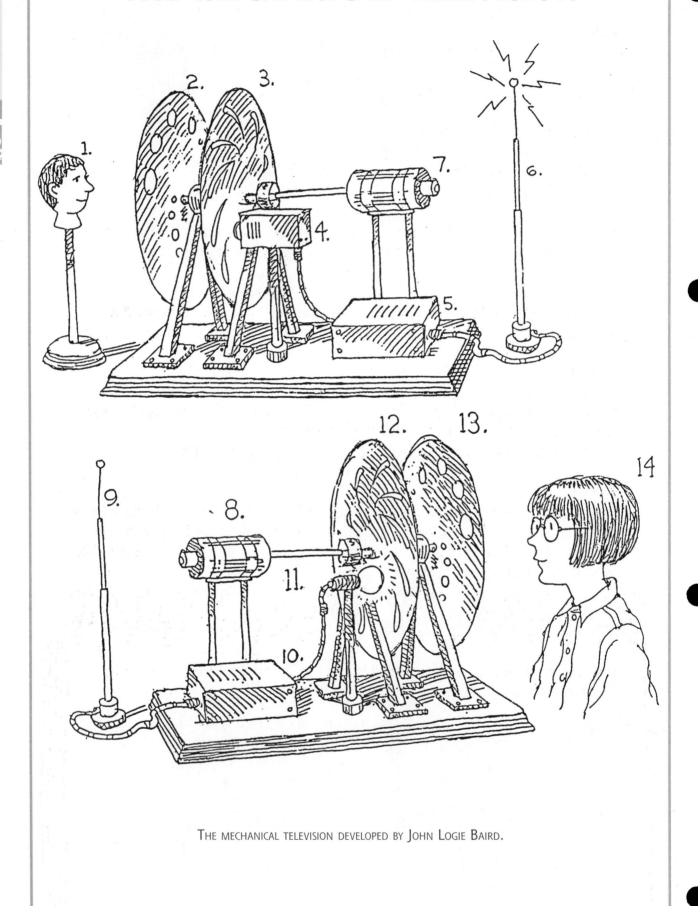

The mechanical television developed by John Logie Baird.

READING COMPREHENSION

PART A

■ Who developed the mechanical television?

■ What discovery was it based on?

■ Explain how this discovery worked.

■ What is the main difference between the
Baird mechanical system and the Emitron system?

■ Look up the word 'synchronized' and explain why you think it is important
that the speed of rotation of the Nipkov disks in camera and receiver are
synchronized.

■ Look up and write a definition of the following words: *pulse, photoelectric,
device, produces, current, amplifies, transmits, rotation.*

PART B

Work in pairs.
■ One person should explain orally (using the diagram but not the text) to the
other how the mechanical television camera works.
■ The other person should explain orally how the receiver works.

PART C

■ Write your own explanation of how the mechanical television works for a book
which will not include a diagram or a picture. This means that each part of the
explanation will have to be given in more detail. An example is given below (the
additional explanation is shown in italics).

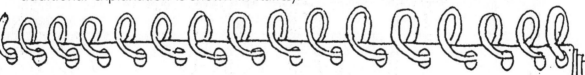

The subject to be broadcast is placed in front of the Nipkov disk. *This is a large
disk with a series of holes going in a spiral to the centre…*

FUTURE TV

OBJECTIVES

UNIT	SPELLING/VOCABULARY	GRAMMAR/PUNCTUATION	COMPREHENSION/ COMPOSITION
WRITING NON-FICTION Explanatory text: 'Future TV Brainstorm'.	Collect, define and spell technical words. Invent words. Understand how language develops.	Understand how writing can be adapted for different audiences by changing vocabulary and sentence structure.	Write explanatory text for two different audiences. Use brainstorm technique for developing ideas.

ORGANIZATION (2 HOURS)

	INTRODUCTION	WHOLE-CLASS SKILLS WORK	DIFFERENTIATED GROUP ACTIVITIES	CONCLUSION
HOUR 1	Use 'Future TV Brainstorm' photocopiable sheet to stimulate discussion and brainstorm ideas.	Explore technical words related to electronics, TV and computers. Discuss language development. Make up new words.	1–4*: All pupils work in pairs within their groups to devise a TV of the future in diagrammatic form with labels.	Pairs join with other pairs to present and evaluate each other's work.
HOUR 2	Select two or three pairs to present their work to whole class.	Investigate how writing can be adapted for different audiences.	1–4*: All pupils work in pairs to produce two written explanations for two different audiences.	Selected pupils present their two versions and rest of class evaluates the appropriateness for intended audience.

RESOURCES

Photocopiable pages 154 ('Future TV Brainstorm') and 149 and 150 ('The Mechanical Television' from the previous unit), board or flip chart, OHP and acetate (optional), writing materials.

PREPARATION

Make enough copies of photocopiable page 154 for one between two children. If possible, also prepare it as an OHT or enlarged version. Copies of 'The Mechanical Television' from the previous unit should also be available for children to use as a model. Write the list of useful technical terms (given under 'Whole-class skills work' for Hour 1) on the board or flip chart. (You may wish to use only some of the terms and/or to add some of your own choosing.)

Introduction

To set a context for this unit, ask the children what they think the TV of the future might look like and might be capable of providing. Write their ideas on the board or flip chart. Then display and read through photocopiable page 154 which provides a brainstorm of ideas about future TV. Discuss similarities and differences between it and the children's brainstorm. Does it stimulate any further ideas? Add any additional ones to the children's list.

Explain to the children that they are going to use some of these ideas to design their own future TV and to explain how it works.

Whole-class skills work

Display this list of technical terms and ask the children to determine what area they are particularly related to (such as electronics, televisions and computers). Use them to focus discussion on the way language develops to reflect the needs of the people who use it.

When and why do the children think these terms came into our language?

potentiometer	headset
transistor	stereo
printed circuit	three-dimensional (3-D)
liquid crystal display (LCD)	virtual reality
light illuminated diode (LED)	digital
electronic scanning	transmission
cathode-ray tube	satellite
high definition	Internet
loudspeaker	video

Do the children know what all these terms mean? Ask them to look up two or three in a dictionary. Are they in the dictionary? If not, discuss why.

Now ask the children to brainstorm new terms for devices not yet invented. A good way to do this is to use parts of existing words, for example:

intervision	TV with Internet access
satellite headset	a headset that connects you directly to a satellite
brainscanner	a device which turns your thoughts into TV images
telebrain	a device which beams TV pictures directly into your brain

Differentiated group activities

1–4*: Children should work in pairs within groups to discuss their ideas for TV in the future. They should then draw a diagram of it, labelling all the parts and inventing new technical terms as necessary.

Conclusion

Ask each pair to join up with another pair. The pairs should then take it in turns to present and to ask questions about each other's future TV – about how things work, about things they don't understand and so on. Children should make notes during the discussion so that they can refer to them when producing the written explanations in the following hour.

Introduction

Select two or three pairs to present their work to the rest of the class. Focus evaluative discussion on those aspects of the work that are particularly successful in terms of the task set.

Whole-class skills work

Discuss how writing can be adapted for different audiences and purposes by changing vocabulary and sentence structures. Ask the children what different kinds of explanation would satisfy a) a TV technician and b) a TV owner, for example:

Content – the owner is not really interested in what happens inside. He or she just wants to know how to operate it.

Vocabulary – the technical term for a volume control is 'potentiometer', but this would confuse the TV owner for whom the term 'volume control' is quite sufficient.

Sentence construction – sentences should be simpler for the TV owner as he or she wants to find and understand information quickly. The technician will be more interested in complex explanations.

Differentiated group activities

1–4*: Children should work in their same pairs within their groups and produce *two* written explanations to go with their diagram. One should be a detailed explanation for a technical audience, one should be a simple explanation for the owner.

Conclusion

Select some pairs to present their diagrams and two different explanations to the whole class. The class should evaluate the appropriateness of the explanations for their intended audiences.

FUTURE TV BRAINSTORM

Ideas for the television of the future:

Digital with much higher definition

All satellite transmission — thousands, perhaps millions
of channels

Table-mounted 3D holograms replace TV sets

Virtual reality — wear a special headset and move around
inside the TV world

Join in the action of your favourite films

Plug-in devices to release scents enhancing the sensory
experience

Wall-sized screens enabling virtual views to replace windows

Used to provide education — no need to go to school

Used as a 3D telephone

In the far future, beamed straight into the brain

Better than real life!

Possible disadvantages could be:

Thousands, perhaps millions of channels — of rubbish

You will probably have to pay for all the extra services —
therefore very expensive

People might get cut off from each other

It might be used as an escape from real life!

NOTE-MAKING

OBJECTIVES

UNIT	SPELLING/VOCABULARY	GRAMMAR/PUNCTUATION	COMPREHENSION/ COMPOSITION
REFERENCE AND RESEARCH SKILLS: Note-making: quotation and adaptation.	Understand meaning of words *quote, adapt, acknowledge, bibliography.*	Adapt text and quote from it.	Understand what is meant by 'in your own words'.

ORGANIZATION (1 HOUR)

INTRODUCTION	WHOLE-CLASS SKILLS WORK	DIFFERENTIATED GROUP ACTIVITIES	CONCLUSION
Discuss issues around 'copying'.	Discuss functions of adaptation and quotation.	1: Practise adapting and quoting from three different sources. 2. & 3*: As above, but using two different sources with teacher support. 4*: Adaptation of a simple text into own words.	Share results of activities and evaluate.

HOUR 1

RESOURCES

Photocopiable page 157 (Research Sheet), a variety of information books on a topic that the class is currently studying (some of these should contain bibliographies and lists of acknowledgements), board or flip chart, OHP and acetate (optional) writing materials.

PREPARATION

Prepare an OHT or enlarged photocopy of an obscure piece of information text taken from CD-ROM or an information book. This should be relevant to a topic that the children are studying, but clearly above their reading level. Make another OHT or enlarged copy of a more easily comprehensible text extract. Make sure that some of the information books that you have collected together contain bibliographies and acknowledgements. Write on the board or flip chart the words: *'Imitation is the sincerest form of flattery'.* Make enough copies of photocopiable page (Research Sheet) for each child in Groups 1–3.

Introduction

Tell the class that this lesson is all about using other people's writing and the rights and wrongs of copying.

Begin by discussing the meaning of the proverb quoted above. Once it has been established that it is about the virtue (or otherwise) of copying, ask the children how they feel if other children copy their work. Would they take it as a compliment if someone copied them or would they feel offended that another person was 'stealing' their words and ideas? Point out that the words of the proverb are not your own words, so you have put them in quotation marks. If you copy someone else's work, it is unfair to pass it off as your own. You can acknowledge the real author by using quotation marks. If you know the name of the author, you should write this too. Ask the class if they know any famous quotations and invite them to come up and scribe them on the board or chart in the format of the following example:

'To be or not to be, that is the question.' William Shakespeare.

Whole-class skills work

Using the OHT or enlarged photocopy that you prepared beforehand, show the children the piece of information text that is above the level of their understanding. If they had been asked to find out about the subject for homework and handed in the information in this form, what would it show they had learned? Explain the necessity to *understand* what you write – or there's not much point in writing it (except for handwriting practice!). Tell the class that it helps you to understand a piece of text if you try to put it in your own words. Use the board or flip chart to model doing this with a part of the selected example.

Now show the children the other, more accessible piece of text that you have selected, and ask *them* to say sentence by sentence what it means. Scribe the most appropriate suggestions so that all the class can see them. Explain that by putting the piece into their own words they have *adapted* the text to show their understanding of it. In a similar way, classic stories (for example *The Secret Garden* and *Oliver Twist*) and complicated books like the Bible are often adapted into simpler versions for children to understand. Can the children think of examples of adaptations from the library corner or their own reading? Stories are also *adapted* for television and film so that they can be told visually and vividly within a shorter space of time than it might take to read them.

When using ideas from books it is still good manners and professional behaviour to name the sources that you have used even if you have adapted the original words instead of copying them. A *bibliography* at the end of a piece of writing is designed to do this. Show the class some examples of bibliographies. Explain that when some of the writing and pictures in a book have been copied, there is usually a list of *acknowledgements* before the start of the book. Ask the children to point out examples in the information books that you have selected.

Differentiated group activities

1: Give out copies of photocopiable page 157. Assign the group a subject to research which is relevant to a topic that the class is currently studying. Each child should locate and adapt information from three different sources. They should include a quotation and a bibliography where shown on the photocopiable sheet.

2 & 3*: As above, but using two different sources.

4*: Work with the teacher to put a simple topic-related passage into their own words and name the source.

Conclusion

Ask representatives from each group to share their adaptations and quotations with the class and name their sources. Have they used quotation marks appropriately?

 # RESEARCH SHEET

NAME:

DATE:

SUBJECT OF RESEARCH:

WHAT I LEARNED (in my own words):

QUOTATION:

From (title of book):
By (author):

BIBLIOGRAPHY:

Title of book:
Author:

Title of book:
Author:

Title of book:
Author:

INVESTIGATING HOMOPHONES

OBJECTIVES

UNIT	SPELLING/VOCABULARY	GRAMMAR/PUNCTUATION	COMPREHENSION/ COMPOSITION
WORD PLAY Investigating homophones through poetry.	Distinguish between homophones.	Consolidate the conventions of 'standard English'.	To write extensions to poems using known structures.

ORGANIZATION (1 HOUR)

	INTRODUCTION	WHOLE-CLASS SKILLS WORK	DIFFERENTIATED GROUP ACTIVITIES	CONCLUSION
HOUR 1	Revise the term 'homophone', then read the poem 'Have you ever seen?' Anonymous.	Investigate homophones in the poem. Read the poem 'Potato clock' by Roger McGough. Discuss poems.	1: Extend verses of 'Have you ever seen?' 2 & 3*: Identify homophones in 'Potato clock'. Prepare poem to read to class. 4: Choose lines from 'Have you ever seen?' and illustrate them.	Groups share their work followed by class discussion.

RESOURCES

Photocopiable page 160 (Homophone Poems), board or flip chart, OHP and acetate (optional), writing materials.

PREPARATION

Make enough copies of photocopiable page 160 for one between two children. If possible, prepare the sheet also as an OHT or enlarge to at least A3 size.

Introduction

Ask the children if they can think of any words that:
■ sound the same and have the same spelling but have different meanings – for example, 'bank' (where money is kept *and* the side of a river); 'pupil' (part of the eye *and* student); 'fly' (to move through the air *and* a type of insect) and so on
■ sound the same and have different spellings and meanings – for example, 'know' and 'no'; 'weak' and 'week'; 'here' and 'hear' and so on.

Write their suggestions on the board or flip chart under the headings 'Same sound, same spelling, different meanings' and 'Same sound, different spelling, different meanings'. Can they think of trios of homophones (for example: write/right/rite; there/their/they're; rain/rein/reign)?

Remind the children that these words are called 'homophones', from the Greek meaning 'same sound'. Tell them you are going to read a poem which is based on word play with homophones. Then read the poem 'Have you ever seen?'

Whole-class skills work

Distribute copies of the poem and/or display it on OHP. Re-read the poem two lines at a time. (You may wish to explore with the children the rhyming couplet and questions format of the poem.) Ask the children to spot the homophones as they occur and discuss them. Although the humour in the poem is based on homophones that are spelled the same but have different meanings, there are also words which sound the same as other words with different spellings and meanings. Which type of homophone are they?

Same spelling, different meaning

sheet	hose	trunk	plot
bed	eye	rake	sound
head	fly	hands	bark
foot	ribs	left	

Different spelling, different meaning

you (ewe)	or (oar)
seen (scene)	all (awl)
hair (hare)	bite (byte)
pair (pear)	right (write, rite)
eye (I)	

Discuss: What is the 'wing' of a building? What is a 'parasol'? Which part of it are the 'ribs'? What is a 'plot'? How can it be 'dark and deep'? Are there any other unfamiliar words? Invite the children to suggest meanings.

Read the poem through again and discuss with the children how the poem uses homophones to make the poem amusing.

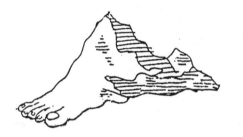 

Now display and read 'Potato clock' by Roger McGough with the children and see if they can 'get the joke' first time round – 'A potato clock' sounds like 'Up at eight o'clock'. Make sure the children understand that although the two phrases sound the same, and this is the basis for the humour in the poem, the phrases are not homophones!

Differentiated group activities

1: Work in pairs to think up more homophones and add more rhyming couplets to 'Have you ever seen?'

2 & 3*: Work in pairs to find words in 'Potato clock' that sound like other words – either with the same spelling and different meaning (*lot, can, state*) or with different spelling and different meaning (*where, site, night, no, one, break, tea, hour, eight*). Then prepare the poem for reading aloud to the class.

4. Work in pairs. Choose some lines from the poem 'Have you ever seen?' and illustrate them, incorporating the written line as a caption.

Conclusion

Select members of each group to share the outcomes of their group work and discuss. End the session by asking some children from Groups 2 and 3 to recite 'Potato clock'.

HOMOPHONE POEMS

Have your ever seen?

Have you ever seen a sheet on a river bed?
Or a single hair from a hammer's head?
Has the foot of a mountain any toes?
And is there a pair of garden hose?
Does the needle ever wink its eye?
Why doesn't the wing of a building fly?

Can you tickle the ribs of a parasol?
Or open the trunk of a tree at all?
Are the teeth of a rake ever going to bite?
Have the hands of a clock any left or right?
Can the garden plot be deep and dark?
And what is the sound of the birch's bark?

Anonymous

Potato clock

A potato clock, a potato clock
    Has anybody got a potato clock?
A potato clock, a potato clock
    Oh where can I find a potato clock?

I went down to London the other day
Found myself a job with a lot of pay
Carrying bricks on a building site
From early in the morning till late at night

No one here works as hard as me
I never even break for a cup of tea
My only weakness, my only crime
Is that I never get to work on time

A potato clock, a potato clock
    Has anybody got a potato clock?
A potato clock, a potato clock
    Oh where can I find a potato clock?

I arrived this morning half an hour late
The foreman came up in a terrible state
'You've got a good job, but you'll lose it, cock,
If you don't get up at eight o'clock.'

Up at eight o'clock, up at eight o'clock
    Has anybody got up at eight o'clock?
Up at eight o'clock, up at eight o'clock
    Oh where can I find up at eight o'clock?

Roger McGough

Term 3

THE CAT

OBJECTIVES

UNIT	SPELLING/VOCABULARY	GRAMMAR/PUNCTUATION	COMPREHENSION/ COMPOSITION
READING POETRY Older literature: 'The Cat' by W Adolphe Roberts.	Find meanings of unknown words. Identify rhyming words with different spellings.	Explore the grammar of poetry. Use punctuation to help convey meaning when reading aloud.	Explore the challenge and appeal of older literature. Investigate the sonnet structure. Compare prose and poetry texts. Explore figurative language.

ORGANIZATION (2 HOURS)

	INTRODUCTION	WHOLE-CLASS SKILLS WORK	DIFFERENTIATED GROUP ACTIVITIES	CONCLUSION
HOUR 1	Read poem and re-read it highlighting the importance of punctuation to aid reading and convey meaning.	Analyse structure of poem.	1*: Guided reading and discussion. 2 & 3: Write a prose version of poem. 4*: Guided reading and discussion.	Selected pupils from Groups 2 & 3 share their prose writing.
HOUR 2	Re-read poem and prose text. Compare the two.	Model ways of turning prose into poetry.	1: Turn the prose text 'The Cat' into a free-verse poem. 2 & 3*: Guided reading and discussion (see above). 4: As for Group 1, adapted for ability.	Selected pupils from Groups 1 & 4 share their poems. Revise features of sonnet form.

RESOURCES

Photocopiable page 165 ('The Cat'), board or flip chart, OHP and acetate (optional), dictionaries, writing materials.

PREPARATION

Make enough copies of photocopiable page 165 for one between two children. If possible, prepare it also as an OHT or enlarged version.

Introduction
Distribute copies of the poem and, if possible, display it also on an OHP or as an enlarged photocopy. Read the sonnet through once to familiarize the children with it. Then re-read it, asking the children to follow the words and to note how you read to bring out the sense, pausing at punctuation marks – *not* necessarily at the end of lines if there are no punctuation marks.

   Examine some of the difficult vocabulary (for example *flanks*, *deigns*, *insolence*, *voluptuous*) and find out the meaning of words with which the children are unfamiliar, using a variety of strategies.

Whole-class skills work
Write the last line of the poem on the board or flip chart and show the children how to scan it:
■ Read the line slowly, exaggerating the stressed syllables.
■ Place diagonal lines where you hear the stresses.

    /   /   /   /   /
She wore when she was worshipped on the Nile.

Ask the children to note that there are five stresses. Tell them that this kind of line is called pentameter (from Greek for five). Do they know any other words with this prefix (for example *pentathalon, pentagon*)?

Next, remind the children how to mark a rhyme scheme using letters of the alphabet:

Pleasures that I most enviously sense,	*a*
Pass in long ripples down her flanks and stir	*b*
The plume that is her tail. She deigns to purr	*b*
And takes caresses. But her paws would tense	*a*

Ask the children to mark the stresses and rhymes for the whole poem.

Finally, ask them to count the lines (14). Explain that this kind of 14-line poem is called a 'sonnet' and that it has been one of the most popular of short forms for the last 500 years.

'The Cat' is an example of an Italian sonnet in which the 14 lines are divided into eight lines and six lines.

Differentiated group activities

1*: Guided reading and discussion of the sonnet and prose text on the photocopiable sheet. Compare the two. The following questions can be used as a starting point:
■ What are the 'pleasures' a cat might feel?
■ Discuss the metaphor: 'The plume that is her tail'. What is being compared to what? How do you see it in your mind? Is it effective?
■ Discuss the metaphor: '...her paws would tense to flashing weapons...' What is being compared to what? How does it make us see the cat?
■ Discuss the last line of the first verse. Explore the meanings of the difficult words. Explore the idea expressed.
■ Discuss the image in line 12. What is being compared to what? Is it a simile or a metaphor? How does it make us see the cat?
■ How does information in the prose text help us to understand the last two lines of the poem?
■ What are the main differences between the poem and the prose text? Which gives us more information? Which is more accurate? Which is more interesting? Which did you like best?
2 & 3: Rewrite the sonnet as a prose text that conveys the same meaning and is easy enough for a young child to read.
4*: Guided reading and discussion of the sonnet and prose text. Compare the two, using the most appropriate of the above questions as a starting point.

Conclusion

Select children from Groups 2 and 3 to read examples of their prose versions of the sonnet. Ask the rest of the class to comment on each one, saying whether or not they think a young child would be able to read it. Encourage them to give their reasons.

Introduction

Re-read the sonnet and prose text. Discuss together the differences between prose and poetry (for example, poetry is set out in lines, often has rhythm and rhyme and makes greater use of figurative language such as metaphor and simile to convey images and emotions. Prose is written in sentences and, in the case of non-fiction, conveys factual information).

Whole-class skills work

Explore how the prose text could be made into a poem. This can be done by:

■ setting it out in short lines
■ omitting connectives and other words to achieve a more concentrated effect
■ adding figurative language such as metaphor and simile.
Model for the children how this might be achieved as follows:

The cat
A small carnivorous animal
Popular as a pet
But like vicious beast to mice and rats...

Differentiated group activities
1: Turn the prose text 'The Cat' into a free-verse poem.
2 & 3*: Guided reading and discussion (see above).
4: Turn the prose text 'The Cat' into a free-verse poem (by using the first two techniques referred to in the skills session).

Conclusion
Select children from Groups 1 and 4 to read their poems written from the prose text. Discuss how these might be collected into a class anthology, with children from Groups 2 and 3 being given the opportunity to produce their poems outside the hour.

Conclude by revising the features of the sonnet form.

FURTHER IDEA

Find similar pairs of poems and prose texts and compare them. This can be easily done by looking in the contents pages of poetry books, and then finding a prose text on the same subject in an encyclopaedia.

THE CAT

THE CAT
Pleasures that I most enviously sense,
   Pass in long ripples down her flanks and stir
   The plume that is her tail. She deigns to purr
And takes caresses. But her paws would tense
To flashing weapons at the least offence.
   Humbly I bend to stroke her silken fur,
   I am content to be a slave to her.
I am enchanted by her insolence.

Not one of all the women I have known
   Has been so beautiful, or proud, or wise
   As this Angora with her amber eyes.
She makes her chosen cushion seem a throne,
   And wears the same voluptuous, slow smile
   She wore when she was worshipped on the Nile.

W Adolphe Roberts

THE CAT
The domestic cat is a small carnivorous animal which is popular as a household pet. It is often kept for its ability to kill mice and rats. The domestic cat has sharp, retractable claws, keen hearing and smell, excellent night vision, and a highly supple body. Domestic cats have been kept as pets for more than 3000 years as pictures from ancient Egypt show. Today there are more than 100 breeds of domestic cat, but they still retain some of their ancient mystery. Cats are often linked to good or bad luck and in the past have been associated with witchcraft. Their unusual eyes, designed to let in as much light as possible in dim conditions, are one possible reason for this. Perhaps that is why they fascinated the ancient Egyptians.

WRITING BLANK VERSE

OBJECTIVES

UNIT	SPELLING/VOCABULARY	GRAMMAR/PUNCTUATION	COMPREHENSION/ COMPOSITION
WRITING POETRY Blank verse: Extract from 'The Prelude' by William Wordsworth.	Develop vocabulary from reading.	Use 1st person in letter writing.	Read an extract from a narrative poem by a well-known 'romantic' poet. Use poem as model for writing own poem in blank verse. Perform poem. Revise simile and metaphor.

ORGANIZATION (2 HOURS)

	INTRODUCTION	WHOLE-CLASS SKILLS WORK	DIFFERENTIATED GROUP ACTIVITIES	CONCLUSION
HOUR 1	Read poem twice – for understanding of theme and to identify punctuation.	Analyse verse form.	1 & 4*: Write blank verse poem based on own experience. 2 & 3: Write letter to friend as Wordsworth.	Selected pupils from Groups 1 & 4 read poems. Class discusses and evaluates.
HOUR 2	Shared reading of the poem aloud. Rehearse and perform.	Revise simile and metaphor.	1: Write an essay about the poem using framework. 2 & 3*: Write blank verse poem based on own experience. 4: Write letter to friend as Wordsworth.	Selected pupils from Groups 2–4 read poems and letters. Discuss personal responses to poem. Review blank verse form.

RESOURCES

Photocopiable page 168 (Extract from 'The Prelude'), board or flip chart, OHP and acetate (optional), writing materials.

PREPARATION

Make enough copies of photocopiable page 168 for one between two children. If possible, prepare it also as an OHT or enlarged version.

Introduction

Explain to the class that they are going to read an extract of a poem by William Wordsworth. Wordsworth was one of the most famous of the English 'romantic' poets (1770–1850), whose works were characterized by emphasizing the emotions and the imagination over reason and intellect. 'The Prelude' is a long autobiographical, narrative poem which shows the growth of a poet's mind, tracing his own life from childhood. In this extract (slightly simplified), he describes how he took a boat out on a lake and was frightened by the looming shape of a huge mountain.

Read the poem to the class twice – first to familiarize the children with its theme, and then again with them following the text and observing how you use the punctuation to indicate how to read the poem aloud and make sense of it. After the first reading, ask questions to check understanding, and to explain words and events in the poem as necessary. After the second reading, identify the punctuation and discuss its function. Emphasize the fact that although the poem is written in lines, the end of a line does not necessarily mean a pause in the reading.

Whole-class skills work

Ask the children to analyse the verse form by clapping and counting stresses in each line and marking these with a diagonal stroke as below.

```
       /      /      /      /      /
One summer evening by the lake I found
   /     /       /     /        /
A little boat tied to a willow tree
```

They will find that there are five stresses per line (lines of this kind are called 'pentameters'). Now ask them to look for rhyme. This is a trick question because there is no rhyme! Tell them that this kind of poetry, written with rhythm and metre but without rhyme, is called 'blank verse'. Blank verse is one of the commonest forms for serious poetry, often used, for example, in Shakespeare's plays.

Differentiated group activities

1*: Children work individually or in pairs to write about one of their own experiences in five-stress rhythm blank verse.
2 & 3: Ask the children to imagine they are Wordsworth and to write a first-person account of the experience on the lake as a letter to a friend.
4*: Children work in pairs to write about one of their own experiences in blank verse.

Conclusion

Select children from Groups 1 and 4 to read out their blank verse poems. The other children listen to see if they can hear the five-stress rhythm and evaluate how effectively the blank-verse form has been used to tell a story.

Introduction

Display the extract from 'The Prelude' and ask the children to read it through aloud as a class, taking note of punctuation as discussed in the previous hour. After the first read, give them a 'performance critique' and then ask them to recite it again.

Whole-class skills work

Revise the terms 'simile' and 'metaphor' (see previous unit, 'The Cat'). Ask the children to find one example of a simile and one example of a metaphor in the poem and to:
■ say what is being compared to what;
■ explain how this adds to the effectiveness of the description.

Differentiated group activities

1: Children work individually or in pairs to write an essay about the poem. The following plan can be used or adapted as required:

Para 1:   Briefly introduce William Wordsworth.
Para 2:   Explain in your own words what happens in the poem.
Para 3:   Explain the blank verse form.
Para 4:   Write about the imagery (similes and metaphors) in the poem.
Para 5:   End by giving your response to the poem: What did you like? Which parts contained the most vivid description?

2 & 3*: Children work individually or in pairs to write about one of their own experiences in blank verse.
4: Ask the children to imagine they are Wordsworth and to write a 1st-person account of the experience on the lake as a letter to a friend.

Conclusion

Select children from Groups 2–4 to read out examples of their blank verse or their 1st-person letters. Ask the rest of the children to respond, saying whether they liked it or not and giving their reasons. Remind the children of the features of blank verse.

EXTRACT FROM 'THE PRELUDE'

One summer evening by the lake I found
A little boat tied to a willow tree
Within a rocky cave, its usual home.
I unfastened her chain, and stepping in
Pushed from the shore. My boat moved on,
Leaving behind her still, on either side,
Small circles glittering idly in the moon,
Until they melted all into one track
Of sparkling light. But now, I fixed my view
Upon the summit of a craggy ridge,
The horizon's furthest boundary; far above
Was nothing but the stars and the grey sky.
She was a lively vessel. Lustily
I dipped my oars into the silent lake,
And, as I rose upon the stroke, my boat
Went heaving through the water like a swan.
Till suddenly a huge peak, black and huge,
Upreared its head. I struck and struck again,
And growing still in size the mighty shape
Towered up between me and the stars, and still
Strode after me. With trembling oars I turned,
And through the silent water stole my way
Back to the safety of the willow tree.

William Wordsworth

COUCH POTATO KIDS

OBJECTIVES

UNIT	SPELLING/VOCABULARY	GRAMMAR/PUNCTUATION	COMPREHENSION/ COMPOSITION
READING NON-FICTION Persuasive writing: 'Are Today's Kids Turning Into Couch Potatoes?'	Develop vocabulary through reading.	Investigate language conventions and grammatical features of persuasive text.	Read a persuasive article and understand the ways in which it seeks to persuade. Distinguish between fact and opinion.

ORGANIZATION (2 HOURS)

	INTRODUCTION	WHOLE-CLASS SKILLS WORK	DIFFERENTIATED GROUP ACTIVITIES	CONCLUSION
HOUR 1	Read the article. Discuss type of text and any difficult vocabulary.	Revise and extend knowledge of discursive connectives.	1*: Guided reading and discussion. 2 & 3: Reading Comprehension, parts A, B & D. 4*: Guided reading and discussion.	Discuss the 'Ten Rules for Potential Couch Potatoes'.
HOUR 2	Re-read the text and analyse how the writer seeks to persuade us.	Investigate the features of persuasive texts.	1: Reading Comprehension, all parts. 2 & 3*: Guided reading and discussion. 4: Reading Comprehension, parts A, C & D.	Discuss answers to the questions on the Reading Comprehension sheet.

RESOURCES

Photocopiable pages 171 ('Are Today's Kids Turning into Couch Potatoes?') and 172 (Reading Comprehension), board or flip chart, OHP and acetate (optional), writing materials, including different coloured highlighter pens.

PREPARATION

Make enough copies of both photocopiable sheets for one between two children. If possible, prepare photocopiable page 171 ('Are Today's Kids Turning into Couch Potatoes?') as an OHT, or enlarge it to at least A3 size.

Introduction

Read 'Are Today's Kids Turning into Couch Potatoes?' on page 171. Discuss what kind of text it is and what genre (an article, persuasion genre). Ask the children to suggest words which they are not sure of and encourage them to suggest definitions or look them up in a dictionary.

Whole-class skills work

Revise and extend knowledge of discursive connectives.

A connective is a word or phrase which connects statements; discursive connectives are those which are particularly useful in expressing an argument. Ask the children to study the following list and investigate which connectives are used in the text.

but	however	this	because	as a result
on the other hand	yet	that	therefore	for
instead	nevertheless	these	so	then

next	in view of	against that it could be said
finally	eventually	to look at it in another way
thus	to begin with	

Differentiated group activities

1*: Guided reading and discussion of text. Use the questions on the Reading Comprehension sheet as a basis for discussion.

2 & 3: Complete Reading Comprehension sheet, parts A, B and D.

4*: Guided reading and discussion of text. Ask the children to re-read sections of the text and give help as necessary. Use the questions on the Reading Comprehension sheet as a basis for discussion, concentrating on part A to ensure basic understanding.

Conclusion

Discuss the 'Ten Rules for Potential Couch Potatoes'.

Introduction

Re-read the text and look more closely at how it persuades the reader. Ask the children what type of argument the writer is using in each paragraph, that is, how the writer is trying to persuade us.

Para 1:   Uses evidence from a survey.
Para 2:   Describes how TV affects one child.
Para 3:   Expresses an opinion.
Para 4:   Expresses another opinion.
Para 5:   Expresses another opinion.
Para 6:   Offers further evidence.

Discuss with the children that the opinions are written as though they are facts, for example is it true that 'the couch potato generation has trouble making friends?'

Whole-class skills work

Investigate the features of persuasive writing. Discuss this definition with the children.
Persuasive writing uses:
- simple present tense
- many discursive connectives
- different types of argument, for example from statistics, individual examples, opinions, facts, facts presented as opinion and so on.

Ask the children to find examples of the above in the text.

Differentiated group activities

1: Complete Reading Comprehension sheet, all parts.

2 & 3*: Guided reading and discussion (see above).

4: Complete Reading Comprehension sheet, parts A, C and D.

Conclusion

Discuss answers to the questions on the Reading Comprehension sheet.

FURTHER IDEA

Conduct a similar survey in the class or school. Here are some survey questions:
- How many hours of television do you watch each evening?
- Do you ever watch a programme after 9 o'clock?
- What are your favourite programmes?
- How long do you spend watching educational programmes and documentaries?
- Do you have a television in your bedroom?
- Do you do any regular exercise (not counting PE in school)?
- Do you have a computer? If so, what do you use if for and how many hours do you spend on it?
- Do you have the Internet at home? Are you allowed to use it?

Compile the answers and compare them with the results given in the article. Are the results different? What do they tell you?

ARE TODAY'S KIDS TURNING INTO COUCH POTATOES?

Children who watch TV for four hours a day or more are less fit and do less well in school than those who watch TV for less than two hours, a recent survey reveals. The survey of 2,000 children aged 8–10 found that 25% watched more than four hours a day.

Darren (his real name has not been used because it would be unfair to single him out) is a typical example. His teachers are worried about his progress. His last school report showed that he was below average in English, mathematics, and almost every other subject except art, for which he seems to have a special talent. His teachers are worried about his lack of concentration, particularly in the afternoon, when he sometimes fall asleep. He dislikes PE and any other vigorous activities, and his physical stamina is well below average. He has no special friends and finds it hard to get on with other pupils. If he doesn't get his own way, he quarrels.

The problem with watching TV is that it is passive. The viewer just sits there for hours on end without making any physical effort. It doesn't need much mental effort, either. All you have to do is watch the images flickering in front of your eyes and if you get bored, press a button on the remote control. Compare this with reading a book. You have to read the words and think about what they say as the story develops. As you are reading you will be increasing your vocabulary, improving your spelling, and developing your thinking skills.

On the other hand, it could be argued that there are educational programmes on TV – but the Darrens of this world don't watch them. Instead, they zap the remote control and tune into a quiz show, a crime programme, or a horror film. Worst of all, if they watch programmes after 9 o'clock, they will see things that are totally unsuitable for their age. As a result of this they can become frightened, withdrawn or violent.

Another problem with TV is that it is a solitary pleasure. This is made worse by the fact that 34% of children in the survey had a television in their bedroom, so they are not even watching it with the rest of their family! It is no wonder, then, that the 'couch potato' generation has trouble making friends and getting on with people!

And it is getting worse! There is another screen that children spend a lot of time in front of – the computer screen. This means more exposure to violence (shoot-em-up games, fighting games, alien-blasting games and so on) and could even allow them to link up to the Internet which is totally uncensored and could be very dangerous and disturbing for children of this age.

So perhaps it is time for parents and teachers to start laying down a few rules. My suggestions are as follows:

TEN RULES FOR POTENTIAL COUCH POTATOES

- No televisions in bedrooms.
- Only two hours viewing per night.
- Spend more time reading.
- No TV snacks.
- Homework must be done first.
- No viewing after 9 o'clock.
- Take part in a healthy sport.
- Join a club such as the Scouts or Guides.
- The computer to be used for serious work only – no games.
- Only parent-approved access to the Internet allowed.

READING COMPREHENSION

PART A
■ Read paragraph 1. What two problems are caused by watching too much television?

■ Read paragraph 2. Make a list of the things that Darren's teachers are worried about. What is his one strong point?

■ Read paragraph 3. Why does the writer think that reading a book is better than watching television?

■ Read paragraph 4. What kind of programmes do children like Darren prefer to watch?

■ Read paragraph 5. Why do children who watch television find it difficult to make friends?

■ Read paragraph 6. What is the 'other screen' that children spend a lot of time watching?

PART B
■ Make a list of the arguments against children watching too much television.

■ Think about each argument in turn, and say whether you agree with it.

■ Do you think children of this age should be allowed to have a television in their bedrooms?

■ Which parts of the article are fact, and which are opinion? Use two different coloured highlighters to show which is which.

PART C
■ Do you agree with the list of 'Ten Rules for Potential Couch Potatoes'? Say which ones you agree with and which you disagree with.

PART D
■ Write a paragraph in which you describe your own TV-watching habits.

FRIENDLY PERSUASION

OBJECTIVES

UNIT	SPELLING/VOCABULARY	GRAMMAR/PUNCTUATION	COMPREHENSION/ COMPOSITION
WRITING NON-FICTION Friendly persuasion.	Investigate the vocabulary of argument, debate and persuasion.	Examine types of argument. Revise discursive connectives.	Write a persuasive article.

ORGANIZATION (2 HOURS)

	INTRODUCTION	WHOLE-CLASS SKILLS WORK	DIFFERENTIATED GROUP ACTIVITIES	CONCLUSION
HOUR 1	Read the article on TV from the previous unit. If this has been the focus of the immediately preceding hours, then go straight on to the discussion.	Revise knowledge of discursive connectives. Plan the structure of the article.	1–4*: Write the first part of the article (introduction and main point).	Pupils read out their introduction and main arguments.Others should listen carefully and try to think of counter-arguments.
HOUR 2	More introductions and main arguments are discussed while others think of counter-arguments.	Investigate types of argument.	1–4*: Finish off the articles.	Read and discuss a selection of completed articles. Finally, ask if the arguments put forward have caused anyone to change his/her mind.

RESOURCES

Photocopiable pages 171 ('Are Today's Kids Turning Into Couch Potatoes?' from previous unit) and 176 (Article Writing Template), board or flip chart, OHP and acetate (optional), writing materials.

PREPARATION

Make enough copies of photocopiable page 176 (Article Writing Template) for one between two children in Groups 1–3 and one per child in Group 4. If possible, prepare photocopiable pages 171 ('Are Today's Kids Turning Into Couch Potatoes?') and 176 (Article Writing Template) as OHTs, or enlarge them to at least A3 size.

Introduction

Read the article on TV from the previous unit 'Couch Potato Kids' (photocopiable page 171). If this has been the focus of the immediately preceding hours, then go straight on to the class discussion.

Discuss further the key issue raised in the article: is television a bad influence on children? Try to bring out both sides of the argument and jot down key points on the board or a flip chart under the headings PRO (for) and CON (against).

Whole-class skills work

Briefly revise the list of discursive connectives (which are printed in a box at the top of the Article Writing Template). Encourage the children to refer to this list when they are thinking of a point and it will help them to express the points and link it to, or contrast it with other points.

Secondly, explain the form the article will take, referring to the template which will provide support during writing.

1. This is an article so it needs to begin with an attention-grabbing first paragraph. The 'Are Today's Kids Turning Into Couch Potatoes?' article did this twice over, first with a paragraph of statistics, secondly with an anecdote about a particular child.
2. Express your main point. Support it with reasons and examples.
3. Express another important point, again supported with reasons and examples.
4. Write a conclusion to round off the article. 'Are Today's Kids Turning Into Couch Potatoes?' concluded with a list of rules.

If the children have done the survey suggested in the 'Further idea' section of the previous unit, they can use the statistics from the survey in the first paragraph. If not, they can begin with an anecdote describing either a child who has benefitted from watching television, or a child who has suffered because of it.

Differentiated group activities
All children should try to write the introduction and express their main argument in this session.
1: Children in this group should interpret the template freely, though they should remember to make use of the list of connectives.
2 & 3*: Follow the structure of the template, but expand each section with additional points.
4: Children in this group should write on the template.

Conclusion
Select some children to read out their introductions and main arguments. Others should listen carefully and try to think of counter-arguments.

Introduction
Select some other children to read out their introductions and main arguments as in the concluding session of the previous hour. Discuss these and ask the rest of the class to think of counter-arguments.

Whole-class skills work
Now that the children have exchanged ideas and expressed their opinions, it is a good time to look more closely at types of argument.

First of all, define the term: an argument, in popular speech, is two people falling out and shouting at each other. Its real meaning is: *a reason given for or against a point.*

So what kind of reasons can we give?
- FACTS. These are usually in the form of statistics. But *beware*: statistics can be made to prove almost anything! For example, a different survey could prove that TV has an educational benefit. It depends what questions you ask. If you ask: have you ever learned anything from television, most people would say they had.
- OPINION. An opinion is usually considered to be too subjective on its own, without supporting evidence. But *beware* of opinions stated as though they are facts, for example 'There are over 50 million televisions in the UK, and they are turning our children into morons!' Is this a fact or an opinion? (The first part is a fact, the second part is an opinion, but because it is in the same sentence it is made to sound like a fact!)
- REASON. An opinion supported by a reason is the main kind of argument that we use, for example 'Watching lots of violence on TV is a bad thing because it makes it seem like the normal way to behave.'
- ABUSE. For example, 'Television is bad for kids and anyone who can't see that must have brains the size of a peanut!' This shows that the writer or speaker has no real arguments left. Abuse should never be used in discussion or writing.

Differentiated group activities
1*: This group (with the benefit of the discussions) should now write a counter-argument to their argument, and then show why the counter-argument should not be

taken seriously. They then move on to their second main point and thence to their conclusion.

2 & 3: This group carry straight on with their second main point and conclusion.

4*: Carry on following the template.

Conclusion

Read and discuss a selection of completed articles. Finally, ask if the arguments put forward have caused anyone to change his/her mind.

FURTHER IDEA

A very good way to help children get used to handling argument is to hold debates. The traditional format for debate has the limitation that only a handful of children are active participants, so the following method is recommended, particularly for this age group.

■ Choose a motion on which opinion is divided (not as easy as it seems).

■ Divide the class into two halves, one for the motion, one against.

■ Each child prepares to express one point supported by an argument (a fact or statistic, or an opinion supported by a reason).

■ One quarter of the class expresses its points for the motion, followed by the corresponding quarter against. This is followed by discussion of the points raised.

■ The process is repeated.

■ A vote is taken.

ARTICLE WRITING TEMPLATE

but	this	as a result	in view of
on the other hand	that	for	eventually
instead	these	then	to begin with
however	because	next	against that it could be said
yet	therefore	finally	to look at it in another way
nevertheless	so	thus	

Article title:

Begin by explaining a fact or some statistics OR begin with a description of a child who has benefitted or suffered from watching television.

Give a good reason why watching TV is good (or bad) for you. Explain fully what you mean.

Give a another good reason why watching TV is good (or bad) for you. Explain fully what you mean.

Write a conclusion (ending). For example, write about how you think children should watch (or not watch) TV.

A THIEF IN THE VILLAGE

OBJECTIVES

UNIT	SPELLING/VOCABULARY	GRAMMAR/PUNCTUATION	COMPREHENSION/ COMPOSITION
READING FICTION Short stories from a different culture: *A Thief in the Village* by James Berry.	Revise use and spelling of possessive pronouns. Make a glossary. Investigate how words can be transformed in a variety of ways for a variety of purposes.	Revise person: 1st, 2nd, 3rd. Investigate differences between standard English and dialect.	Read and investigate stories from other cultures. Identify features of life from text. Compare to own experiences. Identify point of view and how this affects reader response. Understand difference between 'author' and 'narrator'.

ORGANIZATION (5 HOURS)

	INTRODUCTION	WHOLE-CLASS SKILLS WORK	DIFFERENTIATED GROUP ACTIVITIES	CONCLUSION
HOUR 1	Preview the book. Read 'Becky and the Wheels-and-brake Boys', pages 1–7 (approx 10 minutes).	Distinguish between 'author' and 'narrator'. Revise 1st, 2nd and 3rd person. Define point of view.	1*: Guided reading and discussion. 2 & 3: Write about own experience. 4*: Guided reading and discussion.	Selected pupils from Groups 2 & 3 read their work. Pupils from Groups 1 & 4 join discussion with oral accounts of own experience.
HOUR 2	Read 'A Thief in the Village', pages 8–22 (approx 20 minutes).	Investigate difference between standard English and dialect.	1: Tell a story or anecdote about local life using local dialect or slang. Write in note form. 2 & 3*: Guided reading and discussion. 4: Tell a story or anecdote about local life using local dialect or slang.	Selected pupils from Groups 1 & 4 tell anecdotes. Discuss purpose of using dialect and difficulties of writing dialect down.
HOUR 3	Read 'Tukku-Tukku and Samson', pages 23–30 (approx 12 minutes).	Revise and develop understanding of possessive pronouns.	1*: Guided reading and discussion. 2 & 3: Write character study comparing and contrasting two main characters. 4*: Guided reading and writing.	Discuss the two main characters and theme of bullying. Relate to own experience.
HOUR 4	Read 'All Other Days Run Into Sunday', pages 31–42 (approx 15 minutes).	Make a glossary of difficult and dialect words.	1: Write 1st-person description of own Sunday. 2 & 3*: Guided reading and discussion. 4: As for Group 1.	Selected pupils from Groups 1 & 4 read their descriptions. Compare with Sundays in Jamaica.
HOUR 5	Read 'The Banana Tree', pages 89–98 (approx 15 minutes).	Investigate how words can be transformed.	1–4*: Write a book review.	Share personal responses to book.

RESOURCES

A Thief in the Village and Other Stories by James Berry (Puffin, ISBN 0-14-032679-0) – if possible, enough copies for half the class, photocopiable page 182 (Book Review), board or flip chart, writing materials, large world map or atlases.

PREPARATION

Make enough copies of photocopiable page 182 (Book Review) for one between each child in Groups 1–3, and one for each child in Group 4. Write out on the board or flip chart the table of possessive pronouns given under 'Whole-class skills work' for Hour 3.

SYNOPSIS

This prize-winning collection of nine stories by Jamaican author James Berry, portrays everyday Caribbean life from a child's point of view. The place and its atmosphere and people are vividly evoked, making the book an ideal one for exploring another culture through literature. Because the Caribbean culture contributes so positively to contemporary Britain's own, these stories are also very relevant to our understanding of the multi-ethnic society in which we live.

Introduction

Preview the book by exploring the front and back covers and the preliminary pages. Discuss the nature of the book as a whole. What kind of book is it? *(A collection of short stories by one author.)* Discuss the Caribbean setting. Locate the Caribbean islands, particularly Jamaica, on a map. Find out about the author by reading the author details on the first page of the book. Discuss how previewing a book in this way provides the reader with quite a lot of information and sets up expectations about the kind and content of the book they are going to read.

Read the first story, 'Becky and the Wheels-and-brake Boys'.

Whole-class skills work

Distinguish between the author and the narrator. Begin by revising 1st, 2nd and 3rd person. Which person is the story written in? *(First.)* How do we know that the narrator of the story is not the author himself, but a character invented by the author? (For example, *the narrator is a girl*.) Ensure that the children understand the concept of point of view. Ask for their definitions and write these up on the board or flip chart – for example: point of view is the perspective from which the story is told. Discuss how in a 1st-person story the narrator is a character in the story and uses *I, me* and so on to refer to herself or himself. From this point of view, the reader only knows what the narrator does, thinks, sees or feels. How would the story have been different if it had been told in the 3rd person? (For example *the narrator would not have been part of the story and would know what all the characters were thinking and doing. The reader would probably not have been treated to Becky's intensely personal desire.*)

Differentiated group activities

1*: Guided reading and discussion of 'Becky and the Wheels-and-brake Boys'. The following questions can be used as a starting point:
■ Give three reasons why Becky wants a bike.
■ Describe something that you have wanted really badly.
■ What practical joke does her friend play on her and how does she respond? What does this show about her character?
■ What is a girl expected to do in the culture in which Becky lives? What are your opinions on this subject?
■ How does Becky get a bike in the end?
2 & 3: Write about something you really wanted and describe how you felt when you finally got it.
4*: Guided reading and discussion (see above).

Conclusion

Select children from Groups 2 and 3 to read their writing about something they really wanted. Children from Groups 1 and 4 can join in the discussion with oral accounts of their own experiences.

Introduction

Read the second story, 'A Thief in the Village.

Whole-class skills work

Investigate the differences between standard English and dialect. Begin by asking the children what they understand the differences to be and to give examples if possible. Use their input as well as your own to formulate useful definitions, such as:

STANDARD ENGLISH is the language of public and official communication, the language which is used when access to it is needed by a wide variety of English-speaking people. Note that there are several 'standard Englishes', the most widespread being 'British English' and 'American English'. Languages are standardized by definitions in dictionaries and grammar books, usually after hundreds of years of development.

DIALECT is a regional or ethnic variation of spoken language. Dialect can change over time (as can all language!) and is often used in storytelling and writing to add authenticity. There are many dialects of English, some of which differ greatly from standard English in vocabulary, pronunciation and syntax (word order) – for example, the Scottish dialect of English (and, indeed, there are many Scottish dialects of English!).

Ask the children to investigate the Caribbean dialect of English used in the story by making a list of all the non-standard words and sentence structures (the best place to find these is in the dialogue). Make a list of these and opposite each one, write the standard English form.
   Finally, explore the local dialect in the same way.

Differentiated group activities

1: In groups, take it in turns to tell a story or anecdote about local life using the local dialect or slang. Write the story down in note form.
2 & 3*: Guided reading and discussion of 'A Thief in the Village'. The following questions can be used as a starting point:
■ 'A Thief in the Village' is the story which gave its title to the book. Suggest reasons for this. Why, if it is the title story, has it been placed second?
■ The story of the thief is a story within a story. Explain how the two stories are related to each other.
■ Why did people in the village think that Big-Walk was responsible for most of the crime?
■ How did they find out who was really responsible?
■ Discuss Taata Raphael's words to Nenna: 'Folks like when everybody else is like theyself. But the worl' not like that. An' folks not wise to that yet.'
■ Why did Mr Wills ask Maxine to tell the story in her Jamaican voices?
4: In groups, take it in turns to tell a story or anecdote about local life using the local dialect or slang.

Conclusion

Select children from Groups 1 and 4 to tell their stories or anecdotes using local dialect or slang. Follow these with discussion about what the story gains from being told in this way. Discuss the difficulties of doing justice to a local dialect in writing.

Introduction

Read the third story, 'Tukku-Tukku and Samson'.

Whole-class skills work

Revise the correct use and spelling of possessive pronouns. Note that some grammars make a distinction between a possessive determiner and a possessive pronoun. In the table below, words before slash marks would be classified as possessive determiners, and words after as possessive pronouns. However, at this level, the simpler all-embracing use of the term 'possessive pronouns' is best because it emphasizes the important points that the children need to learn:

■ the 'possessive' quality of the word
■ that a pronoun stands in place of a noun.

Possessive pronouns are used to show who something belongs to. Examples from the story are:

> *His* arms are as good as new steel.
> Every vein in *their* bodies go stiff.

Ask the children to copy out the following table, then to find more examples.

TABLE OF POSSESSIVE PRONOUNS

	SINGULAR	PLURAL
1st person	my/mine	ours
2nd person	your/yours	your/yours
3rd person	his, her, its/his, its/hers	their/theirs

Differentiated group activities

1*: Guided reading and discussion of 'Tukku-Tukku and Samson'. The following questions can be used as a starting point:
■ Why did Tukku-Tukku get picked on?
■ What was Samson like?
■ Describe Tukku-Tukku's character.
■ How did he beat the bully?
■ At the end of the story, do you think Tukku-Tukku really grew taller, or just that he felt taller because he had beaten the bully through strength of personality?
■ Discuss the fact that, despite the distinctly Caribbean setting, the story deals with a universal theme – that of bullying.
2 & 3: Write a character description comparing and contrasting the characters of Tukku-Tukka and Samson.
4*: Guided reading and discussion (see above).

Conclusion

Discuss the two different characters in the story. Relate the characters and the situation to the children's own experiences.

Introduction

Read the fourth story, 'All Other Days Run Into Sunday'.

Whole-class skills work

Write a class glossary for the story. Focus on difficult and/or unfamiliar standard English vocabulary (for example *involved, announcement, declaration, proclamation, encircling, hibiscus, precipice*) and use a variety of dictionaries to determine meaning. You could include dialect words and phrases (such as *botheration, marnin', bwoy*), making sure children distinguish these and determine their definitions from content.

Differentiated group activities

1: Write a vivid, 1st-person description of their own Sundays.
2 & 3*: Guided reading and discussion. The following questions can be used as a starting point:
■ What does the narrator like about Sundays?
■ How does he describe his brother?
■ What kinds of thing does he do on Sundays?
■ How does he describe Cousin J-J?
■ What is church like? How does it differ from the church services you may have experienced?
■ Discuss the dialect used in the dialogue passages.

■ What does the narrator mean when he says that all other days run into Sunday?
4: Write a vivid, 1st-person description of their own Sundays.

Conclusion
Select children from Groups 1 and 4 to read out what they have written about their own Sundays. In discussion, compare these with Sundays in Jamaica.

Introduction
Read the last story in the book, 'The Banana Tree'. Discuss how this story makes a suitable final story for the collection.

Whole-class skills work
Write the following words on the board or flip chart (they can all be found on page 89 of the book):

older
merciless
unstoppable
unnatural
warnings
headed

Ask the children to look at each one in turn, identifying the root word and saying how the word has been transformed (such as addition of prefixes or suffixes) and what the change has done to the word. For example, the suffix '-er' has been added to the root word 'old' transforming the nominative adjective into a comparative adjective. The suffix '-ings' has been added to the root word 'warn' changing the verb into a plural noun. Do the same with the other words and then ask the children to identify and analyse more word transformations on page 90 of the story. End the session by emphasizing the versatility of the English language.

Differentiated group activities
Ask all the children to write a book review using the Book Review sheet as explained below:
1: Use the headings for guidance, but aim for the end result to read like a self-contained literary essay, not a response to a series of prompts. Use evidence from the text including direct quotations.
2 & 3: Follow the headings closely, but aim for the end result to read like a self-contained essay.
4: Write on the Book Review sheet itself.
*The teacher supports groups as appropriate.

Conclusion
Select children to read out the final section of their reviews in which they expressed a personal response and allocated a star rating. Ask the rest of the class to discuss.

FURTHER IDEA

The book contains four more stories which can be read and studied in a similar way.

BOOK REVIEW

■ Introduce the book by giving details of title and author. Explain that it is a collection of short stories, and give an overall idea what they are about.

■ Choose one of the stories and write a summary of the plot.

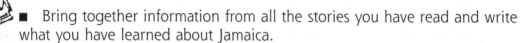

■ Write a paragraph describing the main characters in your chosen story.

■ Bring together information from all the stories you have read and write what you have learned about Jamaica.

■ Explain what you have learned about the Caribbean dialect and how it differs from standard English.

■ Say which story you enjoyed most and explain why.

■ Give the book a star rating (out of five) and explain why you gave it.

FROM BLURB TO BOOK

OBJECTIVES

UNIT	SPELLING/VOCABULARY	GRAMMAR/PUNCTUATION	COMPREHENSION/ COMPOSITION
WRITING FICTION From blurb to book.	Identify and define descriptive vocabulary used in advertisements. Use dictionaries and thesauruses.	Investigate use of punctuation to signpost meaning.	Read and understand purpose of book blurbs. Write a story based on a blurb.

ORGANIZATION (2 HOURS)

	INTRODUCTION	WHOLE-CLASS SKILLS WORK	DIFFERENTIATED GROUP ACTIVITIES	CONCLUSION
HOUR 1	Read book blurbs. Identify ways of stimulating interest. Predict storylines from blurbs.	Investigate use of punctuation to signpost meaning.	1–4*: Pupils work in pairs to develop stories from book advertisements.	Selected pupils share their story ideas.
HOUR 2	Re-read the book blurbs and identify descriptive language of advertisements.	Use dictionaries and thesauruses to define unfamiliar vocabulary and to find synonyms.	1–4*: Pupils work individually to write stories.	Selected pupils share their stories.

RESOURCES

A Thief in the Village by James Berry (Puffin, ISBN 0-14-032679-0) – if possible, enough copies for half the class, board or flip chart, OHP and acetate (optional), writing materials, dictionaries, thesauruses.

PREPARATION

If possible, prepare OHTs of the book advertisements at the back of *A Thief in the Village*.

Introduction

Ideally, this unit should follow on from the previous one as it uses the same text (James Berry's *A Thief in the Village*). It can, however, stand alone. At the end of *A Thief in the Village* there are five advertisements for other books. Each one consists of the title, author or poet and a blurb for the book. Ensure the children understand the term 'blurb'. Then read each one, and discuss with the class the different devices used to stimulate interest – for example:
■ direct description: *Set in Britain, Jamaica, countryside and inner city, this stunning new collection gives us poetry for every mood and occasion*
■ quote from book: *I've seen a ghost. I've seen a ghost through a telescope...*
■ quote from review: *'Guaranteed to send the blood racing through the veins of anyone who loves good writing...'*
■ invitation to reader: *Meet Boy Don...; join the dance...; marvel at...*

Re-read the blurbs and discuss with the children what they think the story might be like and how it might develop. In the case of the story and poem collections, the children could choose one of those mentioned and develop a story idea.

Whole-class skills work

Use this session to revise the use of punctuation to signpost meaning. The advertisements provide several useful examples.

■ *Playing a Dazzler* begins (after the verse) with a complex list in which clauses are separated by semicolons. Compare with the simple list of places in the second paragraph in which single items are separated by commas. The final sentence is a list of two-word phrases separated by commas.
■ The second paragraph of *The Future-Telling Lady* begins with a phrase *(In this sparkling collection of short stories)*. Ask the children to experiment with slotting the phrase into the sentence at various points.
■ Investigate how the semicolon is used in *The Cay*. (It is used instead of a full stop, to show a close link between the meanings of the first two statements of the paragraph.)
■ Discuss the effect of the italics in *A Fine Summer Knight*. (They give emphasis to the words.)
■ Discuss why 'Posh Git' is in quotation marks in *Zowey Corby and the Black Cat Funnel*. (It is to show that it is slang, not standard English.) Examine the use of dashes in the first paragraph. (They are used like brackets to indicate a parenthetical statement.) What do the three dots after 'her problems… indicate? (That there is more to follow.)

Differentiated group activities

1–4*: Ask the children to work in pairs within their groups. They should choose one of the advertisements and develop a story idea together. Remind the children of the importance of story structure and to outline a beginning, middle and end as well as characters and setting. Explain that in the next group activity session they will each be writing their own version of the story they have developed in pairs.

Conclusion

Select children to share their ideas for developing one of the book blurbs into a story. Ask why they chose that particular book.

Introduction

Re-read the book advertisements, asking children to look out for descriptive words and phrases that are used to 'sell' the book to the reader. Make a list of these – for example: *stunning new collection, exuberant language, celebrates the indomitable human spirit, spell-binding, irresistible energy* and so on.

Whole-class skills work

Focus on the descriptive vocabulary listed in the introductory session. Find the meanings of unfamiliar words and list synonyms where appropriate, using class dictionaries and thesauruses.

Differentiated group activities

1–4*: All children work individually to draft their stories.

Conclusion

Selected children read out their completed stories. Compare stories that have been based on the same advertisement. How are they similar or different?
 Ensure that children who wish to are given further time to redraft and finish their stories.

FURTHER IDEA

Experiment with writing blurbs for books. One of the James Berry short stories could be used for this purpose, or children could write blurbs for any of their own stories.

DICTIONARY WORK

OBJECTIVES

UNIT	SPELLING/VOCABULARY	GRAMMAR/PUNCTUATION	COMPREHENSION/ COMPOSITION
REFERENCE AND RESEARCH SKILLS Use a range of dictionaries.	Explore spellings, meanings and derivations of words and phrases.	Recognize and mimic format and layout of entries in different types of dictionary.	Understand purpose and use of different types of dictionary. Compose own dictionary extract.

ORGANIZATION (1 HOUR)

	INTRODUCTION	WHOLE-CLASS SKILLS WORK	DIFFERENTIATED GROUP ACTIVITIES	CONCLUSION
HOUR 1	Display a range of dictionaries or dictionary extracts and discuss their purposes.	Demonstrate the differences between types of dictionary by comparing their entries on the word *children*. Quick questions on where to find what. Search different dictionaries or dictionary extracts to find entries on various words.	1: Work in pairs to produce first part of a Dictionary of Slang or of Scientific or Mathematical Terms. 2 & 3*: Produce a Dictionary of Rhymes with teacher support. 4: Produce a Dictionary of Synonyms using school dictionaries and thesauruses to help with ideas.	Share samples of the group work with the whole class and evaluate.

RESOURCES

Board or flip chart, writing materials, OHP and acetate (optional), OHT displaying sample extracts from different types of dictionary (optional), school dictionaries and thesauruses, copies of a range of specialist dictionaries to include if possible dictionaries of phrases, antonyms and synonyms, quotations, slang, rhymes, idioms, etymology, and technical vocabulary (children's versions of some of the above are difficult to come by, so it may be necessary to borrow examples from the adult section of a library).

PREPARATION

Draw a spider diagram on the board or chart centred on the word *dictionary*, with a spoke leading out to each of the dictionary types listed under 'Resources' above, together with any other examples that you are able to obtain copies of. Prepare samples on an OHT of pages from some of the specialist dictionaries that you have listed so that you can demonstrate to the class what the contents of these look like (optional). Have a short, alphabetically-ordered sequence of simple words ready for Group 4 to use to start them off on the dictionary-writing activity.

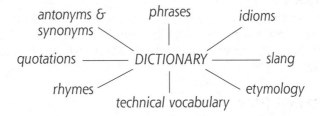

Introduction

Show the class the spider diagram and discuss with them what kind of information they would expect to find in each of the different types of dictionary. Revise the meanings of the words *synonym (a word that means the same)* and *antonym (a word that means the opposite)*. A *thesaurus* is a type of *synonym* dictionary, but may go into more detail about

word meanings. Explain that not all of the dictionaries that you have listed contain definitions. *Dictionaries of quotations* and *rhyming dictionaries*, for example are designed to help with composition rather than spellings and meanings. An *etymological dictionary* contains not only the meanings of words, but their origins and history. As you discuss each type, show the book, or the sample from it that you have prepared on OHT. Talk about layout and organization and ask the children how they would go about finding a particular item in each different type.

Whole-class skills work

Use the example of the word *children* and talk through the entries that might be found for this in the different kinds of dictionaries that you have discussed. For example:

Dictionary of Slang
kids: children, offspring

Dictionary of Cockney Rhyming Slang
kids: *God forbids, Dustbin lids*

Dictionary of Phrases
children: *'Women and children first'. This saying goes back to an accident at sea when a ship called HMS Birkenhead ran aground in 1852 and orders were to save the women and children first. This policy has since been referred to by sailors as 'The Birkenhead Drill'.*

Dictionary of Etymology
Children: A word derived from ME (Middle English) *childre.* The ending *'n'* was added to produce the surviving plural *children* in the 12th century.

Rhyming Dictionary
No words that rhyme exactly with *children*, but **child** rhymes with *filed, mild, styled, wild*.

Dictionary of Quotations
Children: *Children, you are very little,*
And your bones are very brittle;
If you would grow great and stately,
You must try to walk sedately.
(from *'Good and Bad Children'* by RL Stevenson)

Dictionary of Synonyms and Antonyms
Children: boys and girls, infants, offspring, progeny, sons and daughters. **Ant.** adults.

Now check understanding of the functions of the different types of dictionary by asking quick questions of the 'Which dictionary would you use to find . . . ?' variety. To practise using the various types, ask the class to scan for particular items on the OHT extracts or in the books that you have available.

Explain that you are going to ask the groups to compile their own personally written dictionary extracts. They will need to place their entries in alphabetical order and copy the format of the extracts they have seen.

Differentiated group activities

1: Work in pairs to produce a rough page or more of alphabetically-ordered entries for an extract from a Dictionary of Slang Words and Expressions or a technical dictionary of scientific or mathematical terms.
2 & 3*: Work in pairs with teacher support to produce rough drafts of extracts from a simple Dictionary of Rhymes with the sounds alphabetically ordered – for example:
aa *baa ha ma pa*   **ab** *blab cab dab fab.*
4: Work in pairs using simple conventional dictionaries and thesauruses to produce own draft extracts from a Dictionary of Synonyms. This group should start with a suitable sequence of words prepared by the teacher.

Conclusion

Ask representatives from each group to read out part of their work to the rest of the class and discuss how they went about the task. Have all children grasped concepts of format and alphabetical order?

THE CARTOONIST

OBJECTIVES

UNIT	SPELLING/VOCABULARY	GRAMMAR/PUNCTUATION	COMPREHENSION/ COMPOSITION
READING FICTION Modern fiction: *The Cartoonist* by Betsy Byars.	Identify and understand vocabulary from another culture. Understand and identify simile and metaphor.	Recognize non-standard English and its function in reflecting a culture. Analyse sentence construction and use of punctuation.	Read American fiction by significant children's author. Understand different points of view. Explore irony and sarcasm. Investigate characterization. Write in the style of a particular author.

ORGANIZATION (5 HOURS)

	INTRODUCTION	WHOLE-CLASS SKILLS WORK	DIFFERENTIATED GROUP ACTIVITIES	CONCLUSION
HOUR 1	Preview the book. Read Chapters 1 & 2 (approx 15 minutes).	Identify vocabulary from American culture and establish meaning.	1 & 4*: Guided reading and discussion. 2 & 3: Write character sketches.	Share character sketches. Predict what will happen 'tomorrow'.
HOUR 2	Read Chapter 3 (approx 9 minutes).	Investigate non-standard English.	1: Read Chapter 4. 2 & 3*: Guided reading and discussion. 4: Write a character sketch of Alfie.	Pupils in Group 4 relate what happens in Chapter 4.
HOUR 3	Summarize Chapters 5 & 6. Read Chapter 7 (approx 9 minutes).	Investigate the use of irony. Distinguish between irony and sarcasm.	1*: Guided reading and discussion. 2 & 3: Read descriptions of cartoon strips and choose one to draw. 4*: Read description of cartoon strip and draw it.	Selected pupils from Groups 2–4 share cartoon strips.
HOUR 4	Read and discuss Chapter 8 (approx 8 minutes). Summarize Chapters 9 & 10.	Explore and explain similes and metaphors in the text.	1 & 4: Write a description of own room or real or imagine favourite hiding place. 2 & 3*: Guided reading and discussion.	Predict and discuss what will happen next in story. Read Chapters 11 & 12 (approx 10 minutes).
HOUR 5	Summarize Chapter 13. Read to end of book and discuss personal responses to story.	Investigate sentence construction and punctuation.	1–4*: Plan a sequel, according to ability.	Selected pupils share their sequels. Class evaluates for consistency.

RESOURCES

The Cartoonist by Betsy Byars (Red Fox, ISBN 0-09-942601-3) – if possible, enough copies for half the class, photocopiable pages 192 (Similes and Metaphors) and 104 (Story Planner from 'Science Fiction Cards' unit, Term 2), board or flip chart, writing materials, drawing materials.

PREPARATION

Before Hour 2, write the sentences listed under 'Whole-class skills work' on the board or flip chart. If possible prepare an OHT of photocopiable page 192 (Similes and Metaphors) for use in the 'Whole-class skills work' for Hour 4. If possible prepare also page 104 as an OHT – or enlarged photocopy – for use in the 'Whole-class skills work' for Hour 5. Make enough copies of photocopiable page 104 (Story Planner from 'Science Fiction Cards' unit, Term 2) for one between two children.

Note: The length of the selected text means that additional readings will be required outside of the five literacy hours outlined below. If it is not possible to read all of the chapters, selected ones can be summarized as is suggested in the lesson plans. However, additional readings can either be done at other times such as after lunch or just before school ends, or children can complete the readings as homework. The former will work with a half-class set, whereas the latter will require a copy for every child.

SYNOPSIS

Alfie lives with his nagging mum, teenage sister and rambling grandad in a crooked, crowded house. Alfie's way of escaping from the trials of daily life is drawing cartoons up in the privacy of the attic. When Alfie's mum tells him that his older brother and his wife are coming back home to live, Alfie is devastated on two counts. First of all, Alfie has always lived in the shadow of his athlete brother. His mother finds his lack of interest in team games a huge disappointment. But more importantly, if his brother moves back home, Alfie will lose the precious world of his private attic. It is more than he can bear so he decides he has no other choice but to lock himself in the attic, refusing to come down. But he learns that he *does* have a choice – and it is he who must make it.

Introduction

Preview the book by examining the front and back covers and reading page 1. Ask if any of the children have read other books by Betsy Byars. Read Chapters 1 and 2. Identify the main characters (Mom, Alma, Alfie, Pap and Bubba) and their relationship. Establish the attic as an important setting –it is Alfie's special hiding place.

Whole-class skills work

Ask the children where they think the story is set. Establish that the story is set in America and that this is obvious from the vocabulary used in the story. Ask the children to find some American words. List them on the board or flip chart along with their meanings. For example:

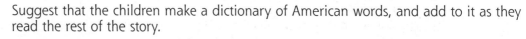

mom (page 5)	mum
yard (page 9)	garden
dollars (page 10)	American currency
hood (page 11)	bonnet
windshield (page 11)	windscreen
pacifier (page 15)	dummy
diaper (page 15)	nappy
principal (page 18)	headteacher

Suggest that the children make a dictionary of American words, and add to it as they read the rest of the story.

Differentiated group activities

1*: Guided reading and discussion. The following questions can be used as a starting point:
■ Re-read the opening and discuss what kind of opening it is and how the writer seeks to get our attention. *(The story opens with dialogue and with Alfie lying. We want to know what he's doing if he isn't studying!)*
■ The four main characters – Mom, Alma, Alfie and Pap – are introduced. Briefly describe each one, and say what their main interest is.
■ Describe the house that Alfie lives in. What does he think is the best thing about it?
■ How can we tell from the writer's description that Alfie is good at cartoons?
■ What do the rest of the family think of his cartoons?
2 & 3: Write a short character sketch of *two* of the following: Mom, Alma, Alfie and Pap.
4*: Guided reading and discussion (see questions above).

Conclusion

Ask selected children from Groups 2 and 3 to share their character sketches. Re-read the last line of Chapter 2. Ask the children to predict what will happen 'tomorrow'.

Introduction

Read Chapter 3.

Whole-class skills work

Investigate the non-standard English used by Pap. Remind the children that standard English is the language of public and official communication, the language which is used when access to it is needed by a wide variety of English-speaking people. Explain that there are several 'standard Englishes', the most widespread being 'British English' and 'American English'. Languages are standardized by definitions in dictionaries and grammar books, usually after hundreds of years of development.

Ask the children to say what is *non-standard* about the following sentences. Note that they need only identify what is wrong, they do not have to give grammatical explanations, some of which require an advanced knowledge of grammar. Grammatical explanations have been included for the sake of completeness, but should not be used with the children unless they request further clarification.

■ "They're going to be six million dollars in debt by the end of the year if the state senate don't bail them out." (page 10)
'Don't' should be 'doesn't' – Pap has used the plural form instead of the singular to agree with 'Senate'.
■ "I built me a car when I wasn't much older than you." (page 10)
'Me' is not appropriate because 'build' is not a reflexive verb. Pap could have said, 'I built a car for myself...'
■ "Wind was whipping back my hair—I didn't put no windshield in the car—I can still feel it." (page 11)
Pap has not used the article 'the' to begin the sentence and he has used a double negative – 'not' and 'no'. Logically, double negatives cancel each other out; however they are used for emphasis in many dialects.
■ "I didn't want to do nothing else for the longest time." (page 12)
This is another example of the double negative.
■ "The government ain't made a law about how we spend that, have they?" (page 34)
'Ain't' is a dialect word not recognized in standard English.

Ask the children to find other examples and add them to the list. Discuss non-standard features of your own local dialect.

Differentiated group activities

1: Read Chapter 4.
2 & 3*: Guided reading and discussion. The following questions can be used as a starting point:
■ How did Tree get his nickname? Do any of the children have nicknames? How did they get them?
■ Describe what sort of person Tree is from the evidence given: what he does, what he says, what Alfie says, physical description and so on.
■ What do you think about Alfie's definition of cartoons on pages 29–30?
■ Alfie was smiling as he approached his house, then 'the smile left his face'. Why?
■ What do we learn about Alfie's dad in this chapter?
■ What did Alfie like about the junkyard?
■ How does mum feel about Bubba? How does this make Alfie feel?
■ What do these words at the end of the chapter mean: 'He was home'?
4: Write a short character sketch of Alfie.

Conclusion

Ask children from Group 4 to tell the rest of the class what happens in Chapter 4. *(Alfie cannot sleep. He is frustrated because when he showed his mother the 'turned-in feet' cartoon, she had not got it. He lies in bed, imagining himself as a famous cartoonist and his attic a famous gallery to which people flock, to see his cartoons. He remembers the only time he made his mother laugh – and that was because he told her about a silly prank Bubba and his friend had played. He falls asleep trying to think of a cartoon to make his mother laugh.)*

Introduction
Briefly summarize for the class what happens in Chapters 5 and 6. *(Alfie gets into trouble at school for drawing cartoons instead of doing his maths problems. He is told to stay after school to see his teacher. Alfie likes his teacher and hopes that by showing her his cartoons, she will understand his passion and talent for cartoons. She is sympathetic, up to a point, but tells him emphatically that school is for school work and not for cartoon drawing. And to make matters worse, Tree mocks Alfie's 'pictures'. Although they have been friends for a long time, Alfie suddenly feels the friendship is going sour.)*

Read Chapter 7. This is a critical chapter, in which Alfie learns that Bubba is coming back to live in the attic, and in which the bond between Alfie and Alma grows.

Whole-class skills work
Read the section on pages 60–61 which includes these lines:
"Did you hear the wonderful news?" she called.
Alfie could tell from the way she said the word wonderful that the news was very bad indeed.

Ask the children to say the words with the same intonation that Alma used. Explain that this is an example of 'irony', which is saying the opposite of what you mean for effect. Explain that 'sarcasm' is like irony, but its intention is usually to hurt or ridicule For example:
Pupil to teacher holding up an untidy scrap of paper:
'Jenkins, this must be your masterpiece!'
Ask the children to think of other examples of irony and sarcasm.

Differentiated group activities
1*: Guided reading and discussion. Use the following questions as a starting point:
■ What news does Alfie hear when he gets home? How does he feel about it?
■ Explain the irony implied in Alma's use of the word 'borrowed' on pages 61 and 62.
■ How and why does Alfie's relationship with Alma change in Chapter 7?
■ What do you think will happen next?
2 & 3: Children read pages 45–46 and pages 49–50 in which two of Alfie's cartoons are described. They should then choose one to draw and label as described in the text.
4*: Read pages 45–46 with the children. Then ask them to use the description in the text to draw and label the cartoon strip about the dog.

Conclusion
Ask some of the children from Groups 2–4 to share their cartoon strips. Then discuss the last comprehension question: What do you think will happen next?

Introduction
Read Chapter 8. What 'home truths' come out in this chapter? Discuss whether the reader's sympathy is just for Alfie. How do we feel about Alma and her mum?

Summarize for the class what happens in Chapters 9 and 10. *(Alfie remains barricaded in the attic. He won't come down, even when his mother threatens to send for the fire department. Alma persuades her mother that she mustn't call the fire department – that it is important that Alfie work things out for himself and come down eventually of his own accord.)*

Whole-class skills work
Revise the terms 'simile' and 'metaphor':
■ Simile: a comparison using the words 'like' or 'as'.
■ Metaphor: a direct comparison, saying one thing *is* another.
Demonstrate how to write about a simile or metaphor using an example from pages 37–38:

'...she had erupted like a volcano' is a simile which compares Alma's sudden anger to the violence of a volcano erupting. Its shows just how mad she was at being told she snored.

Display photocopiable page 192 which contains similes and metaphors from the story and ask the children to explain them using the model above.

Differentiated group activities

1 & 4: Ask the children to write a description of their own room, or a description of a real or imagined favourite hiding place.

2 & 3*: Guided reading and discussion of Chapters 8–10. The following questions may be used as a starting point:
- Why does Alfie barricade himself into his attic?
- How do the family try to get him down?
- What does Alma mean when she says '...there have been other things that I've had to accept and work out for myself, and that's what Alfie's going to have to do' (page 84)?
- What are Alfie's thoughts and feelings during this time?
- How do we know that Alfie has still retained his sense of humour?

Conclusion

Read Chapters 11 and 12.

Introduction

Briefly summarize Chapter 13, up to the last three lines on page 109. *(Tree returns, to tell Alfie of his humiliating defeat: Lizabeth beat him. He sits on the ladder and talks to Alfie through the barricaded trapdoor, giving him a blow by blow account of what happened in the gym.)* Read to the end, beginning with 'Alfie's mother paused at the door' on page 109. Discuss what it is that Alfie has learned from his experience. Solicit personal responses to the book. Did the children enjoy it? Why or why not?

Whole-class skills work

Analyse the author's sentence constructions and punctuation, taking page 104 as an example. You might, for example, undertake the following:

- Count the number of short sentences (6 words or less). Find the longest sentence. How many words does it have?
- What is the difference of effect and rhythm between a series of short sentences, a series of long sentences, a mixture of long and short sentences? (The pace seems quicker when sentences are short.)
- Find the *subject* of the first three sentences. The subject is what the sentence is about. It usually comes at the beginning in the first few words.
- Copy out the four lines of dialogue beginning, "Tree, he's not down from the attic...". Identify and explain the function of all the punctuation.

Differentiated group activities

Distribute copies of photocopiable page 104 (Story Planner) from 'Science Fiction Cards' unit, Term 2. Ask all groups to plan a sequel to the book in which Alfie's skill is recognized and he becomes successful. Before writing, discuss the following questions in groups:
- How does he become successful?
- What is the subject of the cartoon that brought recognition? Is it one of the ones described in *The Cartoonist*?
- What does he do for his family and friends?
- What does his teacher think?
- How does he feel about his success? Does it make him happy?

1: Children in this group should try to capture the style and language used by Betsy Byars, and make the characters consistent with their development in *The Cartoonist*.

2 & 3: Children in these groups should aim to develop characters consistently.

4: Children in this group should concentrate mainly on developing the storyline.

Conclusion

Select children to read out their sequel plans. The rest of the class should evaluate which ones developed the story of Alfie in the most appropriate way.

SIMILES AND METAPHORS

Read the following examples of figurative language from *The Cartoonist*. For each one:

- say whether it is a simile or metaphor;
- identify what two things are being compared;
- explain why the image is effective.

For example:

'... she had erupted like a volcano' is a simile which compares Alma's sudden anger to the violence of a volcano erupting. It shows just how mad she was at being told she snored.

Coming down from the attic was like getting off one of those rides at the amusement park. (page 7)

Then his eyebrows jumped up as if they were on strings. (page 10)

He was like a bundle of sticks in motion. (page 26)

His shoes were eating his socks. (page 29)

The dirt was packed as hard as concrete. (page 52)

The friendship had suddenly gone sour. (pages 56–57)

The slam was like a cannon firing, the first shot of a long and difficult war. (page 68)

STORIES FROM MEMORIES

OBJECTIVES

UNIT	SPELLING/VOCABULARY	GRAMMAR/PUNCTUATION	COMPREHENSION/COMPOSITION
WRITING FICTION Stories from memories.	Use dictionaries to explore meanings of unfamiliar words.	Demonstrate awareness of grammar and use appropriate punctuation in own writing.	Read author's account of own writing. Plan and write a story based on own experience.

ORGANIZATION (2 HOURS)

	INTRODUCTION	WHOLE-CLASS SKILLS WORK	DIFFERENTIATED GROUP ACTIVITIES	CONCLUSION
HOUR 1	Read about the author, Betsy Byars.	Use dictionaries to explore meanings of unfamiliar words.	1–4*: All pupils write about one of their earliest memories.	Share memories. Are any of them similar?
HOUR 2	Teacher displays example of his/her earliest memory. Shared reading and discussion.	Model the process of story planning.	1–4: All pupils plan and begin writing their stories based on their earliest memories. *The teacher works with Groups 1 & 4.	Share selected stories. Discuss and evaluate.

RESOURCES

Photocopiable pages 195 (About Betsy Byars) and 104 (Story Planner from 'Science Fiction Cards' unit, Term 2), a collection of books by Betsy Byars (optional), board or flip chart, writing materials, dictionaries, thesauruses, OHP and acetate (optional).

PREPARATION

Make enough copies of both photocopiable sheets for one between two children. If possible, prepare them also as OHTs or enlarge them to at least A3 size. Write a paragraph describing one of your own early memories. If possible enlarge or prepare as OHT to use in Hour 2.

Introduction

Distribute copies of photocopiable page 195 (About Betsy Byars) and, if possible, display it on OHP or as an enlarged version. If you have done the previous unit based on Betsy Byars' book *The Cartoonist*, remind the children. If you haven't, explain that Betsy Byars is a well-known author of children's books and refer to your collection of her books. Ask if any of the children have read any of her books and, if so, can they tell the rest of the class about them?

Read the main piece on the photocopiable page and discuss the writing process described. Are the children surprised by anything Betsy Byars says about how she goes about getting ideas and writing?

Whole-class skills work

Discuss unusual words and phrases used in the piece. For example, what is meant by 'scrapbooks of her life', 'quirky', 'creative energy', 'fleeting', 'revisions', 'writer's block', 'authority', 'greatest gift'? Use a variety of strategies with the children to find the meanings, including using dictionaries and thesauruses.

Differentiated group activities

1–4*: Ask all the children to read the short 'Do It Yourself' writing activity at the bottom of photocopiable page 195 (About Betsy Byars) and write a paragraph describing one of their earliest memories. Explain that they will use this memory as the basis for planning and writing a story in the next hour. Give support to those groups or children who are having difficulty getting the initial idea.

Conclusion

Ask selected children to share their earliest memories. Talk about how far back these memories go. Are any of the memories similar? If so, discuss why this is. Ask children to suggest how some of these memories could be expanded into stories.

Introduction

Read out to the children the paragraph you have written about one of your earliest memories. If possible display it on OHP or as an enlarged photocopy. Discuss with the children how it might be expanded into a story. Have we got characters? a setting? part of a plot?

Whole-class skills work

Display and give out copies of the Story Planner on page 104. Use it to model how to turn your memory paragraph into an expanded story outline. Explain to the children that the story does not have to be long, but should contain a recognizable beginning, middle and end. Remind them also of the descriptive techniques that help to enhance writing:
■ Use of adjectives and adverbs.
■ Use of simile and metaphor.
■ Use of descriptive details (such as describing particular details to build up the total effect).

Differentiated group activities

1–4: All children should plan their stories. Some children will be able to start writing in this session and should be encouraged to do so.
*Give support to Groups 1 and 4, encouraging the former to get as far with their writing as possible and helping the latter expand their memories into a structured story outline.

Conclusion

Select some children to read out their story outlines and story beginnings if they've been able to get that far. They should also read their earliest memory. Discuss how effectively the memory has become the basis or been incorporated into the story. Do they think Betsy Byars' advice is a good way of getting an idea for a story?

FURTHER IDEA

Ensure that those children who wish to do so are given time to complete their stories, redrafting and producing a finished copy.

ABOUT BETSY BYARS

Betsy Byars thinks of her novels as scrapbooks of her life. 'What do people who don't write do with these details?' she wonders. 'When I see something quirky or real or interesting, I put it in a book.'

When Betsy gets an idea for a book, she writes it down immediately. 'Even if I only get the title,' she says, 'I write the title down.' If she's in the middle of writing another book, she breaks away from it for a few minutes and writes down the new idea, just to get it started. 'I find I have a lot of creative energy at the beginning of a new project,' she explains. 'I don't want to lose that energy.'

Sometimes ideas for a book come to her out of order. If she's writing Chapter Two of a book and gets an idea for Chapter Seven, she writes, 'Chapter Seven', then she writes her idea. 'An idea is fleeting,' she says. 'It's easier to put it down as if it were a chapter.'

'I work on a word processor for the first draft, but for revisions I always print out a copy of the book and do my corrections by hand,' says Betsy. She usually starts by writing the middle portion of a chapter, which takes up about half a page. Then when she does her revisions, she goes back and adds the beginning and end of the chapter.

Writer's block is not much of a problem for Betsy. Still, there are days when she gets stuck. 'If I come to the end of the chapter and I can't think of what to do, I go to the library and pull books off the shelf. I read the first sentence of every chapter. I might go through ten or twenty different books. Finally, I'll find something inspiring, like: "The telephone rang." This has never failed me when I'm trying to start a chapter.'

To her readers who want to be writers, she says, 'When I was in school, the teacher always told me, "Write about what you know." I always thought that the stupidest thing I've ever heard. You've got to make up stuff! But the truth is, the words *author* and *authority* go together. When you write about what you know, you write with authority. Authority is the greatest gift a writer can have.'

DO IT YOURSELF!
Here is a writing activity from Betsy Byars: 'One of my favourite things to give a character is a memory of mine. In *Cracker Jackson* (written in 1985) I gave one of the characters my earliest memory of my father. I'd like to see children try to write down their earliest memories.'

(From *Meet the Authors and Illustrators, Volume One* by Deborah Kovacs and James Preller, copyright © 1991 Scholastic Inc, reproduced by kind permission.)

BAN THE BYPASS

OBJECTIVES

UNIT	SPELLING/VOCABULARY	GRAMMAR/PUNCTUATION	COMPREHENSION/ COMPOSITION
WRITING SIMULATION Ban the Bypass.	Develop new vocabulary from text. Use dictionaries efficiently to explore meanings of unfamiliar words.	Understand conventions of formal letter writing. Revise use of connectives. Investigate the grammar of newspaper writing.	Read and comment on issue presented in newspaper article. Draft and write letters for real purposes. Construct a persuasive argument. Write a newspaper article. Write a discursive essay.

ORGANIZATION (5 HOURS)

	INTRODUCTION	WHOLE-CLASS SKILLS WORK	DIFFERENTIATED GROUP ACTIVITIES	CONCLUSION
HOUR 1	Read and discuss the newspaper article.	Investigate unfamiliar vocabulary using dictionaries.	1–4: Develop arguments through role play based on newspaper article. *The teacher works with Groups 1 & 4.	Groups 1 & 4 present their arguments to the rest of the class.
HOUR 2	Recap on situation presented in newspaper article. Read 'Letter to the Council'.	Work on conventions of formal letter writing.	1–4: Still in role, all pupils write letter to Council. *The teacher works with Groups 2 & 3.	Selected pupils from Groups 2 & 3 show and read their letters. Class evaluates content and format.
HOUR 3	Examine examples of campaign leaflets and posters. Identify features of persuasive writing.	Revise discursive connectives used in persuasive writing.	1 & 2: Write campaign leaflets. 3 & 4*: Write posters.	Selected pupils from each group present their work. Class evaluates.
HOUR 4	Re-read newspaper article, with emphasis on the role of newspaper reporter.	Develop understanding of features of newspaper writing style.	1–4*: Write a follow-up article.	Share articles and evaluate.
HOUR 5	Examine closely one paragraph of article and investigate how detail might be expanded.	Identify and list 'for' and 'against' arguments given, and suggest others.	1–4*: Write discursive essay.	Compare essays and evaluate arguments given.

RESOURCES

Photocopiable pages 200 ('Boreham Bypass Battle') and 201 (Letter to the Council), dictionaries, examples of campaign leaflets and posters (these can be political or based on a recent local issue), board or flip chart, writing materials, drawing materials, OHP and acetate (optional).

PREPARATION

Make enough copies of the photocopiable pages for one between two children. If possible, prepare them also as OHTs – or enlarge to at least A3 size to provide a useful focus for discussion. Before Hour 5, write the discursive essay outline plan (given under Hour 5, 'Differentiated group activities') on the board or flip chart.

Introduction

Explain to the children that they are going to take part in a simulation that will provide opportunities for writing with a clear sense of audience. (Make sure the children understand the term 'simulation'.) The simulation is closely based on issues raised by real-life disputes over bypasses and new roads.

Distribute copies and display photocopiable page 200 ('Boreham Bypass Battle'). Read it together.

Ensure that the children understand what the article is about and discuss briefly the views of the different groups mentioned.

Whole-class skills work

Examine the vocabulary in the text using context and dictionaries to find the meanings of unfamiliar words (for example: *bypass, congestion, outskirts, spokesman, minster, arable, compensation*). The following terms may not be in the dictionary and may need to be explained by you:

activists: people who take political action, in this case, against the new road
eco-warriors: eco- is a prefix meaning 'to do with the environment' – therefore, people who are fighting for the environment
campaigners: people who are also fighting against the new road, but with legal methods
developer: planners, builders and others who are going to build the new road.

Differentiated group activities

Allocate the following group roles. They are in order of difficulty based on the amount of information given in the text. For example, Group 1 has the least information and will have to use their imagination to flesh out the case of the local historians.
1*: Local historians.
2: Farmers.
3: Members of the Action Group.
4*: Residents of Horwood Green and Queen's Park estate.
All groups should re-read the article and discuss in role how the bypass will affect members of their group and what they intend to do about it. The aim of each group should be to prepare a 2–5 minute presentation entitled 'Why we want to ban the bypass'.

Conclusion

Groups 1 and 4 give their presentations. They can refer to an OHT of the planned development (see above).

Introduction

Begin by recapping on the situation about the bypass with reference to an OHT of the planned development. Read the 'Letter to the Council' on photocopiable page 201.

Whole-class skills work

Teach the conventions of formal letter writing using 'Letter to the Council' as an example. Point out the following features to the children:
■ The sender's address is on the right-hand side of the page.
■ There is a comma after each line, but not usually before the postcode.
■ The receiver's address is written on the left-hand side of the page (it is placed here for reference, and is not needed in a personal letter).
■ The letter is dated.
■ The letter itself begins with 'Dear ...,' and ends 'Yours sincerely,' (using small 's').

Differentiated group activities

Ask each group, still in role, to write a letter to Boreham Council expressing its views. The content of the letter can be discussed by the whole group. Each child should then write an individual letter using 'Letter to the Council' as a model.

Conclusion

Ask selected children from Groups 2 and 3 to show and read out their letters. Discuss them in terms of both content and format.

Introduction

Distribute examples of the campaign leaflets and posters that you have collected. Use them to investigate features of such persuasive literature. Look at how they persuade (such as what kind of arguments are used), the language they use and the format they use. The features might be listed under these headings on the board or flip chart. Explain that the children will be writing their own campaign leaflet or poster in the group activities session of this hour.

Whole-class skills work

Revise discursive connectives. These will be a valuable resource in writing the campaign leaflets in this hour and the discursive essay in Hour 5.

Remind the children that a connective is a word or phrase which connects statements, and that discursive connectives are those which are particularly useful in expressing an argument:

but	this	as a result	in view of
on the other hand	that	for	eventually
instead	these	then	to begin with
however	because	next	against that it could be said
yet	therefore	finally	to look at it in another way
nevertheless	so	thus	

Ask the children to find examples in the photocopiable resources for this unit and in the various leaflets and posters that you have distributed.

Differentiated group activities

1 & 2: Write a campaign leaflet. This should do the following:
■ Briefly explain the bypass plan.
■ Give strong reasons against it.
■ Set out a plan of action.
■ Invite people to join the protest.
Children may share ideas but should produce their own leaflet.
3 & 4*: Design a poster. This should do all the above, but more briefly. Again, children may share ideas but should produce their own poster.
Encourage the children to stay 'in role'. For example, the farmers should emphasize the loss of agricultural land, the Action Group should threaten to 'dig in' and hold protests, and so on.

Conclusion

Select some children from each group to show their leaflets and posters to the class. Evaluate them in terms of how well they represent the appropriate interest group and how persuasively they have presented their arguments.

Introduction

Explain that in this session everyone is going to switch role to be a reporter for a newspaper. Re-read 'Boreham Bypass Battle' and explain to the children that they will be writing a follow-up article.

Whole-class skills work

Revise features of newspaper-writing style. Ask the children to note the following:
■ Use of 'journalese' (reporter's jargon) – emotive words such as 'battle', 'eco-warriors', 'determined', 'suffer' and so on.
■ Use of headline and subheadings.
■ Lots of facts and figures.
■ Use of quotations from people interviewed.
■ Layout in columns, illustrations, captions and so on.

198

Differentiated group activities

1–4*: All children write a follow-up article. The various groups have written letters and distributed leaflets and posters, but they might also have done other things such as held a protest march. Develop the ideas that the different groups suggested in their action plans in Hour 1. The children could write individually or in pairs. Less able children, particularly those in Group 4, should follow this article outline:

■ Introduction: 'The latest news about the Boreham Bypass is that the protest groups have written letters to councillors and distributed leaflets and posters.'
■ A paragraph about what each group has to say.
■ A paragraph about any other developments.

Conclusion

Select children to read out their articles. Evaluate them in terms of how well they have taken on board the features of newspaper article style.

Introduction

Re-read the paragraph about Boreham Council's reasons for the bypass (third paragraph). Expand these reasons in discussion – for example, what kind of accidents might have taken place? What other damage may be caused by heavy vehicles going through the town centre?

Whole-class skills work

Explain to the children that they are going to write an essay in which they examine the arguments for and against the bypass. Brainstorm all the arguments for and against and jot them down on the board or flip chart, then try to classify them. It will be found that the main arguments against the bypass fall under two broad headings:

■ The bypass is not necessary.
■ The human and environmental costs of the bypass are too high.

The argument against could be strengthened by suggesting a better alternative – for example, re-open the railway.

The arguments for the bypass are exactly the same:

■ The bypass is necessary.
■ The human and environmental costs of *not* having the bypass are too high.

The argument for could be clinched by demonstrating that there is no alternative, for example the railway was closed because it wasn't serving the needs of the community.

Differentiated group activities

All children write a discursive essay entitled: 'The Boreham Bypass: Arguments For and Against'.
1: Children in this group could be given the freedom to write in any way they wish as long as they examine both sides of the argument and come to a conclusion.
2 & 3: Children in these groups should follow the essay plan below.
4: Children in this group should follow the essay plan below, but omit paragraph 4. They will cover the content of this paragraph in a simpler way in paragraphs 2, 3 and 5.

Para 1:   Introduction. A brief description of the bypass plans.
Para 2:   A statement of the arguments for the bypass.
Para 3:   A statement of the arguments against the bypass (do not use interview quotes).
Para 4:   A discussion of the arguments.
Para 5:   A conclusion, stating a preference for or against the bypass.

Conclusion

Choose two essays. Ask the children to read them out while the rest of the class listen and evaluate the way they have presented their arguments.

BOREHAM BYPASS BATTLE

Activists who want to stop the Boreham bypass stepped up the battle against the developers last night. A group of campaigners, calling themselves the Ban-the-Bypass Action Group, have set up a camp in the track of the planned road. If the eco-warriors dig in as they have done in previous protests, it could take a great deal of time and money to move them.

The bypass, planned to relieve congestion in Boreham, will cost over £30 million and will take two years to build. The planned route goes through the heart of Horwood Green, presently a quiet village, and carries on through hundreds of acres of farmland. It then cuts through the Queen's Park housing estate on the outskirts of Boreham, before rejoining the old road.

Mr Alan Thomas, spokesman for Boreham Council said that the bypass was essential to relieve congestion in the town centre. 'Vibrations from heavy lorries are shaking the medieval minster to pieces, and we've had 26 road traffic accidents in the past month,' he told reporters.

'WE WILL FIGHT TOOTH AND NAIL!'

As council workmen prepared to cut down trees along the route of the new road, the people of Horwood Green village came out to meet them. One resident said, 'We will fight tooth and nail to save our countryside and our village!' The chairman of the Horwood Green Parish Council, Jeremy Nicholls, said, 'We are not the sort of people who go chaining themselves to trees, but we are very serious about fighting this road. We believe that there is a Roman Villa buried under those fields somewhere, and if we can find it, we can stop the road!' A local historian confirmed that several Roman coins and fragments of pottery had been found in the area.

Local farmers were equally determined. Their spokesman, Mr Simon Hodge, said, 'This will wipe out hundreds of acres of arable land. Yes, I'll get compensation,

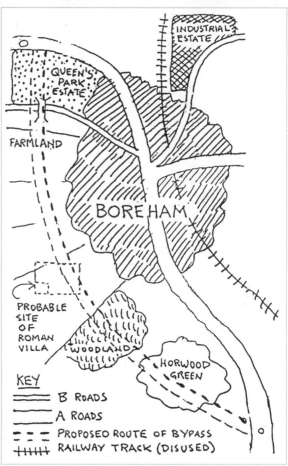

A MAP OF THE PROPOSED BYPASS

but the road will cut my farm in half, and it's not so economic to farm the smaller fields.'

HOMEOWNERS SPEAK OUT

Homeowners in Horwood Green village and the Queen's Park housing estate have received offers of compensation for the loss of their property. The government is offering the market price of the house, plus a home-loss payment of up to £15,000. However, most people would rather stay where they are. Mrs Edna Springer, 75, said, 'I have lived in Horwood Green all my life and wanted to die here.'

But the people whose homes will be knocked down are not the only people to suffer. Mr Barley, who lives near to the proposed route said, 'We are going to go from a quiet, sleepy village to living next door to a noisy, polluting bypass.' Mrs Eileen Dorrington, a mother of two who lives on the Queen's Park estate, said, 'This road means we will be surrounded by roads on all sides. I don't know how I'll manage with the children!'

But Bill Wollman has no such doubts. He said, 'There's only one thing for it. I'm going to join the eco-warriors. Next time you interview me I'll be up a tree in the path of the bulldozer!'

AN ANGRY PROTESTER

LETTER TO THE COUNCIL

32 Roxburgh Drive,
Horwood Green,
Boreham
BH1 2LA

5 September, 1998

Mr. A. Thomas,
The Clerk to the Council,
Council Offices,
Boreham
BH1 1AA

Dear Mr Thomas,

I am a member of the Horwood Green Historical Society and I am writing to express my concern about the Council's plans for a bypass around Boreham. When I saw a map of the proposed route, I was horrified to see that it passed over the site of a Roman villa.

I admit that it has not yet been proved that the villa is actually there, but this is because the site has never been excavated. However, our historical group often visits the site to look for evidence, and so far we have found several items dating from about 300 AD. These include:

■ Five Roman coins, very worn, but one with a clear outline of the head of the Emperor Vespasian.
■ Numerous fragments of Roman pottery.
■ A small ivory figurine of Venus.

May I suggest that the Council has this site properly excavated before building the road? Better still, why not take the road round the other side of Boreham where all the factories are?

Yours sincerely,

Arthur Oman

Arthur Oman

DETECTING BIAS

OBJECTIVES

UNIT	SPELLING/VOCABULARY	GRAMMAR/PUNCTUATION	COMPREHENSION/ COMPOSITION
REFERENCE AND RESEARCH SKILLS Detecting bias.	Recognize emotive language.	Study the function of rhetorical and other questions in arguing a case. Consider and compare form of headline and letters to the press.	Read and evaluate letters to a newspaper. Compose a persuasive reply.

ORGANIZATION (1 HOUR)

INTRODUCTION	WHOLE-CLASS SKILLS WORK	DIFFERENTIATED GROUP ACTIVITIES	CONCLUSION
HOUR 1	Discuss emotive language and 'telegraphese' style of headlines.	Analyse argument and emotive language of invented letter to a local newspaper. Detect bias.	1*: Compare arguments given from opposing sides in letters X and Y. Underline emotive words used in letter Y with teacher support. Compose a reply to letter Y. 2 & 3*: Compare the arguments in letters X and Y. Compose a reply to letter Y with teacher support. 4: Compare the arguments in letters X and Y.	Share and discuss outcomes.

RESOURCES

Photocopiable pages 204 (Letters to the Editor) and 205 (Detecting Bias), board or flip chart, OHP and acetate (optional), writing materials.

PREPARATION

If possible, prepare an OHT or enlarged photocopy of photocopiable page 204 (Letters to the Editor). Separate OHTs or enlargements of each letter would be ideal. In addition, make enough copies for one between two children. Make enough copies of photocopiable page 205 (Detecting Bias) for one per child. Write the following headlines on the flip chart or board (to be used in the introductory session):

SUPERSTORE WILL RUIN LOCAL BUSINESSES say residents.

GREEN CLOSE REC. PERFECT SITE FOR SUPERSTORE argues local mum.

Introduction

Show the class the two different headlines written on the board or flip chart. Ask them where they would expect to see this type of writing *(in a local newspaper)*. Discuss briefly the difference between national and local newspapers. What sorts of news do they each report? Note that the above headlines are written unlike normal sentences. In typical headline style unimportant words are left out. Discuss each one in turn: what do the children think they are about? What is a 'rec.'? (Short for *recreation ground*.) Which words used in the headlines are intended to persuade the reader? Show these by underlining the words *ruin* and *perfect*.

Whole class skills work

Show the class Letter X on photocopiable page 204 and read it aloud to them.

LETTER X

As the Secretary of the Green Close Residents' Association, I am writing to protest about the Council's plan to sell off the old Recreation Ground to get-rich-quick developers who will devastate this lovely area of parkland to build yet another Superstore.

Who needs this Superstore? There are plenty of shops in the area already – all of which give fair value and friendly service. Does the Council care so little about local businesses that it is happy to ruin these as well?

Has anyone bothered to consider the effects of this development on the people actually living in Green Close, who will have to suffer all the traffic noise, congestion and pollution caused by the Superstore and its massive car-park? And where will our children have to play when it is built?

Since this crazy project was first mentioned, property prices in and around Green Close have dropped steadily – and no wonder!

In a time when most people are concerned to protect the local environment, it seems that all that Banfield Council wants to do is destroy it. Please listen to public opinion before it is too late!

Yours sincerely,

Richard Jones (Hon Sec. G.C.R.A.)

Ask the children why the writer is personally concerned about the proposed development. What is a Residents' Association? How does the writer expect the building of the Superstore and its car-park to affect the residents of Green Close? Do the children think he would feel the same way if he were going to work in the Superstore? Why has he asked so many questions in his letter? Does he know the answers to any of them already? Explain that when questions are asked in a way that suggests that the writer already knows the answers (as in 'Who needs this Superstore?') they are called *rhetorical* questions. Asking questions is a way of drawing the reader into the discussion and persuading him or her to side with the writer. Ask the children to pick out all the arguments against the proposed Superstore development that they can find in the letter. Discuss and highlight the emotive words that the writer has used to try to persuade the reader to agree with him (*get-rich-quick*, *devastate*, *lovely*, *friendly* and so on). Does the class feel sympathetic towards the writer's case? Before starting the group activities, read Letter Y aloud. Have any of the children changed their minds now?

Differentiated group activities

1*: a) Work with teacher to read and underline examples of emotive words in Letter Y.
b) Compare Letters X and Y using the framework provided on photocopiable page 204.
c) Compose own letter in role as a child from Green Close replying to Letter Y.
2 & 3*: Activities b) and c) as above. Teacher support with c).
4: Activity b) as above.

Conclusion

Go over the comparisons that the children have made between Letters X and Y. Ask individuals to read out their writing in the role of Green Close children. Discuss the persuasive qualities of their own letters.

LETTERS TO THE EDITOR

LETTER X

As the Secretary of the Green Close Residents' Association, I am writing to protest about the Council's plan to sell off the old Recreation Ground to get-rich-quick developers who will devastate this lovely area of parkland to build yet another Superstore.

Who needs this Superstore? There are plenty of shops in the area already – all of which give fair value and friendly service. Does the Council care so little about local businesses that it is happy to ruin these as well?

Has anyone bothered to consider the effects of this development on the people actually living in Green Close, who will have to suffer all the traffic noise, congestion and pollution caused by the Superstore and its massive car-park? And where will our children have to play when it is built?

Since this crazy project was first mentioned, property prices in and around Green Close have dropped steadily – and no wonder!

In a time when most people are concerned to protect the local environment, it seems that all that Banfield Council wants to do is destroy it. Please listen to public opinion before it is too late!

Yours sincerely,

Richard Jones (Hon Sec. G.C.R.A.)

LETTER Y

GREEN CLOSE REC. PERFECT SITE FOR SUPERSTORE
says local mum

I am delighted to hear that at long last Banfield Council is considering giving planning permission for a Cheapo Superstore in the Green Close area. Banfield is in dire need of somewhere that ordinary people can shop without paying the high prices charged by fancy family-run businesses with no parking facilities.

The waste ground between Green Close and the busy dual-carriageway has been a neglected eyesore for years, and a dangerous place for children to play. There are plenty of safer recreation areas in Banfield for local people of all ages to enjoy, not to mention the excellent amenities of the new Leisure Centre. The old Rec., with its wasted space and close proximity to the main road, is the perfect site for a Superstore.

The prospect of being able to park free and do all one's shopping at minimum cost in the same store is surely one that all local residents must welcome. As a busy mum, I can't wait!

Mary Higgins

DETECTING BIAS

■ Compare Letter Y with Letter X. What do they say about the following?

The recreation ground
Letter X

Letter Y

The local shops
Letter X

Letter Y

Places for children to play
Letter X

LetterY

Parking facilities
Letter X

Letter Y

Prices in the local shops
Letter X

Letter Y

■ Imagine that you are a child who lives in Green Close. Which letter writer would you agree with?

■ Write your own letter to the paper responding to the arguments in Letter Y. Give reasons for your opinions.

IDIOMS

OBJECTIVES

UNIT	SPELLING/VOCABULARY	GRAMMAR/PUNCTUATION	COMPREHENSION/ COMPOSITION
WORD PLAY Idioms.	Enrich vocabulary by understanding purpose of idiom and use of dictionary of idioms. Make a dictionary of idioms.	Understand how writing can be adapted for different purposes and audiences.	Collect and discuss idioms. Distinguish between literal and figurative meaning.

ORGANIZATION (1 HOUR)

	INTRODUCTION	WHOLE-CLASS SKILLS WORK	DIFFERENTIATED GROUP ACTIVITIES	CONCLUSION
HOUR 1	Revise or introduce what an idiom is. Identify figurative nature of idioms.	Share known idioms and their meanings. Discuss how idioms have meaning for certain audiences and also how they develop as language develops.	1*: Use dictionary of idioms to extend knowledge of idioms and their meanings. 2 & 3: Write meanings for and illustrate humorously some idioms from photocopiable sheet. 4*: As above according to ability.	Share idioms, meanings, sentences and illustrations. Discuss how to compile idioms into class book.

RESOURCES

Photocopiable page 208 (Idioms), dictionary of idioms (ideally, several), board or flip chart, writing materials, drawing materials, OHP and acetate (optional).

PREPARATION

If possible, make an OHT of photocopiable page 208; otherwise make sufficient copies for one between two children. It would also be useful to prepare an OHT or enlarged photocopy of one or two pages from a dictionary of idioms.

Introduction

Write the following sentences on the board or flip chart:

It's raining cats and dogs.
He knew that if he told the truth, he would get into hot water.

Ask the children what the sentences mean. What is odd about them? Would somebody who is just beginning to learn English be able to understand them? Explain that our language contains hundreds of common sayings not found in other languages (although other languages have their own!). These sayings are called 'idioms'. They are understood by the people who use them, but cannot be understood just by knowing what the individual words mean. They are not meant literally, but have a figurative meaning, like metaphors and similes.

Whole-class skills work

Display the list of idioms on photocopiable page 208 on the OHP – or distribute copies of the sheet to the children. Ask for the meanings of four or five of them. For example:

Idiom	Meaning
to rain cats and dogs	to rain very heavily
to get into hot water	to get into trouble
to feel under the weather	to feel ill or poorly
to let the cat out of the bag	to give away a secret
to make both ends meet	to live within one's means

How would they be able to find out if they didn't know? Display example pages from a dictionary of idioms and discuss how such a dictionary can be used to find out meanings of idioms. Identify the similarities and differences between a dictionary of idioms and a dictionary of words and/or a thesaurus (note that a thesaurus will often give meanings for idioms). Ensure children understand their different purposes.

Ask the children if they can think of any more idioms. If they can't, give the dictionary of idioms to a pair of children and ask them to find a couple and give their meanings. Write these on the board or flip chart. Then write 'He was cool as a cucumber'. What does this mean? (*He was calm.*) Now write 'He was a real cool cat'. What does this mean? What group of people might understand what it means? Explain that this is a relatively new idiom because the words 'real', 'cool' and 'cat' have developed new meanings among a certain group of people.

Differentiated group activities
1*: If dictionaries of idioms are available, ask children to work in pairs to find six or eight idioms they don't already know. They should write these out, each on a separate piece of paper, with their literal meanings, a sentence using each and a humorous illustration of the figurative meaning. If dictionaries are not available, they should use the idioms on photocopiable page 208.
2 & 3: As above, but using four or five of the idioms on the photocopiable sheet.
4*: Choose two or three of the idioms on the photocopiable sheet. Write them out and then write they really mean. Illustrate the idioms with cartoons.

Conclusion
Select members from each group to share the outcomes of their group activities. You might ask children to show their illustrations only and see if the rest of the class can guess what the idiom is. Discuss how their idioms could be collated into a class book or dictionary of idioms and agree a time outside the hour for this to be done.

IDIOMS

It's raining cats and dogs.

She felt a bit under the weather.

He let the cat out of the bag.

Her name rang a bell.

He bit off more than he could chew.

She completely lost her head.

She was over the moon.

He had a finger in several pies.

I have a bone to pick with you.

The cat has got her tongue.

She was on cloud nine.

He turned over a new leaf.

It was hard trying to make both ends meet.

He was caught red-handed.

Don't worry – I'm only pulling your leg.